Meditations from the Breakdown Lane

Books by James E. Shapiro

On the Road: The Marathon
Ultramarathon

Meditations from the Breakdown Lane

Running Across America

James E. Shapiro

ECHO POINT BOOKS & MEDIA, LLC
Brattleboro, Vermont

Meditations from the Breakdown Lane
by James E. Shapiro

Published by Echo Point Books & Media
Brattleboro, Vermont
www.EchoPointBooks.com

Meditations from the Breakdown Lane
ISBN: 978-1-63561-809-9 (casebound)
        978-1-63561-852-5 (paperback)

Cover design by Kaitlyn Whitaker

Cover image: Joseph Greene

To my teacher, Joshu Sasaki Roshi

Where do you dwell when you are running?

—*Joshu Sasaki Roshi*

Don't work towards freedom; but allow the work itself to be freedom.

—*Dōgen Roshi*

Preface

I can't remember exactly when I first decided to run across the United States, although I have a nagging feeling I ought to remember such a momentous thought. But the transition from admiring those who had taken on such feats to thinking that I could, ought and must try it myself was gradual.

Even now I can barely fathom having run across the country. It was a dream, a painful and exhausting one that I haven't really understood. Perhaps I never will. Although the scale was immense, the experience was only moment-to-moment.

As a schoolboy I ran a fair bit because I enjoyed it, but I suffered my share of last-place finishes on a boarding-school track. Always, I had the feeling that if the distance was long enough, I would come into my own. Feeling overshadowed by the fluency of others in sports wasn't easy, and for a good while my later involvement in running was motivated in part by proving something to ghosts.

Quite by chance, in 1975 when I was twenty-eight years old, I saw the finish of the Boston Marathon. Then it became very simple: I had to run one, too. A few days later I began training around the footpaths of the Charles River, carefully bounding off the balls of my feet as I imagined every distinguished-looking runner would. Later I heard that some other runners who didn't know me at the time had nicknamed me the Kangaroo. Well, it was a start.

Over the next five years I graduated to longer runs in training and in races. I had some success in competition, which was rewarding, but my taste really veered more toward private solo runs, the fifty-mile crunchers. I also wrote two books about running, and meeting people who had run the length of England, across America, whatever, at some point bewitched me with a passion to do likewise.

I didn't quite know how to train for such a step or what to expect in taking it, but that kept my edge nicely honed. Late in 1979 I felt strong enough to think seriously about crossing the country on a mostly solo venture—that is, without accompanying friends and support vehicles. I would carry necessary gear in a backpack, and forage for food, water and shelter.

I spent the summer of 1980 in moderately intense training, putting in an average of twenty miles a day for eight weeks, with some occasional long runs. Of course, this regimen came on top of a reasonable background of mileage over the past few years and the confidence of having weathered a couple of twenty-four-hour runs. Training was at a slop-along pace, which is to say eight to ten minutes a mile forward speed, with frequent soda, candy and stretching breaks, as well as occasional little sit-downs. You can go on forever at this pace, it seems. The question was putting it to the test.

In late July of 1980 I bought a one-way ticket to California and flew out to the West Coast. I picked a little town up the coast from San Francisco in Marin County as the starting point. The very obscurity of the starting point, the avoidance of a roundabout, complicated route out of San Francisco, and the chance to start in a relatively clean, uncluttered rural spot where the waters of the Pacific met the shoreline—all these added to the appeal of picking Dillon Beach as the place to begin.

I got a lift up from the city with Kenneth Lee, a photographer, and Scott Thomason, West Coast editor for *Running Times*. They are pleasant guys and we had a good chat in the car. But like a traveler on his way to the airport who is no longer quite with those around him, or like a condemned man walking down the hall to his last conscious destiny, I felt loneliness settling in between us, blowing in like the heavy mist off the ocean at Dillon Beach where I was to start later that morning. I had made a big promise to myself and the world, and now the only thing left to do was to keep it. It was scary to sense how alone I was going to be and how much I would have to live with myself, and be comfortable doing so. Feeling naked wakes you up. That's what it was all about: trying to learn how to wake up.

Acknowledgments

A number of people along the road gave food, shelter and encouragement to a weary traveler: Don Choi, Mrs. Gwen Storer, Dave and Pat Pedersen, Dr. Robert Donlin, Steve and Esther Arum, Rick and Ginnie Bowers, Bart and Catherine Rocca, John Dwyer and Barbara Willcox.

To my two chief handlers, Donna Hudson and Melanie Marcus, who shared the rigors of the road, I owe a profound debt.

My brother Tom, and his wife, Virginia, were of exceptional help in planning out the run and in appearing just when needed.

Among a number of friends on the home front whose support was particularly helpful are Mike and Kathleen Cleary, Richie Innamorato and Joe Greene.

To my movement and stretch teacher, Gail Stern, go a special thanks for all the preparatory work.

On the literary side I received only the best kind of hands-off encouragement from my agent Peter Ginsberg of Curtis Brown.

Special thanks also go to Fred Lebow and members of the New York Road Runners Club for their reception at the end of the journey.

To all these people and to all the others who are not mentioned I offer a deep bow of gratitude.

Contents

Meditations
from the
Breakdown Lane

The Bear Sets Forth

Down on the beach I announce that I am going to go. As if
something should happen. I, a lone man, am setting off on foot,
about to run across the North American continent, but there
is no crowd and no sign from heaven to cheer me on nor
anyone seizing me by the arm to tell me not to do it (wouldn't
that be nice if I were prevented from going?). All the while the
waves just keep coming in. Just go, I tell myself, don't think
about it. I push off with one foot and then the other, running
a little duckfooted on the uneven, moist sand. I'm on my own
as the sound of the gnashing camera fades out. I run through
a parking lot drenched in heavy mist and then begin the sudden, steep climb up from sea level. Why do I taste such regret
over the end of that ritual swim in the Pacific? But, as always,
the present moment continues to engulf the previous one. It
is just as well I do not guess at how much dying and being born
will take place before this trip of 3,026 miles is over. At the
moment all I notice is that the California seashore is suddenly
behind me. Up in town a few children by the local grocery do
not even glance at me. No one knows where I am headed.

There is no way ever to completely prepare oneself for a
transcontinental run. Only about a dozen living journey runners in the world have taken on comparable runs. And among
those, the solo runners are a minority. You cut your journey as

much from your own personality as you do from the external world around you, so no one can say much that will help you understand what it means to meet your small and large self during the commitment to forward motion that will continue day after day all through your waking hours. From the moment you begin until the moment you finish you are committed to an indivisible problem whose only solution is constant and unrelenting effort. Distance is irreducible. Distance is immense, especially on the three-thousand-mile scale. The scale is too big to dwell on for long. On a high steel beam looking down invites vertigo. There are no shortcuts even on the shortest route from west to east. Whether it's twenty-eight or thirty-one hundred miles, it's still long. The Rocky Mountains cannot be avoided. The desert wastes are an inevitable encounter. All must be swallowed. No matter how free I thought I was before I started, I did not appreciate the compulsive aspect of this challenge—the ineluctable commitment to the word "must." Otherwise, failure.

So at last the climb up the glass mountain begins. The first hour goes well. True, my pack seems a remarkably heavy hump with which to graft myself for the next ten weeks. But really, it is nice just to be underway. Not remarkably nice, not *thrilling* after all, but it is a nice road through nice country with nice things to look at. The eucalyptus trees that grow in steady single-file rank along the edges of the fields are streaked with blond, rawer strips where the bark characteristically peels away. Eucalyptus has a special fragrance, one that seems inseparable from the dense sea mist. The filtered light sharpens the vivid green of the roadside weeds and blades of grass, whose exuberance drives them up through the very asphalt of the road. The aptly nicknamed "elephant rocks," weathered behemoths with creased sides reminiscent of those beasts, stand guard in the foggy dampness at a curve in the road not far out of town. Suddenly, the gray cloud bank ends, long tufted strands helpless against the evaporating sunshine. Last day of July. Barbed-wire fences keep rhythm with the rolling blond hills. Even the quiet of Marin County and the blissfully moronic gaze of cattle could not entirely still some seeping, erosive sense of panic.

"Oh, God, you're really a fool," I say aloud with a small laugh, shaking my head. This ridicule temporarily faces down the fear, but I lose concentration on the road as the unmentionable words—"dropping out"—repeat themselves. When I was in Hebrew School preparing for bar mitzvah, they taught us how one must never say aloud the sacred Hebrew syllables of Yahweh, the word for God. This awesome taboo drew my ever more tempted disrespect until finally obedience melted and I said the word aloud. And waited. No thunder in the heavens. No collapse of walls. And now this low-grade nastiness that I can't shake waggles its demon rump before me, tempting my celibate discipline.

The panic is a familiar feeling from sesshin, the week-long intensive meditation period students of Zen may choose to take on. There is no obligation to sit on your rear with folded legs on a black cushion from 3 A.M. until 9 P.M. with only brief respites for meals and walking, which themselves are a continuation of the meditation practice. It is completely voluntary. Hands in mudra position over your navel point, folded legs consumed by the fire of pins and needles, neck stiff, lower back aching, trying to give up trying. I had met profound panic in sesshin, tramping in the rain in black robes, dreading the return to that Spartan zendo, the meditation hall, where only the groaning of the wooden platforms we sit on and the creaking of bones and flesh would disturb an otherwise unbroken silence. You are up against yourself when five days of sesshin loom ahead with no promise that the seconds will go any faster or slower than they have already. How long is long? I saw my face one day in the mountaintop washroom we all shared. Then I knew how scared I really had gotten. And here I was, sliding into it again. Why, I wonder, did I ever say I would run across the country? How can I do it? And why—worst of all—do I feel so badly *now?* Couldn't I get discouraged a week from now? That would be acceptable. Then it would be easy to say to myself, well, just a phase, old boy.

Other journey runners had hinted that dark valleys had to be endured. A year earlier I had interviewed Mavis Hutchison, who ran across the U.S. at the age of fifty-three in seventy-odd days. "I wondered," she said, "how I was possibly going to do it when I stood on the steps of City Hall in Los Angeles and thought of all that distance I had to cover."

Ken Levy, a broad-shouldered, husky New Yorker who ran from Bangor, Maine, to Miami, Florida, a couple of years earlier, had held a late-night phone conversation with me a few weeks before.

"Oh, you'll really have a great time," he said, his voice abuzz with enthusiasm. There was a pause as he mused, sunk in recollection of his run. "All the same," Ken went on, "my run wasn't all easy.

"After a few days of running down the road I was thinking about this and that until I'd thought about as much as I could. Then I began to realize that pretty soon I wasn't going to have anything left to think about. I didn't know what I was going to do! I'd never been alone with myself for such an extended period before."

Ken laughed while I sat soberly on the other side of the phone conversation, wondering how *that* might be to encounter. The nearest I could come to filling in the blankness was to imagine a massive and solitary roadway through the desert. Alone with myself not for one week but for ten. Ah.

"What I found," Ken continued, "was that you become friends with yourself. And the whole thing led to my becoming a much more religious person and having a clearer idea of my relationship with God."

I had no notion of what to say except to grunt in the social way people have, to indicate my interest in what he was saying, which was certainly keen enough. My own private conclusions went as follows: it isn't uncommon, in fact, it must be fairly likely that you encounter some kind of crisis point in a transcon run, much like a fever, you break through and *then* it's not so bad ever again. "You learn to become friends with yourself." It was one of those lines you don't forget. It sounded reassuring. Perhaps I wouldn't have to go through a crisis at all. I was willing to suffer a great deal to get through the run, but perhaps the whole venture would not be as difficult as I imagined. In any case, whatever comes, I decided, I'll make the best of it.

I started at a place so tiny—it is called Dillon Beach—that it appears only on county maps. It is about forty miles up the coast from San Francisco. Behind me are small resort homes whose tan and bleached woods look even warmer against the fog. Just beyond the homes are eroding hills that plunge down to the beach. My companions, the photographer and the journalist, take pictures and scribble notes. Both pay strict attention to what I say and do. I sense they are really curious about what is driving me to do this and what I might be feeling just moments from death as a civilian and rebirth as a journey runner. I am curious, too.

I want to do the run for its own sake, staying open to whatever there is to encounter in myself and in the territory found between two oceans. It seems best, in any case, not to tempt fate by braggadocio or competitiveness. In the past others have come to grief with their coast-to-coast plans, usually with leg injuries they brought on by going too fast and too far early in the run. In all but the desert regions where a friend will be along in a car, I will be completely on my own. Solo. I will have to find food, water and shelter as I can. I will be my only company for many days.

The translation from saying to doing will demand an effort I can't even imagine. How can I, without ever having tried such a thing? I have run two hundred and ten miles in a single week; as much as a hundred miles or longer in one go three times, all reasonable indicators of being comfortable in this sort of thing. But there's no book with training tables to reassure me. No matter what anyone else says, there always remains a vast difference between having done it and standing on the other side, wondering if you can.

I tend to think it will get easier as I go along and I'll get stronger, transforming myself into a tireless bear lumbering down the highways at the rate of fifty miles a day. I do plan to take a few days off here and there if the mood or scenery seems right, which will bring the average mileage down. Whatever the run wants to be, I will try to let it be. All the same, the racing side in me starts thinking over a conversation I had with Don Ritchie a few weeks earlier. Ritchie, a world-class performer at such distances as fifty and one hundred miles, said he thought eighty miles a day might be possible. Although it was just his opinion, there is something deliciously perverse at speculating on such extremes. Eighty miles a day . . . the mind pauses, quivering with delightful, nay unspeakable, emotions. Sometimes the wider the jump, the easier to leap. Then a sober voice takes the microphone and reminds whoever is listening inside that I am supposed to be out on an adventure, not a race. My speeding heart quiets down. There's already enough to chew on. I would never have chosen this particular bit of folly if it weren't long and difficult. Otherwise, it wouldn't be worth doing.

It was easy in a way to drift along with a casual attitude right up to the day of the run. So much was out of my personal control. Every day I would have to keep myself alive, but the weather, the condition of the roads, the vagaries of geography and commerce and decisions unknown pioneers made eighty years earlier about where to settle meant I would find motels and grocery stores in some places and not others. The United States was not laid out for my personal convenience. Sleepiness, dirtiness, hunger, discomfort—all were inevitable under such circumstances.

Well, whatever was coming could not be guessed at. So it had been easy to say to the reporter over breakfast this morning that I was not nervous. But that had been an hour earlier.

Not that I hadn't had some spasms of fear before—infrequent, but real. During a movie I saw in New York there was a shot at night of a truck stop out West with big trucks parked outside. It pierced me to imagine that in a few weeks I would actually be out there all alone running up to just such a café. Perhaps all that blue American nighttime would swallow me up. Thousands of miles. All those strangers. And could I do it? I sat there in the movie theater, just lit with fear.

And then there was the television crew that came to my apartment. I sat there, a solemn monkey under the hot lights on a blistering July afternoon, when the reporter asked: "What if you don't finish?"

I will never forget the way he watched me or the silence that I couldn't prevent that came up between us. Not anything as simple as hostility or defensiveness. I still don't understand my silence entirely.

I almost hadn't considered not finishing. Certainly, not making it is the long shadow that always lies across any distance run. His question was unanswerable. I wasn't going to try if I didn't think I could do it. I wasn't really afraid of failure. I assumed, in fact, that there was a good chance of it. But you don't ask a warrior before battle where he would like his severed head buried. The question was rude, although in the most unintentional and impersonal of ways. So I said I would crawl if I had to, to finish. Or maybe I said that to someone else, but I still think of the silence sometimes, the way it came up or I came up with it, dry and hard like a stone.

And now here I am averaging a little over five miles an hour plodding down Franklin School Road, Whittaker Bluff Road, Fallon Road onto Bodega Avenue, the sun going up and getting hotter and I'm still getting hot surges of panic. I'm not even suffering physically—everything rotten I feel is in anticipation of what is to come. How do you swallow seventy days in a single gulp? Once in the hospital they did a gastroscopy on me in the special procedures room. They anesthetize the uvula at the back of your throat to deaden the gag reflex and then as you lie on your side, floating up to the ceiling from the shot of Valium, the technicians insert a long viewing tube down your throat into your stomach for a look around with lights and sprays and trick mirrors. The drugs don't provide a complete antidote. Nor does the immensely sympathetic hand of a woman nurse on your flank. Your whole being is in revolt at the intrusion. If you could imagine gagging with your entire body down to your toes, then you can appreciate how desperately you resist what you voluntarily accept because they told you it was necessary for your own good. It is the thinnest line ever drawn to rest on when you hate what is good for you. And now I am gagging on my own ambition, my own inability to relax. It is humiliating to snap from a casual acceptance of the run into this fearful crouch. I don't stop running, however. I just wonder inside how much longer I can pad on. This is as close as I ever want to get to imagining infinity. Bruce Tulloh, who ran across the States in the 1960s, calculated that it takes about 4,000,000 footsteps. How many do I have left—3,985,-000?!

I am simply face up against the terms of a private contract. This is all voluntary. I could stop at any moment. I could lie and say my foot hurt me. I could start again a week from now. But I am committed. What will the photographer and writer think if they see me back in San Francisco that evening? In the privacy of my mind there is no humiliation too small not to consider.

I try to remember how much I can hate the early stages of long training runs and races. It is my own damnable quirk. Used as I am to forty-to-fifty-mile workouts, sometimes the first twenty miles seems no better than a tedious preliminary. I complain in those early stages to myself that I haven't gotten anywhere. Only after twenty-five miles do I begin to savor the stretch of the run and feel like I have *done* something. And I feel a subtle shift in body mood at that distance. The softness, the easiness of the opening miles where I simply don't feel the running as effort is far less preferable than the cut-cut-cut of my strides when a kind of grittiness of effort is demanded. I have to start answering the thirty-fourth mile, say, with a deeper and fuller response. I like being forced up against the wall a little so that I have to fight. There is an incredible pleasure at feeling the weight of the accumulated miles. To go fifty miles is to go somewhere. To go ten miles is not real travel. At fifty miles, perhaps, I am in my third county, tenth township. The landscape has changed. The air is cooler upstate on the training runs. The smell of fields is different from the fumes of upper Broadway. I have gone somewhere different on the earth. Perhaps I am not doing anything any different than when I rode with my mother on the Madison Avenue buses as a little boy, kneeling and staring out the window at the world going by. Even now when I see the backs of small heads and the soles of little feet turned toward me and see both hands laid flat against the window for support, I am with them in their watching. And how much more does one savor the fruit that has taken six or seven or eight hours of patient manipulation to crack open—it is a fine thing to see the Peekskill train station down by the water's edge at the end of a thirty-eight-mile run from New York City.

The real trouble with all this is that I never assume that I am going to finish any run over ten miles until I actually do complete it. I have almost never—or maybe never—not finished a long training run. All the same, I pin a ten dollar bill to my shorts when I run upriver. Perhaps this time I won't make it. It's an absurd mix of confidence and paranoia. I wouldn't wish it on anyone and it is a theme that will haunt me through the coming trip, although at the moment I do not realize it. I think of the impending lunch break as I near Petaluma, a town twenty miles east of Dillon Beach. My worries drop away as I run through the outskirts of my first town, feeling slightly nervous. I secretly expect some unnamed something ought to happen in this California town.

A few old timers, obviously used to their spot on the sidewalk, gaze at me curiously as I rubberneck around. I feel I am newly arrived on the planet and am somberly aware of my responsibility to be a good journalist. It is as if I am hauling a trolley full of future readers behind me. I make mental notes on what I see—a sure way to interfere with just seeing. It's an ordinary, prosperous American town, somewhat rural in flavor. Pickup trucks are parked everywhere. I find a café and step in out of the blazing sunshine and take a counter seat. The waitress is gossiping with some bluff, friendly farmers. When the men leave she tells the other waitress that one of them was drunk. He had been the one pushing their flirtation. I have no appetite, so I get a strawberry soda.

In the brightly lit bathroom, the mirror shows a red face, deep gash lines on each side of the mouth—new since the morning and always a sure sign of stress. Also, I look frightened. I smile at myself, say something snotty, but the grin I come up with is forced. The eyes look too bright against the fierce rose of the skin. If I were someone else, I would put my arm around him. I give up, snap the light off and go back into the world. It is time to get back to work.

Down the main street is a large supermarket. I stalk its remarkably abundant aisles, as broad and cleanly swept as the avenues of a Latin American capital. Under the serene fluorescent hum I choose a white cotton sun hat. Wendy, the clerk, who was marking it down for sale, is the one who suggests I buy it. She has brown hair, clear skin and a low voice, and I suddenly feel how much I miss women. Her firm arms could drive a car alongside me and mix up iced drinks as I run. I want her to take care of me. Of course I say nothing like that. She is quick to extend the conversation.

"Oh, you ran the New York City marathon two years ago!" she says. I am wearing the T-shirt they gave out at the 1978 race.

"It's a long time ago," I say.

"It seems short to me. Well, time depends on your point of view and how much has happened in between."

"A lot," I say. "It seems long to me." I am thinking of how long this morning has been, not to mention the six-hundred-odd days since the marathon.

It is an eerie conversation, since I am just fresh from battle with time. For her it is a casual chat. For me it resonates with heavy implications. I bid her farewell regretfully. I am not sure how much of that sentiment she shares.

Although I am still carrying too much gear, I have chosen each item with care and my worldly stock is greatly diminished. Hence, I examine this latest addition carefully. A small tag announces the hat was made in mainland China. With the fatuous warmth humans attach to their possessions, I turn this information to my advantage. "The hat's made in China, a tropical country, must be lightweight cotton of just the right weight and ventilation. And it has a nice, slightly exotic look on my head. (Much better than getting a hat made in Michigan.) Jeez, it's kind of tight. Actually, that's better because it'll stretch anyway. And what luck to find a *white* cap so fast because that'll reflect heat better than anything else. Besides, white has a tropical, foreign aura." I must have been thinking of pith helmets and African jungles. It's true I don't feel handsome in the hat. I feel funky instead, but I relish even this absurd distinction, highlighted even more when it occurs to me that it would be good to put on sunglasses. I have a pair of mountaineering glasses with black leather sideshields. As I run out of Petaluma I glance at myself in the glass of a store window. I look suspiciously like a lanky relative of Mr. Magoo —white cap, black shades, red kerchief, white shirt, extra large white shorts, white socks, blue shoes, green pack and in between, stretches of spindly giraffe body. The hero advances. People who ask me what I thought about on the trip would not always want to know. The dimension of the feat does not necessarily still the homey chatter of the mind.

Eastward I begin to penetrate the mysteries of Central Valley. This is flattish country, given over to cattle and cropland. Gas stations and grocery stores appear only in the towns. In between it is unprotected running. I ration my drinks and plunge on through the flaming heat. I have no idea how badly the sun is burning me. I thought summer elsewhere had pretty well acclimatized me to what I am going to encounter. No one informs me any differently. Weather forecasts for transcon runners do not exist. An hour in the California sun facing east is not the same as driving through it. So I am feeling wobbly when I reach Ford's Café in Scheelville. Thirty-five miles of ground separate me from Dillon Beach.

The café is at a well-traveled intersection and a number of pickups are parked out front. On the walls inside are dozens of framed pictures of airplanes, many of World War II vintage, photographed in battle formation. There is an aerial shot of the café as well. I pick a corner table, conscious of my ridiculous costume. A deeply buried, almost forgotten attitude from Vietnam War days stirs inside—recollections of rednecks grabbing for my long hair or pitching stones in my direction leave me fourteen years later with some tint of wariness. "Hey, you skinny m.f., what are *you* doing in here with your bare legs showing?" No one says that. I discover as I will repeatedly for the rest of the trip that apprehensions about strangers and odd situations are almost invariably a discredit to the tolerance and sympathy I meet. Not until much later do the last crinkles of mistrust vanish. None of the patrons in Ford's pay any attention to me, so I stare curiously at them instead. They are mostly farmers and they wear nylon hats with big brims, T-shirts, jeans and scuffed work shoes. Their big arms and hands rest on the tables with the kind of enjoyed stillness working limbs savor at the end of the day. They are nursing along their beers.

The waitress, perhaps nineteen years old, comes over with ice water.

"You look like you could use this," she says.

"Oh, great, thanks."

"Maybe I should just pour it over your head," she says. I smile, grateful for the human contact.

I don't feel hungry so I order a salad and French fries. The salad is a vile concoction of iceberg lettuce with brown stains, rotten tomatoes, too many onions and driblets of American cheese. Here and there are outcroppings of mushroom caps already puckered by rot. Even the deeply imprinted habit from boyhood, to say nothing of a natural predilection, of finishing

all the food on my plate cannot compel me to go beyond a few
bites. I worry a bit that the waitress will say, "Oh, didn't you
like it?" And then I will have to lie when I am really angry.
What's the point of telling the truth to people who serve lousy
food when they clearly don't know that they are? It is the start
of another wretched theme on the trip—the clumsy and revolt-
ing attempts at serving palatable food that one finds across this
immense nation. Here in the heartland of vegetable and fruit
production I have been betrayed. I cast an angry look at the
cook through the kitchen door. He is in his early fifties, deeply
tanned, with a high and balding head, a big bristling mustache
and a shirt open partway down his chest and cut off at the
sleeves. I work as a chef myself, so I know perhaps it is not
entirely his fault.

Outside, the Pepsi thermometer reads 96 in the shade; it is
six in the evening. Two teen-age girls drive pickups around the
parking lot, making tight turns on squealing tires. Their gig-
gling faces flash in and out of view. I call my brother and a
friend in New York. I tell them I am fine, happy to be here,
yes, I'm on my way, is it ever hot, and so on. Part of my soul
is back in the city and I feel a little weird going on at an hour
when everyone else's workday is over. I still don't know where
I will find a motel tonight. Far more than I can yet comprehend, I am as yet raw to the life style of the road. Later it means
nothing to know nothing about how the day will turn out or
where I will find a place to stay. Only after a few weeks will
I learn to trust the fortune of the road. Right now, however,
I feel incomplete.

The backs of my legs now glow cherry red from the sun. My
neck is stiff from the unaccustomed weight of the pack and no
amount of stretching can unkink it.

After a trailer park comes a place that advertises cherry cider.
Inside it is clean and brightly lit. A lady with white hair passes
two quarts of cherry cider over the counter. It is really apple
juice mixed with cherry concentrate, but it has a fresh, exqui-
site aroma and taste. I knock back the quarts with long, un-

ceremonious draughts. A blond-haired young guy named Dale, wearing a silver charm around his neck, asks where I am going. He and the older woman get tremendously excited when they hear what I am about.

"I should call channel 7 in San Francisco," Dale says.

"We ought to have a camera around here for people like him who come in," the old lady says. "He's going to be famous."

Dale asks a lot of questions and answers mine about the local farmers, most of whom are shifting over to grape plantings. When I leave Dale shakes my hand.

"God bless you," he says.

I run along high on the flattery and warmth of that encounter until some sneering young guys yell at me. Fuck you, I think, the good mood shattered. Fatigue's first victim is always one's sense of humor. The road gets confusing to follow at one point and there is no one around to ask. Cars swish by with unconcern; how could anyone know that I am a total stranger in this land? It's easy to make grand resolves about enduring grand difficulties, but the little things are the real gnats in the eye.

I begin to climb again over long rolling hills, burnt blond and touched with occasional stands of trees, that now take on a different beauty with the deep shadows of late afternoon. The field grasses have a feathery look. I stop to drink from a water bottle, and two horses, one brown, one yellow, amble over to be sociable. They watch seriously as I run off. A few drivers wave, honk or put on their lights. Could they know what I am doing? Probably not, but it is nice to get the encouragement. I feel important and get a little energy from each of those contacts. Black cattle, fat as bumblebees, low for their dinner. I think of Sasaki Roshi, the Zen master, and his comment that all things in the world are traveling together. The cows, the horses, the motorists, the serene flood of West Coast light, even my stiff shoulders—we all keep running down the world together.

As the sun begins to set I reach a broad flatland intersected by a commercial strip of gas stations, motels and a shopping mall. The lights from that complex glimmer ever more sharply in the soft violet dusk. It is a tremendous relief to have the day come to a successful close. At 9 P.M. I will have covered forty-seven miles. Twelve hours from start to finish. I finally decide to ask where a motel is and find that I have overshot the last one by three quarters of a mile, so I double back. Since I will have to cover the same ground the next morning it becomes actually an extra one and a half miles. True to the thrifty anxiety of a journey runner (acquired that day), I am deeply disappointed by such a waste of energy. The effort needed to run a mile and a half is clearly precious. But I must dodge the temptation to feel angry. In the future, I lecture myself, check sooner. I get a motel room without difficulty and give in to the pent-up diarrhea caused by stress, not enough food and lots of liquids. I am almost too tired to face walking to a restaurant and I am still not hungry, but I know I must force myself to eat.

That night when I finish writing my notes on the day's events, I slip between the sheets. Sleep is troubled, but before I conk out I wonder if I can get up again and get through another day. One day is easy, but two in a row? Yet there is nothing one can decide about the next morning when it is still night. As I lie there in bed, I think about running in under the stars for the finish. There was something special about that. Although I missed human society at the dinner hour, I had had another kind of company. I am comforted by that memory and in spite of a queasy mix of loneliness and fatigue and fear I think it really has been a good day after all. I am alive. It's all right, I think, now you can sleep. And for a little while, I do.

California Is a
State of Mind

Living as I was moment to moment, unsure of my own capabilities, overawed by the scale of the task ahead, battered by the brutality of new physical demands and having only one day's experience behind me, I could hardly envision anything different ahead for weeks to come. Not until much later in the crossing would I see how the run expressed different cycles and seasons. I was so engrossed in the ongoing hour-to-hour demands of running down the road that the past hardly existed and the future did not consist of anything further than I could literally see ahead—a distance of about three miles. It would take time to adjust to my new life as a road hog or a road rat or a road fox—all different terms I dubbed my new persona at different times. They were fondly bestowed nicknames, won at great cost. They were my secret badges, combat ribbons for service performed against the Enemies—the monsters of laziness, fear and fatigue.

That opening day marked one of the great transitions in my life—one of the infrequent times a totally new way of life impresses itself on one's whole way of doing things. Normally we slip through changes quietly; the house we live in remains the same, as do the faces around us and the language we speak. Not always. Working on a freighter as a fifteen-year-old sailor was a profound rupture with the past. The sea, the hard physical labor, the subjugation to a code of obedience to the bosun and the ship's officers, the dependence for one's food and bed on work performed, the danger of knife fights in whorehouses, the immersions into bouts of drunkenness and sexual promiscuity—all that blew apart the irksome gentility forced on me by attendance at a private boarding school in New England. Above all there was the newly discovered immensity of the globe, the sheer vastness of the ocean perpetually unscarred by man's buildings. In those more innocent times I did not know of the undissolved immensity of tiny plastic spheres that were beginning to infest the ocean or of any of the other chemical degradations. I took it then for what I believed it to be—great and terrible in its reminder of things alien, of impossibilities and of death. After all, I stood watch on the bow of the ship from eight to midnight every night, a fine time for thoughtfulness as the ship bucked beneath my feet, the *slop-slop* sound of the steel hull cutting through the random tossings of the waves. Meteorites flashed through the sky, distant storm banks glowed from within with lightning, and the dark surface of the waves promised total anonymity if I should slip overboard. Who at home could save me then? No one in school had ever suggested that I was dwarfed by the galaxy of water that lay a few nautical miles outside of New York harbor.

There was another parallel explosion of internal habits and prejudices that I endured five years later, another blast against the dense clouds of self. At the age of twenty I landed in Brazil to begin a life among peasant farmers. The language, the tropical heat, the smells, the sorrows of the poor, the stories that were told, the way in which living and dying were gone about again snatched up my previous lives and emptied them out. I thrust myself onto a crowded truck filled with fat peasants and squalling chickens and was borne down a dusty red road to a town hidden away under carnauba palms, tucked down among a crinkle of arid land and there received a new name in Portuguese. I could not be who I had been before if I was to survive. I put on a mask with that new language and when it came time two years later to return home I found that now it came off with large patches of skin. I was not the only one who felt lost on returning to an old home back in America. I met other shell-shocked victims, Peace Corps volunteers who thought they could never get over having left. But that becomes another story. I learned it was possible to undergo wrenching baptisms and gain irrevocable insights. But success at lasting through them demanded some dumb, blind faith. Only surrender of the previous life would mean admission into the new one.

The first day in California was an experience, a training run but not the real thing. The second day is when the apprenticeship begins.

I am up at a decent hour, but my things are strewn about in the all-too-frequent cloud of messiness that I create wherever I stay. Only it takes twenty minutes to refold and stuff it all away. So the first good resolve was never to be messy again. In that time I could have been two miles down the road. Of course, I was often to repeat that resolve in the future.

Mornings are always fine. There is not a single morning on the entire trip when I do not want to get out of bed and do not feel that it would all be okay again no matter what has happened before. So I trundle along under the bright sunshine, noting with disgust the heavy local traffic that ends only when I turn off onto Jameson Canyon Road. I decide to establish a system of running and walking to portion out my strength through the day. I run for fifteen minutes (one and a half miles covered) and walk five (a quarter mile covered) for a total of one and three quarter miles in twenty minutes or five and a quarter miles an hour.

Walking plays a sometimes substantial role in many of the great ultrarunning experiences. There is no shame attached to walking after twenty-two hours of a twenty-four-hour race or eighty miles into a hundred-mile training run. Up to what point does one literally run without a single walking step? And does such a boundary matter? Clearly it doesn't. Most journey runners do some amount of walking, either to get through a period of injury or as a standard part of their mileage. In America, partially due to the example of Tom Osler in New Jersey and partially to its perpetual rediscovery by every weary, desperate soul who overextends himself, walking periods are common among participants in track races of twenty-four hours and an inevitable feature of the newly revived six-day races now being held in this country. When Don Choi covered two hundred miles in forty-eight hours in 1980 (the first hundred were his part in an annual hundred-mile race in Queens, New York) he walked a substantial portion after the first sixteen and a half hours. The newspaper accounts said he "ran" the distance; people said, "Don *ran* two hundred!" The issue of walking drops away when the performer pushes that far beyond the ordinary. It is a reversion back to the mixed method first used and developed by pedestrians in six-day races here and in England from the 1880s to the 1930s.

All the same, it is unsettling for me trying to decide in advance how much to actually walk. For years the walking record for crossing the U.S. was faster than the running record. Running is more stressful, more tiring and increases the risk of muscle and tendon strain. I'm not sure how I am going to find these consecutive days of heavy mileage, so I opt for a tentative solution. I will "mostly" run and keep walking as minimal as possible. And for the rest of the trip walking anything more than a few minutes at a stretch is always accompanied by guilt. In any case, I rarely walked more than three miles a day. Only today I am to find myself smack up against the issue in an extremely unpleasant way.

At the moment, I am hemmed in by steep hills on each side. When cars approach from in front, I must pick my way along an exceedingly narrow shoulder, facing traffic. I do not dare run with traffic coming from behind with so little margin for error. But the sharp curves are hazardous on the left-hand side of the road because the cars come barreling into sight with no expectation of seeing a runner, so as I approach curves I look behind me and lumber over to the right. Then once through the curve I head over to the left side again. I think of the extra steps involved and wonder how much extra running I will do by the end of the day. Steps are getting precious. I have become a miser of energy. I almost resent the motorists, but it is too patently absurd to blame anyone. I am an uninvited member of the roadway.

My water supply gets low and houses are infrequent. I am made shy by the way the few that there are sit in off the road, hidden by fruit trees. Something about seeing only part of the white plaster wall of a house, a random section cut out through a break in tree branches, intimidates me. The hell with it, I'll get by somehow.

Finally, at a farm outbuilding there is a telephone company truck parked nearby. The driver is sitting in the cab having a smoke. We fall into conversation and in the kind of litany that is to become so familiar, we make a fair exchange. I tell him what I am doing, which rouses his heretofore sleepy interest, and he tells me what I want to know, which is what's coming on the road.

"You want good food?" he says. "Try the Red Top Diner just off of I-80 up a few miles. And you can fill your water bottle over there." He gestures to an outside spigot. "Go ahead, no one will mind."

Just the name—the Red Top Diner—sounds classically funky. Perhaps Bogart and his truck-driving compatriots in the old film, *They Drive By Night*, would have eaten at such a place. Now I am getting closer to the real thing! And there is an immediate goal a few miles ahead rather than having to choke on the cosmic swallow of the twenty-nine hundred miles that are left. Musing on a good lunch always dissipates the blues. Unfortunately, your expectations, based as they are on fancy, can never really tell you what's ahead. The wrinkle this time is that the Red Top's sign juts over the trees, a quarter mile off this local road. I literally stand there debating whether to go ahead or not and all the while each minute, worth on the current energy market one tenth of a mile of forward progress, clinks unused into the barrel of wasted time. Hunger and romance win out over road thrift.

Just in front of the diner is Interstate 80, a bright heedless spillway of traffic. California sunshine ricochets off the speeding cars that gnash through the brown sizzled-out hills. Interstate 80 is the shortest route between San Francisco and New York and the special magnetic sense you get near great terminal points of travel is still strong. I am running east, slowly penetrating into the great western spaces, but by car I am only an hour and a half from where it all began. I feel pride at being part of this great east-west interchange, a loving sense of travel for its own sake.

The Red Top is big, blowzy, efficient and the food is just fine. The telephone-line man taps my shoulder as he walks by and we smile. Many diners have plump faces, big heads, open mouths. My precious dollars buy me the privilege of sitting here on some nameless midday in the summer of 1980 where I can listen to the clash of china and silver and watch the brisk legs of waitresses hurrying steaming plates of food to the many hungry who flock in. Like an Indian squatting in the sunshine against the mission church, I have my right to be here, but the comfort of the leather plush is temporary. It is a precious thing to sit down. I rarely sit down any more.

The sense of being a road vagabond cut off from others deepens in little ways. When I reach the nearby town of Suisun City, I avoid taking an exit ramp that would add another hundred yards and opt for a shortcut through the industrial back end of town. I slip cautiously through a barbed-wire fence and trample through weeds past the anonymous litter that always accompanies the straggly bits of land no one ever tends on the edges of plant and warehouse buildings. It might as well be Bruckner Boulevard in the South Bronx. There is a beauty even in the subworld of mankind's litter.

I stop again in a supermarket. A tall black man, thin as a stork, wearing old shoes, his crispy hair streaked with white, is losing his driver's license, as he announces to several shoppers he knows.

"It's not fair if you're not responsible for the accident," says an older woman with red hair.

She lets me go ahead of her in line. She is shopping for a family; I am temporarily winged by thirst, hemmed in by the fleeing minutes. She does not know how much I appreciate not having to wait. Outside there is nowhere to sit down and the only shade is by the wall of the market, so I drink standing up. This part of town consists of very simple homes with small yards and no sign of air conditioning. It is the first day of August and the temperature is already at 100°—eventually it will go seven degrees beyond that. It might as well be some Peruvian coastal town. I automatically switch to the shady side of the street. I dodge inside a combination bait shop and bar. After the white glare outside it is a blue cave of darkness and tobacco smoke. A bunch of young fellows are sitting at the bar. It is midday on a weekday. Things must be slow.

"Where you going?" someone asks.

Like a traveling salesman, I give my snappy pitch.

"Shit, I couldn't even run down the block," someone says. The laughter is friendly, the reception friendly if a bit bewildered and their information is depressing.

"No water 'tween here and Rio Vista," one man says. "Nope, nor gas stations. Nothing out there. No water no place."

It's twenty lonely miles to Rio Vista and the hottest part of the day is yet to come. Whatever clouds there were in the world have gone astray, but I can't quit after twenty-odd miles on the second day. It's ridiculous to give in just because I don't know how I'll manage it. Luckily, I have one of those last-minute purchases that turned out to be a godsend. It was a combination mouth-inflatable air pillow and one-gallon water tote bag. It could also be hung from a tree branch and used as a portable shower! Now that it was close to full, it weighed at least six pounds and simply would not fit in the pack. Nor could

I run with that kind of extra burden without dramatically increasing my need for water. So I have to set off walking, shifting the tote bag occasionally from hand to hand as I tramp along. And the pack tugs in a different fashion walking rather than running. Very slowly the world begins to drift past again and I am underway, thinking bitterly that I will not see Rio Vista before nine or ten o'clock that night.

Traffic is fearsome. Lots of campers and cars pulling boats streak past. Grit and dust lash my skin from the air blast every time the trucks pass; my hat flies off my head. Some people yell at me, obscenities that the howling wind of their speed blurs into unintelligibility. Only the insulting, abrasive tone remains like a slap in the face. Nor do I react much better than they behave—I curse and indulge in insulting hand and arm gestures. I can't believe how little I have to think about. In the distance, farm trucks cut their way hither and yon over the distant sunbaked roads, raising plumes of dust that linger and only slowly dissipate into the trembling immensity of the sky, itself as hot as an open gas oven.

To the left is Travis Air Force Base. Slowly the condominiums and ranch houses plunked down by the hundreds in spanking new grids disappear and my view of the base is unobstructed. Immense bombers, perhaps B-52s, rise silently off the runways, levitating slowly like monstrous helium-filled creations through the shimmering air. They seem to rise through my skull. When the planes bank, the fuselages blaze. Only once in a great while does the thunder of their engines become audible. The pantomime show might have been made by a savage-humored dwarf. I am running on pigmy legs myself, unable to get very far on this deadly horizon. I drink and mumble aloud, curse and walk, dodge the trucks' air blasts, worry over so much walking, give up and then expect it to get easier. It still doesn't. A man in a world without water.

Several hours of this go by and then I spot a cyclist ahead of me, pushing a bike east. I run over to his side of the road. He is dressed in straggly fashion and when he turns toward me his face is puffy and indecisive, shifting and uncentered, but he is a human being and I am warm in my greeting.

"Where you from?"

"Queens," he says. He seems to take it for granted that I am here, a tall Martian who's just checking out the planet. He doesn't realize what a miracle our meeting is, but I don't mind. His story is simple. Living on the West Coast for a while, he is on a trip down the coast, but he has leg troubles. He, too, is low on water, but eventually we reach the California Railway Museum, where locomotives are caged behind wire fencing like zebras. The place is closed and signs warn against trespassing, but survival takes precedence over bureaucracy. A dog barks nearby as we turn on an outside tap and gorge on water. God knows when the next relief is coming. We say farewell, he rides on and I begin to run again, not minding the frequent swells of hills. Trucks swarm down the road; they carry milk, crushed rock, fruit and oil. As cars approach, the motorists have their sun visors down and they have trouble seeing me. I calculate a half pint of water for every two miles; it is way too little, but having a plan helps counter the physical pressure of a thirsty mouth. My feet ache and my lips are sunblistered, but I will make it now.

Around eight in the evening I trundle into Rio Vista, which is baking away in the blue dusk. It is a clean and pretty town, tropical looking. At the Striper restaurant, marked outside by a red neon sign showing an open-mouthed fish jumping, I fight down my nausea over fried foods and pick at a pork chop. A middle-aged man in shirt sleeves plays the bartender a dice game for small change and drinks. A big mounted fish hangs over the bar: under it is the notation, "61 lbs., 8 oz., caught by Joe Papetti." There is also a small sign: "I'm not a fast bartender. I'm not a slow bartender. I'm a half-fast bartender."

Out on the street two young girls walk side by side, one of whom is particularly pretty. She is barefoot, has smooth, pretty skin, blond hair and wears short blue-jean shorts. Under her white ribbed T-shirt she is braless. There is a sweet look about her; she and her friend are perhaps seventeen. She holds a drink with a soda straw projecting out. The two girls brush defiantly past a group of blond teen-age boys who are hanging out in front of a couple of cars. No word is exchanged. A little beyond is another local boy standing in the shadows by himself.

"Hello," she says, a friendly lilt in her voice.

"Hello."

"You from here?" she asks. She says it kiddingly.

"Unfortunately."

"I can understand that," she answers.

The night is blue and still. In my hotel room I shut out the lights and lie down naked on the bed. Even a single sheet for covering would be oppressive on a night like this. I feel as fresh and crackling from the California stove as a newly made baked potato. I have covered thirty-six miles today; eighty-three altogether. It is comical how much effort it is taking. Ah, well.

The next day the transitions are easier. My attitude brightens. I leave early after dining in my hotel room on warm apple juice and a partially rotten cantaloupe. Just on the edge of Rio Vista is the Sac River, the first real one that I get to cross. It is a pretty, flat, calm piece of water that even in the early morning is a very bright blue. I am running just north of the San Pablo Bay and the entire day's run will take me over the flat marshes and snaking cuts of water that divide up this hot stretch of country. Rio Vista's elevation is nine feet and I can expect more of the same for hours to come. The only relief from the sun will be when I reach the Sierra Nevada mountains. It is possible to just begin to think that the day after tomorrow I will almost be there. It is not a thought I can cling to, but the flavor of hopefulness makes me behave with more common sense. Now instead of waiting to be battered by events, I am trying to anticipate things. Sunscreen goes on first thing in the morning to reduce the potency of the sun's rays. I have just escaped getting badly burned. The white zinc oxide ointment, although it gives me a clownishly gleaming lower lip, prevents the already blistered flesh from getting any worse.

Now when pebbles get in my shoes, I stop and remove them immediately.

Such maneuvers might seem so obvious as to defy any rationally apparent reason for picking them out as noteworthy. The sad truth is that long-distance running encourages a certain pigheadedness. The perpetual talk endemic to the breed about injuries and troubles with joints, stomachs and bowel movements is a mere surface hypochondria (your body is your only means of expression in running), while any variation for the worse speaks as loudly as it does to any athlete or dancer, which is to say louder than to many people who merely inhabit their bodies in a vague fashion and hope for the best for fifty years until it gives out. But the attentiveness of the runner is toward wringing performance out of the body in spite of the ailments, creaks and strains. A certain breezy stoicism is standard.

In my own circle of running friends, we all take turns criticizing each other's abuse of the limits. So out of such a context, the notion of stopping in a race merely because your feet are blistered or a knee hurts is not easy to address. It's tough not only because runners are needy folk seeking to measure themselves in races but also because the habit and the attitude needed to persevere in tests of endurance use all the delaying psychological techniques that getting through discomfort teaches you. "Well, just a little longer and *then* we'll take care of it," is the basic ploy. But now I am *not* racing anyone. It is not just running my heart out for a few hours and then repairing the damage by resting for a week if need be. I am not only going to be running for the next few hours but all day, for many hours. And then I have to get up tomorrow. I can't afford the luxury anymore of getting a new crop of minor ailments. Not only are some unavoidable no matter what I do, but suppose they become worse? It's not like missing a few days of training at home where the loss is only thirty miles out of my total mileage; out here it's a hundred and thirty miles or so— *half* a state, for God's sake—that I could lose. Or the run might be over if I step in a pothole and get a bad strain. This entire venture depends on staying healthy. Ted Corbitt's lugubrious assessment of why some transcon attempts never succeeded repeats itself at frequent intervals as if my mind is a radio station pausing for frequent repetitions of a public service announcement: "They go off too fast, get too excited and then they hit the mountains. They get leg problems." It conjures up images of stark-faced runners stumping along steep mountain roads until at last, their project and hopes in vain, they slink back to their points of origin. How terrible it seems not to finish. The past failures gleam in the distance like plane wrecks on the mountainside. I am only the latest in a line of aspirants and as yet, a mere bush-grabber at the base. I am not even a one-stater yet, so I cannot gloat over how others crumbled. Greed for results and misjudgments of pace and distance are always harder to spot in yourself than in others. I cannot afford pride so I trot like some philosophical Aesopian ass down the California roadways, sorry not to cut a handsome running figure, but hoping that this humble pilgrim's gait will carry me all the way home.

The land now is flatter than a dinner plate. The crops grow in precise rows at a ground level a few feet below the road, which runs above like a levee. Here in the San Joaquin Valley there is an ever-present smog on the horizon, sometimes pinkish, sometimes bluish gray. Sheep grazing in hay stubble look up placidly. Something about their long jaws and that look, at once imbecilic and profound, is reminiscent of ancient Greece.

I don't look around much. I am inhaling the present moment with closer attention now, not minding the slog-along gait. Although my shoulders and neck are stiff and sore, it doesn't really matter. As the sun rises, sweat streams from every pore, beading on my eyelashes and then dripping down off my nose and chin, falling between my legs with bright flashes down onto the roadway pavement that mutely swims past beneath. My shadow travels off at an angle to the left. It must be my own because I recognize my shape in it. There are no shop windows to glance in anymore on this kind of running and the dark grotesque that is my own is the closest I can come to seeing what I must seem like, but self-flattery is not helpful these days. My problem has only one answer: speed. I hope earnestly that the worst panic is over and that only work will hold my attention. Hour after hour I become an aching but reliable steam engine. A minute equals a tenth mile. I think of saving a penny for every tenth mile. I need to save for a long while to grow rich enough to retire.

I accomplish great things and run five and a half miles without stopping. This takes me to the end of Bouldin Island. At the river channel is a kind of fancy parking garage for fancy boats. Nearby is a coffee shop. I order a few glasses of milk from the waitress and knock them back quickly like a serious drinker knocks back shot glasses of whiskey.

A state trooper is sitting near me on one of the counter stools. He has black hair brushed straight back, big brown hands and the manner of a rural person. He is in the middle of a story.

"Those hippies from San Francisco were back out here," he is saying to the waitress. She might be nineteen. "You know those two from before, *that* kind!"

"Yeah," says the waitress.

"Well, they looked like they couldn't wait to do it together, those two guys!" They both giggle. The trooper is angling to hit it off with this charmer and he is chewing up lots of people, hooking his words into fragments of people, drawing them up bloody and grotesque out of the conversational pool. They both sneer at the easy prey and pitch the remains back. The talk seems on the edge of indiscretion between an older man and a young woman, especially the way they use the behavior of others to raise the whole unspoken issue of sex between themselves. You could hear doors slamming and see the corners of curtains lifted inside their small minds. But then in atonement for finding them so distasteful and as a kind of challenge, too, to see if he will treat me, a stranger, rudely, I ask the trooper directions. He is cold and I realize suddenly that way deep down he is frightened. I leave a small tip and once out the door, sigh with relief. Not only the good but the bad gets left behind when you travel.

The drawbridge lowers itself down as a sailboat with a furled mast purrs serenely past. I start up just before the backed-up line of cars do, trying in a mildly competitive way to beat them. A moment later I lose to the superior power of engines and the cars stream past and vanish. I run on anyway until an hour later I reach Terminous, population fifty, elevation nine feet.

At the Tower Park marina lots of blond young men in cut-off pants stand around exposing their husky barrel-chested bodies to the sun. Their girlfriends are silent while the boys horse around. The young women placidly apply suntan lotion, but their motions are at best only languidly narcissistic. They are all on vacation and have probably been up late the night before. I maintain my confidence sitting at a nearby picnic table by feeling like a grubby road hog. I pride myself on my offhanded macho to counterbalance the threat of other men and the reminder at seeing other women that I am without one myself. They discuss water skiing and since I have no private life of my own anymore, I eavesdrop as I sit there pretending only to be swilling orange juice. Dozens of boats are about, their ridged plastic hulls as fat and brightly colored as Caribbean fish.

One pretty nymphet wearing terry-cloth shorts and a brief halter top is talking to two of her friends. She has a genuine teen-age pout on her face, but her lacquered nails and the slim quick motions of her arms make her as graceful as a swamp heron. All the same, I console myself, she may be impossible to live with in twenty years.

"It'd *kill* me to walk all the way back there," she says, wherever "back there" was. A grim smile twitched up about the corners of my mouth. They and I did not live in the same world. That was okay, but it reminded me I had business afoot.

The rest of the morning I run past plantings of asparagus, some of which had been left to grow into unchecked fuzzy exuberance so it could go to seed. As I near Interstate 5, the distant trucks rolling north and south look like children's toys. The wheels of the trucks beneath their underbodies are seen against a backdrop of open sky that adds to the unreality of their scale. The flatness and breadth of the landscape, new to my eastern vision, make such a view uncanny—things so easily seen from afar take a long time to approach.

I push on toward the town of Lodi and the three hours of running required to get me there bring a special reward, for as I go beneath a railroad underpass I can see at last the faint blue of the Sierra Nevada mountains to the east, straight ahead. The mountains offer the blessed prospect of cooler weather. The temperature is around 98 degrees. At least I am in a county filled with peach groves. Big trees by the side of the road afford lovely regular pockets of shade. The things that give pleasure in this new life . . . The small, tightly prosperous homes are frequent now and it is not easy to find a secluded spot to take a piss.

Finally I reach Route 88, the road that will lead up into the mountains. From having studied the map, even the names of the towns had looked more interesting and, it seemed, why I don't really know, the part where the trip really began. So I glow with satisfaction at getting here, even though the "here" is about to be replaced shortly. Well, I may have expected great things from getting onto 88, but the terrain is much the same. Transitions are earned slowly in this business and I am still running past groves of fruit trees with the blackish soil furrowed up for irrigation channels. The farm work is immaculate and the tire tracks of the tractors and cultivators swirl neatly around the end of each row.

At Clements I stop in a fairly posh air-conditioned restaurant. I walk in with a touch of defiance at looking the way I do, but two of the waitresses quiz me in the friendliest way. I bask in their admiration. I can see them telling some of the other help, and quick, appraising looks from the other customers as they are served show that they, too, get the word on the star attraction. I pretend not to notice. A man going out with his wife stops and shakes my hand.

"I just do four or five miles a day," he says. "Nothing like you."

Funny how so many people deprecate their own abilities. I'm not quite able to submerge myself in the praise; I feel too sorely mortal to feel very sure about much. What have I proven yet?

Don Choi is coming out tonight after he gets off work from his mail route in San Francisco to meet me on the road; he will be my handler tomorrow. I have at least gotten somewhere decently far away so that his trip will be more interesting for him. What if I had done only ninety miles in three days? I have not shamed myself so far.

As the sun goes down, the field grass on the rolling hills burns brightly. Traffic dies away. It is the world's hour for home, supper and rest. I have this open stretch of country to myself. The barbed-wire fence makes a sharp line against the sky and the infrequent groups of trees, two or three at a time, are black against the orange horizon. The furnace of heat empties out and I am left with a feeling that I am a curl of unbroken white ash, consumed by the day's effort, at peace finally with my work in life. Once in a while there is a bird calling. The long white stripe looks fine against the belly of the road as it rises, subsides and rises against the curling hills. It is pure roadway, good roadway, leading on through this crystal region. I don't have to get anywhere for a while it seems; I can be content padding along, letting the night arrive as it pleases. There's no clock anymore; just the gray velvet blur of dusk and the scurrying of field mice from underfoot. It is nice to see them as if I'm running back home by the Hudson River at the same hour, startling the rats off the path into the dry weeds. Once in a while car lights flash like cat's eyes. At dusk an approaching car makes an odd echoing sound, as if the atmosphere were as dense and opaque as a tunnel. It has a domineering, restless quality. There is an afterbite of exhaust, a few turned heads. They are wondering why I am in the middle of nowhere, but I feel less lost than ever, only with the mildest and easiest kind of sadness, more distinct than ever from their own world. They must travel somewhere. I am just going on. Running at night has a special romance, but not when the hour of rendezvous with a friend comes and goes. All the same, the very helplessness of my position made it easy to accept the fact that maybe Don had missed me. I wasn't near any towns or pay phones or houses. I couldn't leave the road because he might shoot past at that very moment, so all I could do was run on and wonder with a detached curiosity if *that* car approaching from behind were the one. A car flicks its high beams and then with its right tail light pulsing ahead in the blackness, pulls off on the shoulder. A familiar figure lopes up and Don and I wrap up in a big hug. We might have been two stray rowboats bumping noses in a fog bank. I mark the end of the day's run by tying a rag to some fence wire. Then we speed off, seeking shelter. For a minute, seeing the pavement spin past has a dizzying effect—the space I intend to cover to New York *can* be covered at high speed. This whole venture is a voluntary condemnation of self to a very slow rhythm. For a moment regret at making myself impure by riding in a vehicle saddens me, but I suppress my guilt and finally relax against the soft cushions.

Don Choi is a phenomenon of sorts, addicted in a high-spirited way to tremendous feats of legwork, which he usually gets through with uninterrupted good humor. Good humor is an inadequate term for a man who is really a laugher. Bursts of laughter punctuate his sentences as frequently as commas are sprinkled through other people's sentences. Conjurings with fantastical imaginings will set him off as will his appreciative sense for the zany—he is capable of one of those mutual cacklings with a friend that start on some innocuous conversational step and then race round the circular staircase until collapsing on the top level of uncontrollable laughing that becomes its own regenerative sense of amusement long after the original joke or twist has been forgotten. His long, mobile face is framed by an immense swatch of straight black hair. He is of average height and although on the slight side, his legs and

arms look supple, not prone to the somewhat stringy delinea-
tion of some of his peers. Under the gaiety is an emotional,
sometimes deeply serious side that I glimpsed in looking at
photographs taken during the finale of a six-day running race
held later that summer in New Jersey. At the end, the battered
knot of runners, who survived ankle-deep cinders, clammy August weather and 144 hours of on-again, off-again walking and
running, were thoroughly exhausted. Don's face, partially hidden by his hand and by someone else's shoulder, was ripped by
weeping. For a while I used to think that, in a way, running
was a child's game, but not now. Anything that cuts this deep
is not a game for children. Hanging on beyond ordinary reason,
ordinary comfort and ordinary standards makes it something
no child would ever do.

We camp out at Comanche Lake where the sharp prattle of
children and rock music pierces the air and makes sleep hard
to slip into. The tent is so small I feel like a grasshopper in a
snuff box two sizes too small. Don's breathing, bless his luck,
is soft and regular. I cannot even turn on my side because my
hips are too sore to bear the pressure. The foam pad that I
hacked down to this tiny square with misguided zealotry is
inadequate protection against twigs and stones. How could I
have ever conceived of camping out? I have not bathed, written up the day's notes or had a hot meal. I want a bed to sleep
in. Once I decide that this is the last night of the trip I will
camp out, the resultant peacefulness of mind allows me a
semblance of decent rest.

Loving as he is to come all the way out on his day off, Don
still arouses my technical ire. He is cheerfully disorganized and
somehow as he drives us out of camp, we get lost. The morning's run begins at 8:30 A.M. The day before I was five miles
farther along at that hour in the cooler part of the morning.
On the other hand, we start late because I wake Don late
because I need to write my notes because I have a book contract due and if I miss doing my daily notes just because I'm
tired then there'll always be an excuse. I steam for a while

about my editor in New York, about Don, about this person and that person. The irritation is just hen scratching in the dust, but two things are clear: dependency on others has its burdens and for the duration of this trip, anyway, I am a raging perfectionist. I can be sloppy enough about other things people consider important, but not about this run.

The day goes quickly since the changes are rapid and dramatic. Soon after crossing into San Joaquin County, the land changes abruptly. Low shrubs appear on the hard-packed soil that is a variegated blend of white and red. It is easy to imagine cowboys riding through the hilly terrain. A wooden trestle railroad bridge seems older and more "western" as well. The town of Jackson comes later in the day. It is set down in a smallish valley and Route 88 does a sharp dogleg left up toward Pine Grove. Beyond town the forested hills really begin and although the trees throw long shadows, it is still smotheringly hot. Pine Grove is a small town settled in the 1850s and the references to the bygone days of the gold rush survive in the names of housing developments. Odd and sad. The hills keep coming and we go through Pioneer on up the road until the day's run ends at a lodge in the middle of a steep and forested mountainside.

Don is a guardian angel of the first rank. He drives up about two miles at a time, runs back with a water bottle in one hand, a mist spray bottle in the other. I stop for a few steps to drink, hand the bottle back and then he runs tight circles around me as I stamp doggedly on, spraying the icy water over my bare skin in a fine mist. I feel like an insect being zapped by an aerosol can. I notice Don more carefully; he has wide shoulders and a crinkled nub of scar tissue high on his right shoulder blade from a biking accident. His skin is very brown. Somehow road life sharpens the impressions people make; details of speech and appearance cut more deeply.

Since breakfast was minimal and I feel weak because of several days of eating poorly, Don feeds me a little at a time —a few peanuts, a little fruit. He remembers in a vague way how he ran a fifty-mile race over some of that same stretch of road a few years before; funny how important the races seem at the time and how quickly they blur. I can't imagine forgetting a single moment of this transcon, but I shall forget much.

Don applies pressure in his polite but iron style. My own way is to baby myself along with frequent little breaks and ditherings over food and maps. Now my excuses for stopping are stripped away and even a lunch break is diplomatically postponed. Beneath this easy demeanor is his own version of relentlessness. I am tired a lot of the day so I look to see him coming, his tiny figure loping in that familiar easy style. When he runs up he always begins by saying: "Okay."

He is really thrilled about the scope of the transcon. It appeals to the artist in him; the scale stirs him the way a painter of immense landscapes would feel at seeing a respected peer sketch in the opening lines. There are only two or three people who *really* know what I am doing. Don's praise for me is unstinting, but it is special coming from an equal. I don't feel that our kind of obsession makes us special, but it is itself special in the sense of not being easily met. We are not twins, however, so I can learn from his own attitudes. In a Cantonese restaurant the week before I was waxing on at great length about specific body maneuvers I use to relax and lengthen muscles, how to align organ groups, how I breathe, and so on with a good many et ceteras. Don laughed finally and said, "I just try to relax." It wasn't a put-down and I didn't feel I had to snap shut my case of snake oils and slink off, but it did remind me of the danger of getting too verbal, too fussy. And I knew I had been trying to sound impressive.

Don is stimulated by the transcon to talk of what he might try to do next. Apart from his interest in long-distance speed skating, long-distance ski racing and ultra bike racing, he wants to do a few things in running, such as a nonstop from Death Valley to the peak of Mt. Whitney, a good hundred and seventy miles. There is race around Lake Tahoe every year, seventy-two miles long. A different approach would be to run around the lake five times in as many consecutive days with the fifth day being the actual race. And if he runs across America he would like to do a double.

"Imagine how that would blow people's minds," he said, "if you get to New York and then just turn around and head back again. I don't like the word 'ultimate.' People are always saying this thing or that is the end point. I like to show what you can really do."

At the end of the day we eat at a roadside place whose interior is decorated with police sew-on badges from all over the country. We order Texas jailhouse chili. One forkful and my raw lips feel like a midday pavement. Luckily, Don is a relentless eater. He says one last thing, that the route would have a certain aura for him because of my running over it.

"Someday I want to finish off this section on 88, starting from where you began at Dillon Beach. I want to really appreciate what you've done."

We exchange farewells and then he is gone. It seems more real to be alone than to have company. I go to sleep surrounded by pine forest. Already life in the flatlands is behind me. Somehow the trip has rounded the first real curve, because when I look around now I am no longer reminded of where I began.

Mountain running was supposed to be the worst. Everyone had warned me how tough it would be, not because they had run over mountains themselves, but because running uphill, everyone knows, is harder than running on flats or downhill. In my innocence, I thought the same way. In fact, running uphill now and over every range I pass for the next three thousand miles will be the easiest part of the trip. The horizon is much closer in the mountains. Switchbacks in the roads, the incessant curves and flattenings and new rises in the roadway constantly change the angle of one's relationship with rocks and shadows, sunlight and trees, as well as the skyline of far-off snow-capped mountains. Mountain sky is unusually blue, just as it was when Kit Carson wrote about it in these same hills a hundred years earlier on a cold winter morning. It is midsummer now, but the thin air gives the sky an extra vibrant richness. And apart from all this stimulation, there is a sense of achievement. For every thousand feet of climb there is a new elevation marker. Up, up, up, I urge myself, not caring for the why of it, but finding within an anticipatory sorrow that I cannot run through here forever.

Mountainside meadows are alive with wildflowers—some have light violet blossoms; others as yellow as corn. The rest are soft blue. Sometimes horses graze among the wild grass, a green whose purity and intensity matches the sky's. It seems especially poignant in light of the brief season between snows.

Car and truck traffic is heavy, but now comes a new phenomenon—transcon cyclists. I meet a father and son from New Hampshire. They are twenty-four days into their trip. They report on weather conditions in Nevada and Utah. We speak the same language. We know what weather means.

The stretches between water are very long and I am pushed to heavy feats of concentration to ignore my thirst. When I finally reach Silver Lake thirty miles out from where I began, I am too blasted from dehydration to feel much emotion. I meet two couples down by the water's edge. They are very quiet and I feel quiet, too. What bliss to wade slowly into the cool water and wash off the grime. The couples watch as I prepare to leave, absorbed in my now-familiar routine, swabbing on sunscreen, smearing on zinc oxide, shaking out shoes, dousing head and cap with ice water, cleaning sunglasses. I move with the intensity of a surgeon.

The mountains and I climb up toward Carson Spur. I run for twenty or thirty minutes and walk about five. There is deep quiet in the pines. I yearn to lie on my back and listen to the wind and the mountain streams. At Caples Lake, named for a pioneer who stopped on his way to the gold fields and later returned to open up a traveler's stop, there is a place to stay for the night, but to quit at thirty-seven miles! On! Throw it all away.

Up near the top of the spur off to one side is a gray stone

shaft, four sided, broken off at the top. With a wry disdain I muse on how poorly California maintains its monuments and at the depravity of vandals. When I reach the marker I read the sign and then understanding breaks out. The memorial is in honor of John Tostensen, also known as Snowshoe Thompson.

> There ought to be a shaft raised to Snowshoe Thompson; not of marble; not carved and not planted in the valley, but a rough shaft of basalt or of granite, massive and tall, with top ending roughly, as if broken short, to represent a life which was strong and true to the last. And this should be upreared on the summit of the mountains over which the strong man wandered so many years, as an emblem of that life which was worn out apparently without an object. . . .

On a nearby tree a sign says "Carson Emigrant Trail" and if I remember correctly, on another tree is a replica of the initials Carson himself carved in a tree trunk.

A little farther down the road is a small grave made of heaped-up rocks. A sign at the base near where the feet should be reads: "Maiden's Grave/Historical Landmark No. 28." The stone marker at the head says: "Rachel Melton Died Oct. 4, 1850/Native of Iowa/Erected by guests at Kirkwood 1908." On the ground is a broken-off piece of styrofoam with the following inscription in childish handwriting: "Shannon Brownie and Colette Jones cleaned up the grave."

It is quiet at seventy-eight hundred feet. I sit down on a ledge looking out over a tumbled wildness of stone, rock ridges and pines. On some far-off mountains is unmelted snow.

I run on for another six hours. On a steep two-mile rocket-ship downhill the high bluff faces of rock on the left are exposed through all the centuries of strata. The sun dips behind the clifftop, but illuminates the top part of the hills on the right. At such a height one practically emerges off the mountain into space; the vast scale is immensely tranquil. I fill my water bottle from an icy mountain stream.

At Hope Valley only grazing cattle and a few houses break the solitude. Past Picketts Junction down the hill to the lodge where I come to rest for the night is fifty-one miles for the day. It is cold up here at six thousand feet when it gets dark, especially after the furnace of central California. This is my last full day in California. Two hundred and sixteen miles lie behind me.

The woman who rents me my cabin is a bit cool at first, then gradually warms as we talk. For a change I do not announce what I am doing until she asks and then when I tell her, she says: "I was *afraid* you were going to say that."

For four hours I chase sleep. The altitude has my head buzzing and my legs and hips hum with soreness. The pain is searing. Now that I am loosening up emotionally, my body is unable to let go. It's like getting eye drops that dilate the pupil; for hours afterward the eye remains black and staring, even in the dark.

The next morning is bright and sunny. There are twelve and a half miles of downhill running to reach the Nevada state line. Coming out of the mountains on this side, the rock faces are drier, sandier, yellower. The sun floods across the road, uninterrupted by trees. California is dying out. License plates say Utah, Nevada, Oregon. The last town, Woodfords, seems hardly more than a single blinking yellow light suspended from a drooping cable at an intersection.

My handlers from New York meet me, tooting the horn of the rented Toyota. There was hardly time to consider the significance of the change. There are pictures we take of each other at the state line, but really the anticipation was better than what I feel now. Getting here still leaves ever more. So when I run on into Nevada I think, well, if I die now, at least I will have run through *one* state. Shortly after, I work myself into a violent depression. I had expected something to happen just because I ran so far and did so well. Like the running is supposed to get easier and I'm supposed to be immune to bad feelings for ever afterward. Maybe I think I'm running into happiness, running to some spot in the future of my life where

I will always be happy. Not that I think so at such a grossly naïve level, but that in a subtle, permeating way I think achievement means happiness. Further, it sinks in even more deeply that no one can do it for me. I feel more alone with friends around me than I did before. I could almost hate them for being here. As usual, there is nothing to do but feel bad and just run on. The only alternative is to stop.

Okay, I think, okay. I'm not sure if anything's okay anymore at 11 A.M. in Nevada with 2,750 miles to go, but I go on anyway.

Carrying Weight
and Living Light

In some ways the first few days were the most difficult if for
no other reason than the weight that I carried on my back
transformed me from a runner into a species of human donkey.
I had run with a pack many times before. Years earlier I had
started commuting to a job in Cambridge, Massachusetts, with
a day pack and continued doing so at various jobs in New York
City. I became a shameless quick change artist, a kind of Clark
Kent of the roadways, dodging behind potted plants in the
front of buildings or into shadowy doorways to slip into or out
of my pants. It could be more than a little embarrassing in
pre-runner-infested days. At first, unzipping my pants and un-
buttoning my shirt for no apparent reason passers-by could
discern was not an easy process to commence with a cool heart
on busy midtown streets. While employed at an office at Park
Avenue and Forty-seventh Street, I was for a few months too
bashful to feel like reporting for work in my shorts (although
that came). I would change out in front of the building where
the wide plaza offered a kind of spiritual anonymity. A friend
told me later he saw a woman nearly die because of me. She
had stopped, frozen, in the middle of the Park Avenue intersection, mesmerized by the sight of my disrobing. She failed to
notice the light had changed. A cavalcade of taxis just missed
trampling her. I simply shut it all out, concentrating so

thoroughly on dressing up or down that eventually I achieved a kind of serenity only partially dimmed by the fear that someday someone was going to call the police.

But the loads I carried were relatively light—pants, shirt, sweater, a bag lunch. Sometimes returning from baking class at night school in Brooklyn and later, from a chef's job at a French restaurant in the same borough, I would ply my way homeward with heavy containers of leftover kasha, potato salad, breads, and if I were lucky, dense slices of coulibiac. Sometimes greed would incite me to a five- or six-pound load, but for a handful of miles, what kind of burden was that?

On long training runs with Richie Langsam or Richie Innamorato, we would often set out from my West Side apartment with a good deal of friendly bickering about who was carrying how much weight because one or two of us would usually go without a pack and his brother of the roadways would have to carry an extra change of clothing for four or five hours. Innamorato was inordinately fond of hip or fanny packs —a kind which is held in place by a belt around the waist. Innamorato, a veteran of a Maine-to-Florida solo run, would stuff his pack with what seemed to be an absurd amount of clothing and minor goodies. I found such weight too heavy for my thinner legs and would remind Richie forcefully that only his immense bulk allowed him to carry such stuff.

Not until later in the transcon did I remember his incredibly slow opening shuffle at the start of such runs, the peculiarly fascinated yet practical way he had of looking at road maps, something both dreamy and sharp-eyed at once and as different from the way you or I would look at a map as a landsman is from a tar when they pluck up a nautical chart. Innamorato talked about the road differently from the rest of us, elaborating on the specific locations of fast-food joints, restaurants and grocery stores along Route 9 as if they represented the true spiritual landmarks of the course. But what he really displayed in all this was perhaps characteristic not so much of himself as of the road hog experience. I, too, developed the shuffle, learned to pull a map out of my pack and dream over its potentialities while wringing from it hard-nosed clues as to survival. At one level, crossing the United States was a tour devoted to nothing more than ascertaining the location of convenient stops for food, water and shelter.

I knew the matter of weight would be critical. I made a schematic drawing of the contents I wanted in my day pack with a column to the right of the aforesaid items showing weight in pounds and ounces. Actually, for years I had been fascinated by the idea of ultralightweight camping gear and the impending run simply honed my interest to a finer edge. It wasn't so much the fascination of the gear and gadgets themselves. My older brother, Tom, is a magnificent example of that kind of obsession. We would sometimes discuss various items to be found in the REI, Early Winters or EMS catalogs. His tone was filled with the raptures of a devotee of technology for its own sake. What fascinated me was the minimal weight, the minimal bulk, the very lack of presence because underneath was the one captivating theme—how close can you live to the bone's edge on a long trek, how completely self-sufficient can one be with a handful of pounds?

It was not just the attraction of traveling light only to see if it could be done—my soul was not lit by a passion over technique. The motivation flowed from a deep source, one tangled over and hidden in part from my own understanding even now. Although I am no contemplative who has completely severed his ties with the world of possessions and attachments, perhaps I can say that apart from my books and a pile of running shoes in my apartment as big as a heap of firewood I am not owned by what I own. It was important for a long time to sleep on the floor with as little as possible—sometimes just a sheepskin and a blanket. The closer to the floor, to true surface, the less dependency on anything outside of myself. It has a bracing effect. I am not a fanatic who never sleeps in beds and eats only handfuls of brown rice—I relish comfort as keenly as anyone. But the theme of endurance on the barest terms has always held an inexplicable fascination. Little stories resonate for years. A *National Geographic* article about Tibet, I think, mentioned a man encountered in the marketplace who slept outdoors without blankets on even the coldest nights. There was the study done on Scandinavian lumberjacks who adapted to sleeping on cold nights with less and less covering. Tarahumara Indians walk about with bare legs and feet in frosty weather—although a young Indian boy I asked about it said his people felt the cold the way others did. Clearly, they endured cold from the necessity of poverty. There was a story a mountaineering friend had about Reinhold Messner, the great solo Alpine climber. Supposedly, Messner was able, through some type of Yoga exercises, to lower his metabolic rate and breathing so that he could outlast a storm on a mountainside while holed up in a snow cave. Alexandra David-Neel, a French woman who traveled in the Himalayas in the early part of this century, told of undergoing the trial that Tibetan Buddhist monks endured—draping one's naked body in wet sheets on icy, windy nights and then summoning up powerful channels of heat by reciting a special mantra.

Such stories inflamed my admiration and desire to do likewise. Here was a chance to test my own capacity for adapting to whatever rigors the world might offer. If I could break from ties with motels I could live closer to the kind of experience I was seeking, living as close as possible to the land I would be crossing, as well as saving money. Such a slow crossing, plus the expense of paying a handler's air fare, car rental, gas, food for two, et cetera, meant the run would cost thousands of dollars.

Now I was determined to be realistic about such a thing. I would need a bath sometimes—I did not fancy sponge baths in grimy gas-station bathrooms. But surely there would be times when an open field under the vast dark sky would be a great comfort to lie down in. Maybe one night out of three, or two nights out of three. This whole theme turned out to be a vast miscalculation. Innamorato was skeptical from the start. I secretly dismissed his objections, feeling he was too tied to creature comforts. Not knowing, of course, what was to come, I continued to study the catalogs for a solution to the problem of shelter. The issue was weight. I could not conceive of carrying anything over eight pounds at the maximum. Commercially made sleeping bags generally weigh several pounds. I needed something better than that.

During my search for the perfect pack, I remembered a small storefront in Manhattan's SoHo district. Streets in New York change character in a handful of yards. This section of Spring Street is a darker, bleaker piece. The old cast-iron buildings show more of an as-yet-unredeemed bleary commercial character that dominated these work-stained streets not so very long ago, before the nearby influx of the fashionably offbeat. So you dodge into the shop as a kind of cozy nest. The name, Down East, conjures up pine forests and cold winters, a sense of genuineness and honest craft. Well, I smelled no pine needles and the place was well heated, but the qualities of workmanship turned out to be as substantial as I imagined. Behind the counter were work tables, a sewing machine and shelves filled with rolls of material, blues and greens, practical khakis and olives. Hanging from pegs were an assortment, in sharp nylon pastels, of day packs, purse-type bags with skinny shoulder straps, parkas, sleeping bags—the whole tumble-up conjuring of sewn camping goods that a needle could devise.

"Can I help you?" asked Leon Greenman, the owner. He was a short man with glasses and a hint of acerbity in his tone. I did not feel rushed, but I sensed he was a professional in his craft and not a great explainer. Or not at that hour of the afternoon after going through a concentrated fifteen minutes of exchange of opinion with a difficult customer. I was next. I knew with an internal calculation that if I presented the problems and demands of the transcon run, he would give me his best attention.

I explained I was looking for a superlightweight sleeping bag and a custom-made day pack.

Greenman's eyes sharpened and he stood more easily as he

became grounded in the problems I laid out. No exclamations of admiration for my physical derring-do escaped his lips— clearly he thought I was setting about this with a potentially loose judgment. But how his sleeping bag and day pack might endure the run—well, it is always easy to lure the pros into enthusiasm.

"I have a man who custom-sews bags for me," Greenman said. "I think he can put any amount of down you want into a sleeping bag."

Greenman explained the technical options in the way the bag would be sewn as they related to the amount of heat it would retain. I nodded sagely. There was one troubling variable neither Greenman or anyone else could answer: How light would be too light? The amount of body heat you lose by the end of a day of running is considerable—a mild autumn night to a householder out for a stroll can be a tooth-rattling experience for a tired runner. And what about the drop in the blue hour around 4 A.M. when the earth turns its coolest and one's own body temperature drops to its lowest as well? And what precisely would be the average temperatures in different states as I crossed them? I didn't know and somehow could never quite get around to finding out. And now Greenman was casting a skeptical eye over my lanky six-foot-two-inch frame and saying:

"You want a one-and-a-half to two-pound bag? Okay, I'll try to see if this guy will do it."

After a phone discussion he returned to the counter, giving me an affirmative nod. Greenman decided to try a 1.1 ounce-per-square-foot weight nylon on the top and a slightly heavier fabric on the bottom. If the top cloth were any lighter it would either rip too easily or the down would bleed through.

For discussion of a day pack, I was introduced to Rosemary, the seamstress, a tall bony woman with a fine quiet face and a long unadorned fall of straight brown hair. Probably in her early thirties, she had a shyness and reserve so palpable it was reminiscent of deep country folk. Her hands were well-formed, large and capable. She was nice about the run and my concerns; she asked a few questions, careful not to be intrusive. She suggested modifying a basic pack design they already had. I chose the wonder material called Goretex, a waterproof but breathable synthetic that they had in pine green. I provided a drawing of what I wanted and a week later the call came: my orders were in.

Back down at the store Greenman shook the sleeping bag out to full length—a handsome 4 P.M. sky blue on top and navy on the bottom. The material caught the light in a sheen that was true to its slippery, silky feel. A small tag from the sewer said: "Top of the World." It was a nice touch, but my general exuberance dimmed at the next remark.

"The weight is two pounds, three ounces," Greenman said.

My face looked somber.

"When he sent it in, he said he couldn't make a bag any lighter than that. He said to tell you that if you want a bag any lighter then you might as well just sew two sheets together. The point is there's so little down—maybe a pound and a half— that if you stretch it any further it just won't keep you warm at all."

I didn't say anything. I have trouble sometimes being up front when I am angry. I expected to get what I paid for, but what if the stubbornness of the custom-bag maker was saving me from my own stubbornness? I was certainly capable of making a mistake. How could I know for sure? Too warm was better than too cold. Perhaps I would be grateful later. But the thrill of thinking I had summoned into existence this ultralight marvel was soured by those extra ounces. Three ounces meant little to anyone else, but for me it represented thousands of miles of extra effort and possibly the difference between having camping gear or not. They were *my* ounces to be responsible for and I felt betrayed. It was my risk. Eventually, the beauty of the bag, its undeniable lightness and my determination to camp out reconciled me to its weight.

Also, the beauty of the day pack made the three ounces

easier to accept. The padded straps promised freedom from chafing. Sometimes my other packs, whose straps are made of black webbing, cut so deeply that they leave my neck raw and scabbed. Side pockets with cover tabs fastened by Velcro strips were to hold cans of soda; the closure flap had a map compartment; two major pockets inside the body of the bag; and a long hidden compartment that would hold the foam pad I had planned to use for stretching and sleeping. It would also cushion the pack's weight on my shoulders and blunt the sharp corners of any protruding toothpaste tubes. Adjustable drawstrings could reduce it to a smaller size. A clip-together chest strap grounded the sides of the pack and reduced its side wobble and any aggravating pull if I hit heavy side winds. A yellow-and-gray reflector tape ran like a distinctive if narrow sash across the back so that motorists would be warned of my presence.

I loved the pack, not only for its convenience and craftsmanship and for being a new thing that I owned, but really I loved it most of all for being completely mine. I mean that it became part of the trip, it made the trip possible, it was the single most important item outside of my own body. It would carry all that I needed. Like a snail I, too, would make my laborious way over the ground, yoked to this single frail protection upon my back. Already I felt anticipatory sorrow at how the indifferent and dirty concrete of a hundred towns would abrade and stain its bottom when I set it down on the ground. One fear plagued me in the midst of this pleasure—would the stitching along the seams hold? I had had seemingly well-made packs disintegrate in mid-run before.

Then came the real test, stuffing it with goodies at home and testing its ridability. I jogged down the street and it was clearly a Rolls-Royce of packs. It had a smooth, well-distributed sense of stress points. It nestled in against my back with just the right balance between firmness and softness. The sleeping bag, which took up a good deal of room, had a comfortable plumpness that dominated the feel of the entire pack even when

loaded with all the items I thought I would need. I was especially pleased by the outside pockets for water bottles and soda
cans. It meant not having to rummage every time I wanted a
drink. Also, the smaller and denser an object, the more difficult
to pack. Packing itself is an entire subart a road hog learns in
order to achieve a fine quality ride.

The two other items needed for shelter were a tent and a
foam pad. Without going into the long by-pass of possibilities,
I ended up choosing a one-pound tent, which was really a
weatherproof shelter sack barely big enough. At the head section, a panel of mosquito netting doubled as door and ventilation port. The tent, manufactured by a Northwest camping
firm, was made of Goretex, so even if I were caught in a
downpour, body heat could still escape, avoiding the build-up
of condensation on the inner walls. The green-and-yellow shelter rolled up into a stuff bag. For a foam pad I just cut up an
old one I had lying around and reduced it to as narrow and
short a rectangle as I dared. Now all those months of sleeping
on the floor would pay off, I thought.

My other major investment was a Goretex running suit. A
number of manufacturers had suddenly burst on the scene with
their versions and I chose one through mail order. A few years
earlier I was entered in the Mechanicsburg, Pa., hundred-
kilometer (62.14 mile) race. It went off on a fickle spring day.
Wet snow, rainstorms, driving wind, bursts of sunshine, all
followed one another in a relentless mélange. I was dressed in
longjohns, a cotton zip-up parka and gardening gloves. The
misery of running in sodden, heavy clothes while getting colder
and dizzier all the time was grueling. I realized for the first time
that a blithe devil-may-care attitude was fine only for shorter
distances. I had forced myself to run in windy eighteen-degree
weather in February with only a singlet, shorts and gloves,
working on the experimental principle that cold was primarily
a psychological phenomenon and that if I imagined myself to
be the thin edge of a knife, I would be able to survive without
warmer apparel. Such runs only lasted four or five miles and

they laid me low with flu two winters in a row. Mechanicsburg then added a new twist—a loathing for the wet and cold that lasted into the following year. I felt during those nine hours or so it took to complete the run that I would never get warm again. The danger of hypothermia in wet, windy weather, even at 35 to 40 degrees when the core body temperature drops and the victim can go into shock and eventual death, is not an unreasonable thing to worry about.

Until the introduction of Goretex a few years ago, rain garments were either waterproof or water repellent. Waterproof garments tended to be heavier sportswear designed for general use, not for running. No water came in, but the condensation build-up on the inside left you soaking anyway. Water-resistant fabrics would hold out against a penetrating rain for only a few minutes. Over a short distance the discomfort of weather doesn't matter; over a stressful long haul, it does.

Then one year I ran up to the start of the annual Yonkers marathon about twelve hilly miles north of Manhattan. I drank one can of soda after getting to the check-in and then set off a few minutes later with the rest of the field. It was a gray, cold morning and when the chilling rains came, I was entering the roller-coaster hills that mark the closing miles. I began to wobble, eventually sank to my knees, and was plucked up by a police car. Shortly after, under warm blankets and the protective wail of a siren, I was taken by ambulance to a nearby hospital. After a couple of hours the constant spasmodic shivering eased and I was released into the world again. That taught me for the second time that it was an absurdity not to run with the proper clothing.

The final proof came the following spring when Innamorato and I set off to attempt a hundred-and-five-mile run. It was one of the rainiest days of the year and we got off to an evening start. My companion wore shorts and a water-resistant nylon shell. By 3 A.M., fifty-five miles upriver deep in the Putnam County hills on a twenty-mile stretch without a single place to get a cup of coffee or get in out of the rain, Innamorato was a trembling mess, threatening to break in the glass of a Burger Hut to get in and get warm if we didn't get help. I found a pay phone and finally managed to convince the local police to come. A sullen policeman drove us to a nearby hospital where we both fell asleep sitting up in a lobby. My Goretex rain suit had left me feeling fine. No more proof was needed.

Now with a newly arrived maroon Goretex rain suit and my new pack, I ran down to a stretch class with my teacher, Gail Stern. I burst into the apartment she shared with her friend, Philip, and in a matter of moments had disgorged the contents of the pack, shaking out the tent and sleeping bag. I popped inside it while Betty, the dog, wagged her tail and looked on eagerly, awaiting an invitation to crawl in as well. Gail and Philip looked down at me as I lay on their kitchen floor. Recalling the scene later, I felt a certain embarrassment wondering if they had really understood. Perhaps I seemed—as I was in part—as infatuated as a child by all the new things I owned, but it wasn't so much giddiness as delight in being free at last. The equipment allowed me to do the solo; it was the final deliverance. The only thing that remained now was to get to California. I knew perfectly well that the seductiveness of this stuff could be a trap. The fanciest garb could not help me. It was will and gritting of teeth, physical hardness, that would make it possible to run forty a day. Okay. But now I could go. I was no longer a prisoner in the city. It was like an open window on the first warm spring day.

So after all this to-do, what did I carry out to the West Coast?—two pint-sized Austrian water bottles; one small Swiss Army knife; an Army issue can opener the size of my thumbnail; toothbrush and toothpaste (small size tube); a one-ounce container of zinc oxide; one bottle of sunscreen lotion; one small size (and almost empty) jar of Vaseline; four pairs of socks; three T-shirts; two running shorts; one singlet top; one bandanna (red); one Goretex jacket and pants; one sleeping bag; one tent; one foam pad; $3,000 worth of traveler's checks; a passport; a pad of paper and pen; envelopes; a California road

map; one log of towns and roads I planned to follow. Probably
there were a few more odds and ends since forgotten. And after
all that fuss, I never did weigh it all, but maybe it came to eight
and a half or nine pounds. It was too much. I slung the pack
on in my apartment, talking out loud to myself.

"Okay, okay," I said. "It's okay."

I didn't really know how it would be. I ran with the pack on
some training runs, but I resented doing it. It was hard work.
I was planning to run myself into deep road shape on the run
and I didn't want to press too much now. I didn't think it
would help. The pack weighed less in New York than it did in
California. In New York it was just a dream; out West the
weight was real. Had I figured it right? Had I chosen right?
Whether I had or hadn't, only the run could answer. The hell
with it, I thought. Too much planning got on my nerves. So
when I stood on the beach and saw how cram-full the pack was,
I no longer cared. It *was* too heavy. I knew that, finally, but
for now, until I got to the Nevada border, I was going to
become a species of human donkey. I was going to ride myself
and whip my flesh as hard as I needed, but I was going to make
it to Nevada! At the border, I thought, with a semi-serious
sarcasm, at the border I can quit. Little did I realize that in
exactly the same tone I would urge myself on toward each of
the following eleven state lines. At the moment all I do is spit
whenever I feel the dig of shoulder straps reminding the man-
turned-donkey that he is bearing weight against the inclination
of the earth.

Goin' Down
the Highway

Interstate 80 is a beautiful thing.

There is a child's game—"Animal, Vegetable or Mineral" —where in twenty questions that require a "yes" or "no" answer, the interlocutor must determine what the object is. I got to spend a thousand miles on I-80 and although I cannot classify it by the rules of the game any less crudely than to call it a "thing," it *is* a beautiful thing. Even after coming off I-80 for the last time at the Nebraska border, I was to run so closely parallel to it that I glimpsed it, if only from afar, in all the other states.

Some people need to hear only a certain strain of music from a beloved piece of Bach to feel a rush of emotion that comes with that intimate friendship. As for me, the sight of rushing cars and trucks on that four-lane highway and the peculiar whine and hiss of the traffic evoke a deep, secret kind of feeling in my heart. Without embarrassment and in perfect tranquillity at the prospect of being misunderstood or of not being understood, I can say that I love I-80. In fact, I adore it. I gave myself up to her too thoroughly ever to recover myself again. I paid a price for every mile I ran over her and in return was borne through the sacred mysteries of the desert and the mountains. Interstate 80 was part of the trip, was the path onto other roads, was the path itself. My truest seasoning as a road fox came in the Far West. After enduring the heat and flatness and altitude and solitude of the desert, the rest of the trip would never be more difficult than that—*as* difficult yes, but never worse. I learned hard lessons out there.

It is with a certain ruefulness that I muse over my state of mind in the early days on I-80, remembering as I say this that each day seemed an immensity in itself, a vast epoch of change and emotion, hell and paradise both, that obliterated the memory of all the previous days. So the three weeks on I-80 were like a multitude of lifetimes. I cannot quite say what this retrospective sorrow is. Perhaps I thought then that because I was struggling so hard I would be rewarded in the closing stages of the trip. I thought I would become a superman, a super ultrarunner. Interstate 80 was a prelude to a physical labor that never grew easier. Perhaps the nostalgia is simply for the youthfulness I had then. I am now on the other side; the run is over and it might never have been. Then it existed and like all parts of one's life that take one to extremity, it may be impossible or wiser not to try to repeat them (which would be impossible even if one wanted), but they will never be forgotten. The very thing that makes them difficult makes one more keenly oneself.

I have to say that I had never particularly heard of I-80 until I made plans for the trip. I have traveled on it before, but as a Greyhound bus passenger freed from the obligation to notice or care what specific route led where. My brother, drawing on his experience out West as a mining geologist, had general suggestions about which parts of which states to travel through, so I had an approximate idea of the route. All the same I thought a visit to the Exxon travel center in mid-Manhattan would be worth a visit. I ran down there one jolly morning in June and waited in line with other motorists. There were a number of men ranged behind a counter, modestly attired in blue blazers. They deftly flipped open crackling fresh maps, smoothed out the starchy lines of the folds, and with the accompanying squeak of magic-marker pens, picked routes around the country for the various petitioners. Soon my turn came and I announced my need.

"What is the shortest possible way, please, to get between San Francisco and New York?"

I was afraid if I suggested I was going to cover it in other than a car my request might seem too frivolous.

"I'm sorry, sir," they might say, "but only motorists might find out such information."

I felt an absurd, but all the same real, guilt at the implicit misrepresentation, but my disguise as a car owner must have been passable, for the request raised no suspicions. In fact, in the friendliest way, the man in the blue blazer spanned the two coasts with a swoop of his orange pen. He needed two maps to do the business and handed them both over.

"I-80 is the most direct way," he said.

Now at home, my own fumbling calculations had come up with a thirty-four-hundred-mile course. The next question was critical.

"How many miles?" I asked.

"About 3,096," he said.

I nodded sagely and withdrew. I walked through the shuffle of midtown crowds feeling free and easy, intensely connected to the city and perfectly happy at the coming separation from it.

My task then was simple. I would remap the course, keeping as close as possible to I-80 on local roads. Running on highways had always been a deadly experience, so I wanted to avoid it completely if possible. I wanted to see America up close, off the busy tourist routes, but I found I would have to compromise. Given the kind of choices I wanted to make so that I would not hang myself up unduly running over too many mountain passes, I-80 was the only way to traverse Nevada, Utah and Wyoming. No other local roads ran parallel to the highway. With an easterner's belief that surely many small local roads were present that weren't on the map, I called my brother to check.

"What do you expect?" he said wearily. "I've told you before, this is desert you're running through. There's nothing out there except what's on the map."

"Oh," I said in a very small way.

Sometimes I had a hearty dislike for this map business. The temptation to just go out to California with a few maps and pick my way along haphazardly, generally heading east, was a strong one. But I had to plan about handlers. I had to make arrangements about my apartment, about monthly bills; had to not frighten my editor at Random House into thinking I was launching myself on a kamikaze mission; had to reassure my family that plans were being set afoot in a coherent and reasonable way—and, most important, I had to be responsible to myself. But it is easy to look at a large colored swatch of territory never glimpsed by oneself and say—"Oh, I'll get through it somehow." But when I bent my face closer to the roadways and found that fifty-two miles separated Fort Bridger from Little America and there were apparently no gas stations in-between and August temperatures were likely to be punishing, why then I just kept at it. But it was an irksome business spreading out separate state maps of the U.S. on my desk while my two cats tried to rest their large selves under the heat of the desk lamp without caring that their furry flanks were obliterating scores of miles in my future.

Then, laying out one course commits one to a certain set of road options that may or may not be longer or shorter than the previous attempt, but there is no way of knowing that until the entire potential route is charted. And the tiny mileage figures, confusing sometimes in their placement, made the calculations not so precise as needed. And how do you decide, raw, far-off from the reality of those roads just what to do? How much traffic on that county road? Too little or too much? What kind of shoulders? Were they concrete or asphalt roads? Concrete would demolish my legs far quicker than asphalt. And those towns strung out like infrequent dewdrops on a spider's strand —were they intersections with nothing there or did they have motels? Cabins? Tourist rooms with pleasant old grannies rocking on the front porch? All I could do was guess as best I could, relying on instinct and some practical experience at that sort of thing. It was incredible, finally, how well I chose and how little I deviated from the blind bargain I struck with the devil.

The next hassle was to be sure I would not be thrown off I-80 by the highway patrol. Visions of going several hundred miles out of my way because of some such snag actively gnawed at my tranquillity. After undue procrastination I finally called the Departments of Transportation for Nevada, Utah and Wyoming. Everyone was most obliging. In their regional drawls various men and women shunted me from one hold button to another and said I was sure welcome to just come on through.

"My, we've never had a request like *this* before," said one woman in Utah. I had a feeling my request might merit repetition in the employee cafeteria.

A lot had changed since those long-ago days a month or two earlier. Now I had a profound respect for this mysteriously complete roadway. Interstate 80, too, was in the business of spanning the continent. I understood the simple vastness of its reason for existing. We were linked for that reason, dedicated as we both were to travel for its own sake.

There is always anticipation built into a run. No matter how rigorously I tried to ground myself in accepting the present ground, I was always looking over my shoulder or worrying about what came after the next rise. The very premise of the trip was that I would ever move from this point to that. And now I was arriving at I-80 and I knew with a sure instinct that it would mark another important shift in my life on the road.

Coincident with most of my time on I-80 was the experience of having a car and a handler. Having company about did not alter the basic solitude of the task, but it did soften the loneliness. The price for companionship was like that which comes in any relationship—I just couldn't have it my way all the time anymore. I found that I was a raging perfectionist and that I could reserve occasional bouts of temper for friends that I would never presume to show strangers I encountered along the way. Even at the time, however, it was nice to know that a few other people had shared the run and had a sense of what it was like. I just assumed that in future years it would be nice to talk it over, the way people recall past history together, as if leafing through an album.

No greater love hath a journey runner than a handler. After yourself come those who help you. Handlers are the quiet ones found at the margin of ultraraces. They are wives or husbands, friends of either sex, on foot or on bicycle, sometimes in cars. They wait long periods in hot weather and cold, rummage frantically in tote bags seeking a fresh change of socks or that piece of moleskin the impatient darling of the roads is demanding, keep special drinks and foods ready for the periodic handoff. And they wait patiently at the end for the whole thing to finish, the last award to be handed out and the last bit of shoptalk to be exchanged.

Handlers are often expected to do more than just be glorified carriers of water pails and lunch buckets; they cajole, fuss, criticize, keep their runner informed of the competition's progress; but they must be astute judges of individual psychology and adjust their presence to what's suitable. In the closing miles of a hundred miler, some runners are grateful for company and others flinch from it. A good handler must be thoughtful, patient, loving and well-organized. Also, the more unflappable the better, because there's always bound to be a crisis. All these qualities are not frequently housed within a single individual.

Now on a journey run the scale of various complications, burdens and pressures is much greater than in a race. Day after day the handler must sit, drive ahead a few miles, sit, drive ahead, exchange a few words with the runner and then go back to the solitude of the car. How many times can you listen to the top ten country-and-western hits, interspersed with the drivel of disc jockeys? Reading is difficult in such short fragments of time and all day there is the steady hum in one's conscience and heart for the fool who is pounding down the roadway. If they don't show up in the accustomed time slot, where are they? Talking to someone or flattened by a truck?

And where is the reward other than in seeing your own job well done—it is in the accomplishment of another. Who gets the admiration and the attention when the outside world asks what is going on—the journey runner, not the handler. The runner may know that without the handler the whole venture would founder, but no one else is interested in that.

I was lucky in the two different handlers I had crossing the desert wastes of the Far West. My first supporter was Donna Hudson, a close friend, who had promised earlier to come out for the Nevada and Utah section. The distance between towns, the heat and the lack of water made it impossible to run without help. However, those very factors plus never having attempted anything similar made me fret at having to predict precisely how long Donna would have to be absent from her job. It was just words, just paper plans, just guessing.

"I ought to be able to do it in two weeks," I told Donna, "but what if it takes longer?"

"I'll try to take some more time off from work," she said. "Don't worry about it."

I had great confidence in Donna. Not only did she run ultras herself but she had been a handler for a number of her Millrose Club running mates. She is the kind of person who cannot help being generous. When she comes for dinner, she wants to wash the dishes. Sharing a cab ride home on a cold night with her fellow workers at Hisae's restaurant in lower Manhattan where she tends bar, someone wanted to get the Sunday *Times*. Everyone shuddered at the idea of leaving the warm sanctuary of the cab, but Donna jumped out and ran to get it. The host of nieces and nephews that her nine brothers and sisters have brought into the world are the objects of her wildly partisan and adoring attention. Donna is a believer and a cheerer-on of her circle, so when I called and said I would be getting to Nevada a day earlier than planned (I left a day ahead of time) she said without hesitation she would try somehow to get out there.

Also along for two days was Joe Greene, a photographer who

had collaborated with me on two previous books and had promised to do a shot out West that might be suitable for the cover of the book. Joe is a friend from Peace Corps days when we lived in neighboring towns and we now live on the same block on the Upper West Side. Joe had been along for some of the other high (and low) points in my running career, so it seemed only fitting that he be out for part of this venture as well.

The little rental car is chock full of suitcases, newspapers, cameras, running shoes, bags of food, an ice chest—a regular dispensary of delights. In a day it looks as if we had been gypsies in it for weeks. Somehow the change of having company, and both Joe and Donna to run with in occasional spells, seems as natural as if it had been going on forever. I am still sleeping badly, am deeply troubled by a very sore right foot and shin, and am just plumb tired. All the same, the legalized prostitution, the plethora of slot machines and the wild contrast between the purple-and-brown desert and the tackiness of Carson City provide ample topics of conversation for the three of us. We tack north and then east and then northeast heading through a long lonely stretch for the town of Fernley where I will get onto Interstate 80 at last. How I yearn for that encounter!

At the end of the seventh day I trot into the relative oasis of Fernley, rejoicing in the presence of actual roadside trees. I have covered three hundred and two miles in a week, the most ever in my life. Previously, I had run over two hundred miles in a week a few times, but they were strenuous and seemed the outer limits. At the entrance ramp to I-80 the inner push to go on is tremendous and I debate whether to end the day's run there.

"I don't think you better get on here," Joe says. "You only want to do a few miles, but what if we can't turn around until the next exit? It'll take forever to get back to our motel."

I don't want to hear that. Screw it. Screw Joe's caution. Undoubtedly, he's tired, he's leaving tomorrow on the bus and wants an early night and Donna is certainly tired also. I know insistence will get me on the highway. Reasonableness would vote for retirement, but I do not feel generous. The relentlessness of ambition has me screwed up to a high pitch. I pose for a few photographs under the road signs, but my clowning seems stale and—well, perhaps disrespectful is the word. There is something about the seriousness of all this that I really feel inside. But sometimes the child in one behaves a certain way and the rest of oneself follows behind, slowly shaking its head.

I am thoroughly overtired and my first good fit of temper soon follows. Frayed patience always snags on twigs. We are all in the motel room. It is a blessing to close the blinds and shut out the desert light.

"Where shall we eat?" I ask.

"I don't care," Joe shrugs. He is fresh from the shower. He blows on his glasses and cleans them with his shirt. The air from the bathroom is saturated with a damp and soapy smell. I want to be—well, not alone, but just not so crammed in with all of them. I feel we've been together for two weeks, not two days. My friends come all this way to help and already I'm in a snit. I condemn myself, too. We all stink.

"Well, I'm famished," I say. The glaze of politeness on the pig is about to crackle off when he gets up on all four trotters. I try to keep the suggestive tone in my voice subtle.

"Well, I'm ready," Joe says.

"I just have to put some more ice in the cooler," Donna says. Who can fault her for that? I don't even offer to help her lug the green case out of the trunk. I am a sacred god of labor whose energy must be reserved for the road. But the emperor wants his servants to be perfection itself. I grind away, quietly mashing fingers between millstones. It is not my hunger that swamps me—it is *the* hunger, a force, an elemental craving. In formal Zen training we eat carefully, with attention, hedged in by chants, by an offering of food to the hungry ghost. One does not grab and stuff. One waits and maintains control. As a gobbler, I had always appreciated the stiff rules, but now I am out of control. I am possessed by the demonic need of the hunger. And it isn't ordinary hunger. It is survival to eat. Everything on the run revolves around expressing strength, dipping the ladle with your own hand and arm into your own brimful gut, hearing the clack of the metal dipper against your ribs hour after hour as you feed yourself into motion. Slowly one learns the rhythm of eat and drink, learns the soothing whispers and conspiracies that soften the grinding labor, but woe betide this slight interference that threatens that stability. I do not have until tomorrow to eat. I am a beast now, a beast of labor, and at last I pull off my gloves and unsheath my nails like a savage housecat so crazed with need it now stalks its owner. Still no one says anything and soon enough we are in a shopping mall, another crappy shopping mall with drab-looking restaurants. One is Chinese and the other is an American place, offering barbecue specialties.

"Where do you want to go?" Donna asks me.

I ask her the same thing. She says she doesn't care. I insist she must.

"Well, Chinese then," she says. That was her mistake. How can she be so boorish, she of all people, a Manhattanite, a companion on trips to various Chinese eateries, a possessor of the knowledge of how much good Chinese food means to me, how could she imagine that outside of San Francisco or New York it is even worth considering? Loathsome images of my days as a reporter in Pawtucket, Rhode Island, when I used to be served lumpy masses of chow mein aquiver with viscosity, swam before my enraged vision. And here in Fernley, Nevada, we are to eat Chinese food! My sacred meal, regenerator of my flagging energies, was to be composed of this!

"I think it'll be a shitty choice," I say, my voice charged.

"Well, let's eat at the other place then," Donna said, carefully not commenting on my stripping away any pretense of a choice.

We march in, take trays and silver when Donna suddenly balks, a cow on the runway, head lowered.

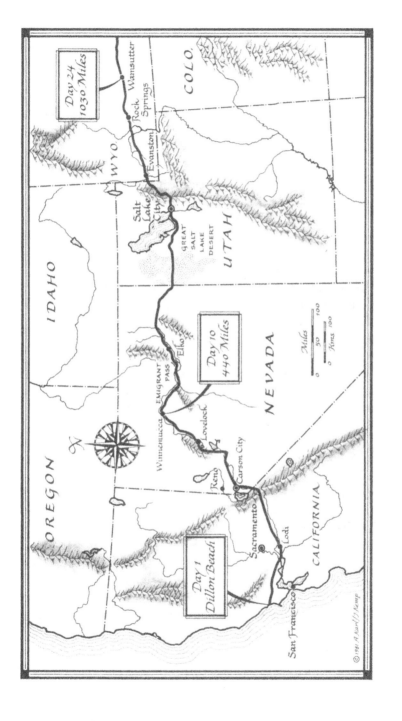

Day 24
1030 Miles

COLO.

Wamsutter

Rock
Springs

Evanston

WYO.

IDAHO

Salt
Lake
City

GREAT
SALT
LAKE
DESERT

UTAH

Elko

EMIGRANT
PASS

Winnemucca

NEVADA

Day 10
440 Miles

Miles
0   50   100
0   Kms 100

Lovelock

Reno

Carson City

OREGON

N

Day 1
Dillon Beach

Sacramento

Lodi

CALIFORNIA

San Francisco

© 1981 R. Karl / J. Kemp

"No," she lows in protest. "It looks awful." The cafeteria-style decor had set all *her* expectations ajangle.

We tramp outside. Now the sky is dark. Families come and go in the shopping mall. The three of us are tied together in dogged misery. Joe takes a neutral refuge in pipe smoking while Donna and I argue for a while. Most of the arguing is a ferociously gloomy silence. At last we agree to go back into the barbecue place, which turns out ultimately to have wonderful hickory-smoked beans, delicious cole slaw and savory ribs, even if the sauce was on the sugary side. We even managed to joke about it, but a half hour had been squandered. There was no lasting damage, but the warning was clear—never get so far behind on eating that you can't think straight, and beware of letting the whole enterprise dominate so much. But such thoughts were useless. The strain for both of us was occasionally enormous. Though bouts of temper were relatively infrequent, they continued to punctuate the next two weeks—most, if not all, precipitated by me.

I think one reason I now look back on I-80 with such intensity is that in Nevada the mastery of the craft was forged. The road was the anvil, the sun was the hammer and my self was the hapless metal caught in-between. Ambition reclined nearby, having put down a payment for a blade capable of slicing from coast to coast.

On the second day in Nevada I turn weary. I am used to everything but the weariness. I am simply tired. I am relaxed and adjusted enough to eat well, to be full of jokes for my handlers and myself. I chew dutifully on my two-mile segments and swallow them manfully, but I still feel tired. A transcon cyclist rides alongside on Route 50 for a while and as the brown mineral wastes, long since abandoned by gold miners, stretch away on each side, we chat about this and that. I forget my fatigue, but soon my new friend, John, vanishes after lunch in another direction. I cannot nap in the cramped front seat, although a full meal leaves my eyes feeling puffy. On impulse, born of resignation, I get up and run after a short meal break.

Slog, slog, slog. I think about writing this book. What can be said to people who ask "What did you think about?" because for a long time I do not think about very much except doing what I am doing.

The sun finally breaks through and the hills all about are remarkable for their subtle browns and purples. Green sage. Dead yellow grasses. Sometimes lizards dash for cover. Here are the hills waiting all day. They just keep on waiting and I keep on moving and slowly the soil turns a hard-baked white and the green dissolves away mostly so it is just chunky layers of rocks that express a variation on the wide rolling flanks of the land. Way down at the bottom of a gully by the road embankment is an armchair whose cloth has faded to white. The armchair faces off to infinity. I consider posing in it with the desert for my living room, but the energy it would take is not worth it. I consider Sasaki Roshi's advice—breathe in the world, breathe out the self. Maybe that will help. So I work on that and then uninvited comes a different understanding of what is happening and what is going to continue to happen.

For the first time I appreciate the fact that endurance is not transcendence over pain, but simply *is* enduring pain. Endurance means accepting things as they are. Now it is not the first time I have mulled over this point of view, nor the first time it has saved me through a tight spot, but never before did it seem definitely to alter what is going on. I am not thinking now about being trapped in a zendo with legs blistering off for another ten minutes or ten hours. I am thinking about how to get through the seventh day out of seventy. I might as well be in that armchair. But the romantic, basically naïve viewpoint I had cherished till then suddenly seemed outmoded—I was never going to be able to just dash through fifty miles in ninety-degree heat as if it was five. Fifty miles is fifty miles. It's a piece of distance. Eight, nine, ten hours of running—it would always take that long. It was just a long day's work every day. I wasn't going to get through this kind of fatigue either by disassociation (as some psychologists call it), where runners fantasize about building houses or making love to get their minds off what they are doing. I wanted to stay in touch with it all, even when it tasted boring. Why after all should it be boring? Who is it who speaks of boring? Who clings to such a rag when there is all that sky overhead? I talk about seeking quiet and now when I am in the middle of a literal desert, I am still trying to count my fingers and toes. So there will be no birthday cake. No Mummy and Daddy leaning down out of the sky to tell me how well I did. The work won't change just because I accept it, either. No god will reward me with a blissful shot of transcendence. The pain won't be something that I will burst through into some higher state where I can abandon it. It is simply mine and what I know now is that the real meaning of being an endurance specialist is that heroism is not feeling less than others, but is feeling more perhaps by just taking it. Endurance is not a road to anything but endurance; it means only not to finish, not to dodge, not to ask for anything other than the price, not to make more or less of it than what it is. It then changes and does not change—it means that fatigue is easier to accept because you can go on indefinitely accepting it. The worst fear was the fear that I might find I could not go on, not of the taste or bite or weariness of the pain itself. Others have said it before me and to me—take it step by step. Easy to state and too easy to forget. I had to go wrong all by myself to find it out again. But you don't discover it without guessing that the heroics of others come under the same sky that others now call your heroism. Praise is just words. So I feel better because I feel calmer. I'm happy enough now to eat stones, and to live my life on a ribbon of tar that goes as far as eyes can see.

At Home
on the Road

Whether in jail or in the jungle, life always has a routine. The word "routine" has a humdrum, domestic sound, but regardless of how or where we spend our days, the hours are filled by meals, toilet, cleaning, work and rest. And what comfort routine has! At least I know it offered hope and solace on the road. Everything else was in flux—the scenery, the people I met, the state of my body and mind, but at least my own needs would never fail to be a source of worry and entertainment.

There was, first of all, slumber. After resorting to the aspirin bottle I could blunt the worst edge of the soreness and get some sleep. Before leaving New York I bought one of those digital marvels, a lightweight wristwatch framed in banker's black. By squeezing various buttons I could call forth upon the tranquil watchface various soundings on my position in time, in the calendar, stopwatch my progression from this point to that, and have an alarm go off. The alarm itself made a peeping sound like an insistent electronic chick. But in all those days I never slept too late. No matter how tired or wretched a day might be, the next morning always began with a rush of energy. I never regretted having to get out of bed. I never hesitated or moaned over my fate while I lay in bed. Later, yes, during the day, during my work I would have a bad hour almost every morning. In any case I was too high-strung ever to really let go so much that I could simply yield to sleep. The norm was five or six hours a night. The body drew energy from its invisible sources for that period and then suddenly switched off. Like a Styrofoam keg released from ocean-bottom bindings, I shot to the surface, bobbing, hopelessly awake, on the bright surface of a fresh new day.

Donna would be sleeping, her thick sandy hair fanned out over her face. I hardly had the heart to awaken her, but the rules of the game were strict. Somehow once we were both dressed and ready to go, had picked up the room that we had strewn with belongings, looked under the bed for stray items, loaded the car and driven off toward the day's starting point, the morning was well along. The sun was up around 5:30 and we rarely saw it happen. I would sit in the car, balancing a camping saucepan on my knees, eating Rice Krispies, canned fruit and milk. Around 7:30 we would find the marker for the end of the previous day's run.

With no ceremony, no grand thoughts or preparatory drawing in of breath, I would simply begin trotting down the shoulder of the highway. At that hour traffic was relatively light, the air was cool and the glare from the sun not yet sharpened to the full measure of the wickedness it had yet to unsheath by 11 A.M.

One of the little-appreciated factors in choosing whether to run east-to-west or west-to-east is the consequent choice of which side of one's carcass one wishes to have broiled. Facing the sun meant the morning's glare came early, but that the strongest heat fell on my neck, shoulders and backs of my legs in the late afternoon. I also had my back to a lot of sunsets. Someone running to California has an easier time at the start of the day, but gets both glare and heat late in the day when they're getting tired. Then there is the matter of slope. Running toward the east means climbing swiftly, staying at altitude for a longish while (most of Nevada, Utah and Wyoming is over five thousand feet in altitude) and climbing on an uphill bias. From the Continental Divide in Wyoming onward, the gradual predominance of downhill running takes effect. There is also the definite advantage of running with prevailing winds coming from the west, pushing one down the road.

My last words to Donna were, "See you in two miles down the road."

She would sit and presumably watch as I dwindled down the shoulder of the road, look at her watch, start the engine, and ease into the flow of traffic. A short while later she overtakes me, gives a beep. I wave without turning and watch with unflagging interest as my little house away from home goes on ahead. The blinking right-hand turn signals the two-mile mark and the immediate goal of the next minutes of running. If it was farther or closer than I imagined was right, I would think about that. Usually in the cool of the day, I would run four-mile segments without water, and sometimes Donna, then in training for the London-to-Brighton race, would run back to meet me, car key in hand, run up to the car and beyond and then double back again.

Then I was back on my own and the segments progressively dwindled until in the heat of the day I needed water every mile or mile and a half. It was time consuming. I run up, Donna gives me a drink of ice water or fruit juice. I grab a cookie. She nags me lovingly to douse my kerchief and hat in ice water (they turned bone dry in twenty minutes), sprays me with the plant mister, reminds me to put on more sunscreen or zinc oxide. I wipe the sweat off my glasses, say something glib or friendly and shove off again. The car is a precious raft I haul myself up onto for a pause. As the day progresses and I get tired I will sit in the front seat and listen to some song on the radio. Once in a while I take my shoes and socks off. Feet emerge, blunt, pale, creased with lines from the ribbing of the socks. The toes express gratitude for the airing. I roll my feet over a small sponge rubber ball to massage them.

Sometimes I study the map. A squiggle means an hour more to Lovelock. Where is that pass? How many inches to go before liberation into Utah? Slowly it comes. But it doesn't help to linger over it. I stuff the map up onto the dashboard and get cracking. Time is like an arrow, Kozen Daito said in his final instructions just before his death. *"Ben sen, ben sen,"* he concludes in the chant. "Work hard! Work hard!"

Slowly, the gravitational tug of the day focuses around lunch. Where shall we break for that precious repast? It is no small question. We quickly discover the desert is an uncomfortable place for a picnic. The wind backlash from the trucks makes the little car jump, and blows a cloud of grit over an otherwise toothsome sandwich. The wind off the desert, relentless and shrewish, teases everything loose into motion so that half the mealtime is spent grabbing things before they dance out over the glaring roadway. And the heat is fierce.

"Shall we fry an egg?" Donna asks.

"Why not?"

She cracks one against the fender and places it on the roadway with a little butter. We stand over it, but it cooks very slowly indeed. We leave it for some lucky coyote. All the same, it is ridiculously hot. The inside of the car is even hotter. After six hours on the road and immediately after finishing a meal, I am in no mood to step out again, so all we can do is swelter in the front seat. Crossing the country on a budget isn't always easy. These small pieces of discomfort, such as an overly small car for someone with legs as long as mine, mean I lose a chance for a half-hour nap. I am playing the edge for all I am worth anyway, so that extra buffer of rest means more than a nonjourney runner would imagine. It isn't the sleeplessness I mind, it's the body's need to heal in sleep that nothing else can replace.

Donna soothes her frustrations by watching campers and rec vehicles stream past, selecting and choosing an imaginary future transcon home.

"That's a nice one," she'd say. "It has space in back for a bunk bed. I could keep the ice cooler in there as well and . . ."

So she rambles on in her dissatisfaction.

Green dots on the map represented rest areas and even when it meant driving twenty miles down the road and then back again at the end of lunch, it seemed worth doing so. On ideal days I would simply run off the road onto the exit ramp that led to the knoll. There I would find Donna with instant Japanese soup mix bubbling merrily away on the camp stove and a plate full of sandwiches and salad ready for consumption. A few handfuls of cookies, a quart or so of milk and juice, a container of yogurt and a couple of pieces of fruit, some peanuts and raisins would top off what was, compared to dinner, a light meal break. Then groggy with sleep, I would shake out my sleeping bag and stretch out on the concrete, oblivious to chatting children or the road traffic noise. Forty minutes later, my mouth stale and my legs stiff, I would roll out. Back to work. If Donna was lucky she got some sleep herself. Lunch breaks usually came no sooner than twenty miles, most often at twenty-five or twenty-six miles. Then all that faced me would be fifteen miles for a "decent" forty, twenty miles for a "good" forty-five and twenty-five miles for a "great" fifty.

The flaw in the routine was that lunch came in the vicinity of one to three in the afternoon. Exactly at that point the fullest heat of the desert was torching the air. The heat was an overwhelming presence, a palpable psychological and physical pressure. It took strength to go back into it and some days it was simplest, really best, to run just another hour or so until four or four-thirty and then drive on to find a motel room in the nearest town. Then we would head back out again about six. The temperature was beginning to drop and a late surge of energy would make those two hours of running into the dark a delight. By the time we drove to a restaurant, ate and returned to the room it would be nine-thirty or ten. Stops for gas and groceries and ice came every night and even though I sat in the car while Donna did it all, it meant more precious quarter hours of rest slipping past. On the other hand, I wasn't just a wind-up robot, indifferent to the new territory and new people all about me. What was the point of running in a mental closet? Usually it seemed better to be alive and tired by doing more, not less.

Back in the room I had to write my notes on the day's run, study the map for tomorrow, do some stretching, eat some more (usually a pint of ice cream, handfuls of peanuts and cookies, fruit, milk and fruit juice) and then squeeze in some blah time to unwind either by talking to Donna or by watching TV or reading a book. I could hardly just go to sleep. An extra hour (and they came rarely) seemed as luscious as a day's vacation. Sleep always came late, and then with a start, as if every window in my body flew open at once, I was sitting up in bed. Twenty-five hundred to go! Let's go, pal!

The truckers loved Donna far more than they loved me. Although I had insisted that I didn't want publicity or fuss, I did yearn for attention at first. It was good to see just how childish I really could be. The first day on I-80 I hoped that big cheerful air blasts would come from the large diesel trucks welcoming me aboard, so to speak. I might have thought they were all mind readers, or subscribed to running magazines or would be expecting me. Any day now we'll see him, they'd be saying. In fact, some truckers did find out what I was doing, but they were tired men hauling their loads for hour after hour without sleep. And as a perfectly polite bunch of fellows they were not necessarily going to hail me with a toot; a truck's air horn when you're not expecting it is an invitation to jump sky-high. I think they realized that. But the sight of Donna in her green running shorts, with her fine legs honed by long-distance training, evoked a series of blissful and yearning toots, taps, beeps and wails. Donna, as a former New York cabbie and a present bartender, was not notably impressed by such rough tokens of gallantry. She just maintained a neutral stance about it all. My own presence at times did nothing to hinder the toots either. Whether they assumed she was my wife or not, perhaps they felt I would take it all with a due measure of pride.

The first truck that stopped came up behind us just as I was nearing Donna and the car. The trucker's wife beckoned me from her high perch. I grabbed ahold of the recessed handholds and pulled myself up to window level.

"Ya in trouble?" the woman hollered over the massive purring of the engine.

"No!" I yelled, explaining the whole venture.

Then her husband signaled me, so I went around to the other side. He hadn't heard what I'd just said. He was a rough-cut small fellow with graying hair and tough, gnarled hands.

"You lookin' for rocks?" he asked. "I can tell you where some good places are to find rocks."

I explained.

"Oh," he said. He looked disappointed.

"Coulda told you where to find some rocks."

He looked sadder, not really hoping that I would change my plans and get on to something interesting like rocks. My answer had just caved in his interest in me.

I jumped down and stood clear as they rolled off, his wife waving and their little bulldog barking defiantly from the safety of her lap.

In general the code of helpfulness out in the Far West was remarkable. Every day on I-80 perhaps ten trucks, vans, cars and campers would pull over to offer help.

"Car broken, lady?" they'd ask Donna.

"You running down the road looking for a gas station?" they'd ask me in dead seriousness. It is no joke to be stuck out in the desert thirty miles from the nearest town. Everyone knows that and they look out for their roadside neighbors. I tried to explain quickly and offered thanks to spare people the embarrassment they often felt on feeling they had intruded or misread the situation. Even women offered me rides once or twice, a remarkable degree of trust.

A few old men in beaten-up pickups or sedans would offer me a ride and something about the graciousness of them cut very deep. I was a lonely man in a way, my work was lonely and I tried to expect nothing from the world, so such small gestures seemed so rich.

Trash

Zen Master Shunryu Suzuki Roshi once said that one should not leave any traces of one's passage.

I never threw anything away on the road that would not decompose without trace. It wasn't always easy to haul tin cans and plastic trash for dozens of miles before finding a trash can, but how could one not? The levels of debate it inspired were of so mundane and petty a spirit that perhaps it is instructive to see how I struggled with erasing traces in the most literal way.

Extra cans always have a residual bit of liquid left in the bottom, unable to have penetrated through the thin lip that separates the teardrop snap-open top and the actual edge of the can. Those last few drops resist even a nudging set of plinks from snapping fingers. Yet without fail, if I simply put the cans in my pack, these driblets would jounce their way out and stain my clean T-shirt or goo up my note pad. For someone as dirty as I was and as pummeled as I was to become by rainstorms, who would have imagined such fastidiousness would merit transmission through my mind? And yet, alas, such themes would fill my field of concern. To avoid involuntary soilings of my pack's contents, I would give the can or bottle a series of sharp downward flicks to spray out against the roadside the last gasp of whatever corn-syrup-and-water commercial concoction

I had seized on for refreshment. The ability of the mind to cut the thinnest slices of thought over the tiniest actions is quite astounding.

The other troubling factor was weight. Only the truly obsessive can appreciate the ludicrous aspect of knowing in your heart that the two to four ounces of dead container weight you will carry for fifteen extra miles will not matter in any measurable degree, but will inescapably bother you all the same.

"Every ounce you save helps you," I told myself. "Throw the damn thing away."

"No," came a deeper reply.

"Oh, all right," was the sullen acquiescence.

There was actually a stretch of a hundred and fifty miles in eastern Wyoming where I had laid out caches of food and water for myself every twenty miles in advance by driving over the route beforehand in a car. A couple of two-gallon plastic containers, even when folded up, and a day's supply of cans added up to a couple of extra pounds and an awkward-fitting pack. Trash cans appeared every fifty miles out there. But by then I had become determined not to yield. How could I criticize the rest of the world if I behaved as they did? How could I say how deeply it offended my own view of things if I gave in so quickly to inconvenience?

For it was the sight of eight hundred miles of trash that had been a revelation. There was a comical, even utilitarian aspect to the massive strewing along the roadside of America all the various detritus with which people had briefly amused themselves or satisfied their wants.

Combs? There for the asking.

"Donna, do you need a comb?"

"Sure."

I go back to work. In two miles a comb shines up from the black tar of the road. It was a funky, teen-ager's comb, made of red-and-blue plastic in a swirling marble pattern familiar to lovers of bookplates.

"You want a toy for your nephew?"

"Sure," Donna says. She constantly talks about Andre, her two-year-old, blond-headed nephew from Nyack, New York. Finding a toy is not as easy as a comb, but within an hour I report back with a small plastic figurine. Later in the trip when I was thinking how I ought to have a road atlas of the continental U.S. I found one, its pages riffled apart and a few states missing, but otherwise serviceable. I lost a red handkerchief, but quickly found another. I needed a cap and shortly found a brand new one with a fine brim and a bright yellow-and-green pattern that included a California logo. Wrenches, hammers and screwdrivers were useless to me so I let enough to fill a bushel basket go by.

Later in the trip I found reading material, the most promising catch being a hardbound edition of *The Thirty-Nine Steps,* a jolly English mystery. As I read it, I ripped off pages and discarded them in order to save weight.

Pornographic material was not lacking either, although I felt about as much stirring as a sun-dried pea when I looked through their contents. I was too tired really to feel deprived and the sodden pages (I always seemed to find them after rainstorms) were unreal. Admirable, admirable flesh, but the insubstantiality of it was hilarious. Like all species of trash, you had to wonder how and why it all came to rest just there. Did some husband buy it and read it before nearing home where it had to be ditched, or did some angry girlfriend fling the offensive material from the car? If you buy something, why discard it, except under fear or duress? I conjured up various scenes, but how could I determine what had happened? Mad ideas marched through the brain. An advertisement I would place in a Nevada paper, asking if anyone with information about a discarded copy of *Musk* at mile post 212 would come forward. Discretion assured. Vast tomes of the recorded history of every event in the world had yet to be written. What an undertaking! As I glanced down the black spines of the books stretching off toward the horizon, the immensity of the task seemed desperate. Even if one wanted to, how could one account for everything? And who would account for the accounters?

Not being able to answer that problem hardly prevented me from further discursions. Who could resist the problem of the ladies' shoes? True that an occasional pair of men's cowboy boots, sadly worn at the heel, would appear, first one side's footgear and then the brother leather article a dozen yards farther on. But far more women's shoes than men's were discarded. Sometimes underpants from both sexes appeared, rather frail and gamy items after exposure to the desert weather, but rarely alongside shoes. The obvious sexual connection seemed to be missing. More sinister possibilities abounded; especially murder or assault. Or were western women simply a more high-spirited variety with a penchant for pitching perfectly good footgear into the sagebrush? Shoes are more affecting discards than worn clothing whose collapsed sleeves and legs suggest only vaguely the human form that once filled them. Women's shoes maintain their spatial integrity and the suggestive femininity of the straps is half of what one admires on a woman's foot so that the rather humble, entrancing toes and arches of strange, never-to-be-seen women haunted entire half miles as I ran along paying homage to the long-since vanished owners.

Since the desert did not yield answers of this variety, the easiest stance was simply to fulminate vainly over the piggish inclinations of what is probably a sizable majority of the driving population. It is one thing to see someone pitch a cigarette butt out the window, especially at night. The skidding shower of sparks adds color to an otherwise humdrum blackness. But what possible aesthetic excitement could I squeeze from the sight of hundreds, nay thousands, of Pampers along the roadway? Perhaps since my notions of motherhood are based in part on the formal, purified scenes of medieval Italian painters like Fra Angelico and such modern-day interpreters as Mary Cassatt and Norman Rockwell, I associate the mothers of infants with a rather hazy and blissful outlook. What snarling, unhappy wretches would fling their children's soiled panties into the roadside? Vile plastic things they were, too, flattened by the sun, the cursed dark streak of the now shriveled feces proof positive that the Pampers served their function. Once I came across a baby bottle, baby shoes and Pampers, each item separated from the other by fifty yards. It would have been no surprise to find a baby next.

Quirky details lent themselves to easy solutions. In California the busy hum of trucks laden with fruits and vegetables explained the occasional appearance of a white onion in excellent condition along the shoulder of the road. One leaking onion truck. But there was the candy-corn case that still remains an open file. In Utah an individual candy corn, the kind colored yellow, orange and white, would appear on the road as bright as a semiprecious gem. About a minute later by my watch another one appeared and so on for several miles. Perhaps some perverse child flung them at regular intervals from the open window.

There was the matter of money. Donna began its collection by giving little cries occasionally during her run when she would stop and pick up a penny from the road. A long-ago running companion had also displayed the tedious habit of discovering fair-sized sums in the streets of Boston, which, to my impoverishment, I never saw. Donna's habitual cry and stoop for copper bits seemed miserly, given the reality of an inflationary economy.

"It brings luck," she said.

"Oh, for God's sake," I muttered. All the same, childish jealousy spurred me on. Instead of gazing at the tar shoulder with the grimness of a prisoner looking at the same stretch of yard, I now scanned it for what became the minute but instantaneously recognizable blemish of metal coin. Later I forget to look on a conscious level, but even on country roads where the pickings were smaller and a week might pass without a single spotting, I would stop and scoop up the find. Total findings for 3,026 miles probably equaled three dollars. The coins were often nicked and scarred, but of recent vintage. Much of I-80 was laid down in the last ten or fifteen years, so there was no surprise in that. But why would coins appear at all? Perhaps lost when people bend over to check their tires or squirm beneath the underbodies of their cars? I have yet to come up with a completely pleasing solution.

There were still two more categories of roadside leavings that were far more forgivable than mere trash; one was shredded tires. I can say as a student of the subject that there are scraps of discarded tire as often as every few feet and rarely separated by as much as ten on the nine hundred miles of I-80 I covered. They seemed, poor hapless pieces, to have been truck-tire blowouts. Perhaps truckers skin flat tires off the rim like useless pelts—I do not know, but the result was a kind of rubber carnage. There was an appreciation I came to feel for these savaged shapes, an affinity that only solitude could have taught me. Since many tires were reinforced by steel threads, the frayed edges had a kind of clumsy stiff fringe. Diamond patterns on the treads would gleam up from anonymous pieces that my own speed of foot doomed to solitude once again. All the odd coincidences and stories of what came to be, where the rubber first came from, the hand of the industrial draughtsman who decided one morning that a certain tread pattern would look the best, the trucker who bought the tire, the tire's fatigue brought on by trips here and there over great bouts of highway road—all ending at a particular stretch of desert roadway where the final footsteps of inspection in this morgue of industrial waste would sound. If I did not appreciate these ganglialike fragments, then who would? Sometimes the crescent-shaped pieces filled with water or sand. Sometimes I gave them a kick with my foot, almost to see if they were still alive. After four hundred miles I finally bent down to pick one up. What a surprise! How heavy such a small piece was! Visions of a rubber reclamation project pleased some tidy impulse, but I have a feeling these humble servants who bear us on our errands are still fallen, unburied soldiers of the roadways.

Finally, there was the literal carnage of animal death. In Nevada, Utah and Wyoming I saw thousands of jackrabbits smashed into oblivion by those selfsame tires. I don't suppose it really bothered me at first. Although capable of great sorrow for any animal killed by a car or for sport, I have no tint of squeamishness over the odors or look of animal carrion. As a small boy in upstate New York I spent many hours armed with bushel basket and work gloves as I scoured the woods for cow bones to add to an immense collection. In lieu of dinosaur bones, it was the best I could do. I had armed myself with a .22 rifle and whacked away with some success at chipmunks. But the simplicity of boyhood had yielded to a sense of gratitude, as one chant puts it, "for the warm flesh and blood of Buddha." I prefer not to eat meat, but do eat it at times without a trace of guilt. After seeing people die in Brazil from hunger, it is clear that we must eat or die. The point is not to forget at what price it comes for someone or something. Grass, air, water, sun, muscle and work—none of it comes from nothing. We are lucky that we can eat. But you can die without ever knowing just how lucky you really were to share energy. Sometimes I thought of the microorganisms squashed by my stride. As it was, I tried to avoid stepping on insects or hapless beetles or ants crossing the roadway. Fellow travelers. Once in the *New York Times* there was an article about an Indian holy man of the Jain sect. I believe he walked with a light broom so that he might sweep any insects out of his path rather than inadvertently kill any. There were other extraordinary lengths he went to, but now they hardly seemed that—only an exceptionally clear sense of how strong a commitment one might make, not out of ideology or fanaticism, but inspired instead by gratitude. It was not my way to run with a broom, but I did what I could.

So when I ran down the road and saw perhaps a thousand rabbit carcasses by the end of the day, I could not help but feel sorrow. There was no blame attached to that emotion. No one deliberately ran the rabbits over, but I was close to the carnage,

as no one else was. Some died more or less whole, sometimes
with a froth of blood now caked around their mouths. More
often the limbs were scattered and severed in every conceivable
pattern. Paws, tails, heads, ears, spines, bits of fur and bloody
grime were scattered every which way by the impact. Entrails
blackened and dried up under the sun. Open eyelids, so that
the black pupils gazed somewhere. Nose whiskers. And the
feet. My god, who ever thought that a rabbit's foot brought
luck, the loss of such an appendage being a distinct piece of
evil luck for the original owner. The paws, clipped, broken and
severed, were strewn everywhere. Less occasionally I saw deer.
Their eyes were always open, too. Even cats and dogs. The
dead animals changed with the land. Approaching the Mississippi in Iowa the following month, dead turtles and snakes
announced the arrival of a more humid flora.

I felt the animals were myself.

"Sorry," I'd say, if some rounded fur body caught my gaze.
The way the sun baked the carcass. The hapless posture. The
simple testimony of intestine and blood. The victim of the
auto. The sufferer on the roadway. The grim hazards of life,
if life could be separated from death, though, of course, it
can't. Those were some of the things that helped explain why
it was suffering that I understood. Perhaps it sounds as if I was
out alone on the roads too much. I think not.

Just beyond the Imlay exit on I-80 in Nevada, I run along,
still feeling aggrieved at the litter in the desert. Cellophane
wrappings, tin cans, plastic six-pack rings, all resting on the
surface of the soil. It might have been one of those moon shots
where urine bags and discarded landing pods will remain in a
stark state of arrested decay for a thousand generations. Then
I notice an odd clump in the distance. The idea of reaching
a building that was not where anything was marked on the map
quickens my interest and the next hour is greatly lightened,
suffused as it is by anticipation. The structure grows stranger
as the reducing distance makes it grow larger, some unknown
manifestation slowly inflating with helium. After discarding

various interpretations of what it is, the buildings and sculpture finally reveal themselves in clean and remarkable detail.

Odd, looping structures that resemble the girding beams of a modern sculptor arch over a few of the simple buildings beneath. Sculpted faces and heads emerge from the creation and the bright uncanny colors wink in the early morning sunlight. Crude, handhewn statues of Indians with stern faces stare silently at the whizzing traffic a dozen yards beyond the fence that separates the property from the interstate.

A sign announces that this group of weathered gray buildings is the Rolling Thunder Mountain Temple. Another massive sign announces: "Educational, Recreational, Philanthropic." It has the home-cooked flavor of a serious and untutored genius. Although a few "no trespassing" signs seem at odds with the other public invitations to travelers to come camp and visit the site, I go up to the fence and read a copy of a magazine article that had been pinned there. This is what I recall:

Frank von Zundt, born 1911 in Oklahoma, a full-blooded Creek Indian, had gone to serve in a tank battalion in World War II, where he took part in a number of major battles and won many decorations. He went through a variety of jobs afterward, including one as a policeman in Yuba City, California. He and his first wife raised wild kids from the city and gave them some stability and love. They also watched nuclear tests from their home out West; she later died. He since remarried a woman half his age and had several children. One of them had a long and unusual name that I have since forgotten.

"Wasn't a name like that a burden for the child?" the reporter asked.

Frank, whose own name now is, I think, Rolling Thunder, answered to the effect that names can be changed, but for a child love is what he cannot do without.

He ended up in the middle of this desert because when he drove by and saw Thunder Mountain in the distance he knew, as people do sometimes, that this is where he was meant to be.

His home and museum are, as he sees it, a monument to the earliest men of the West, both whites and Indians. Everything is made from castoffs in the desert—scrap metal, lumber, wrecked airplanes, whatever.

It is a long way to Winnemucca, I decided. The parked cars at Rolling Thunder are still asleep. The houses are closed up. I look at my watch and decide to go. Maybe someday I will come back. I don't really want to meet Rolling Thunder in person. I've seen him as clearly, in a way, as I can. He is crude, powerful, original. It doesn't matter how one ranks a statement like his in terms of conventional aesthetics. It is as pure as art can be because it is honest. Anyone who can value trash, who can love the humblest thing for what it offers is . . . well, I can't say what it is but I feel gratitude.

For the rest of the morning I judge the motorists severely, so smooth and insulated as they whizz past in their little worlds. They just go through the desert, they don't respect it. They are probably like the bicyclist I met recently who was "bored" by it. Rolling Thunder Temple must seem like a zany, tasteless trap they would never stop at. Rolling Thunder. The houses out here look like they are held down by carpet tacks when a typhoon of death lingers below the horizon. Houses bear no relation to the lines of largeness and space.

Dry sage bounces on its yellow, spongy fingertips, cavorts across the road. Sometimes cars connect with them for an instant and the fine yellow branches shatter. More sage bounces in, singing with the wind, not wondering where they are going, skittering for an instant over this thin track of blacktop that, though it is but a scratch beneath the sky, is the roadway we call home.

False Expectations

We cannot predict the future. And yet I let myself have expectations. I didn't have many, but the ones I did have were so much what I thought would be true that I barely realized that they might not be. No matter how one schemes there is no way to imagine the future accurately. We will never own what we never reach. Either we look for what we want or what we fear. It isn't easy giving up hope and fear. Being, fairly frequently, on an earthy and imperfect plane, I worked myself into a real pit about the upcoming rite of passage. I decided the hellhole of the trip would be crossing the Great Salt Lake Flats in Utah. My brother assured me dispassionately that it would be a nasty bit.

"Even driving through, it's boring," Tom said. "There's a radiant heat that makes you feel like you're suffocating. It's like an oven. Even at night it's bad, but it's definitely at night that you should run across it."

I looked at the map of Utah for a long time, but any detour meant lots of extra miles. Although I had nothing to base it on, I said with the breezy self-assurance of a fool whose bluff no one calls:

"The worst part of the entire trip will be the flats. I'll have to run them at night."

Although my blasé attitude was mostly unfeigned, I suppose

I hoped for a bit of my-my head shaking and listener's eyes that glazed slightly as they imagined the fearsome flats. But what did my East Coast friends and I know about such places? What guidebook would describe them from a runner's point of view? What would it *look* like, *feel* like, *be* like? The whole thing was wildly imprecise. Perhaps someone else could not have endured such vagueness. I didn't really care. I just assumed the worst. Well, doing so was easier in New York than in Nevada. If it's the worst part of the trip, I now thought, how can I endure heat much worse than what I'm getting? I realized within a hundred miles of this rendezvous that I was afraid.

"How were the flats?" I asked different transcon cyclists I met heading for California.

"Not too bad," said one fellow. "But we had cloud cover going across so the weather was a little cooler. Nineties."

That was three days earlier. Weather is never constant and the cycle was bound to shift into higher temperatures. I groaned inwardly, imagining the inevitable fried-alive encounter. It was easy to say beforehand that I would run it at night, but now that disruption of schedule seemed a gruesome prospect. Car headlights would light my way as I ran in an endless hell of asphalt, nothing visible but the swath of shoulder. All this imagining was not as foolish as it might have been. If it was going to be bad I had two choices. One was to take it moment by moment simply as it came. The other was the way athletes are fond of: the classic psyching up, reviewing the ordeal, making promises to oneself, tasting the quality of it so much so repeatedly that simply to begin it becomes a relief. It's possibly a waste to do the latter, but to do the former . . . not easy.

What worried me even more than the heat was the unbroken flatness and the unbroken straightness. (On the maps, the thirty-eight miles of road between Wendover and Knolls was like a string stretched taut between two push pins.) Each feature requires an explanation. Running perfectly flat terrain never gives the legs a break; hill running, contrarily, alternates the use of different muscles. Physical tedium is exacerbated by the sameness of the terrain.

As for that straight-ahead road (so common in flatlands), being in a spatial plane that stretches off into shimmering vastness of the starkest kind of desert would afford nothing with which to distract myself. No matter how fast you run, the road mocks the effort. "Where are you going in such a hurry?" it asks. "Not until you run for hours will you earn the right to be somewhere else, out of my clutches."

I faced a day and a half of running to get through this wilderness of eighty-odd miles. Up till now I had enjoyed the desert, but now . . .

Take it in segments, I thought. Run ten to fifteen minutes at a time and just try to reach the car. Four such segments will equal one hour. Two hours of running will merit a five-minute break. Four breaks equals a night of running. Not so bad! If real heavy-duty panic sets in, there is always walking. I always dangle the prospect of walking in front of me as one of the backdown emergency relief plans. (I don't have many.)

"If you feel *really* bad," I'd say to myself, "then you know you can always walk for hours and hours."

On the sixteenth day of the trip, just shy of the flats, the first rainfall I had encountered came with the violence and rapidity of western thunderstorms. Black storm clouds gathered over the rocky Nevada plateau. Vegetation here was almost nonexistent. Brown and gray rocks littered the long rises and falls of the roadway. Lightning bolts began to drop out of the sky with alarming frequency. The ground rule of never stopping for any reason, playing the edge, suddenly went down with a big gulp of fear. For someone who had decided he was ready to die to finish the run, I looked like one of the roadside hares in full flight. It was one thing to get creamed from behind by a truck driver. It was another to die simply because I was an ass.

A bolt fell about eight hundred yards away. Under that vast cataract of gray air, shimmering with clarity in a range of land where I was the tallest object for forty miles in every direction, the closeness of the lightning was enough to make me involuntarily jump. The clouds boiled overhead and gray dull-hearted banks of rain marched like patient soldiery from the southwest across my path.

Gone now were all brakes as I flung myself into a mad dash toward the car. What folly to have told Donna to drive on two miles ahead! Every time a lightning bolt fell, the purity of its deadly spirit put an extra charge in my stride. There was a sort of jiggle at the bottom of the stroke as if it flashed briefly a second time. Like a thread of molten glass, it dribbled a little thicker at the point of contact.

As I neared the car I yelled furious obscenities at Donna— "Back up for Christ's sake! Help me!" Couldn't she realize what it meant to be so alone and so exposed! I knew she couldn't hear. Didn't matter. "Donna!" I shrieked. Rain was falling as I yanked open the car door and leapt inside.

"You ran the last part very fast," Donna said mildly. She found my sprint comical and we exchanged some spirited opinions as we waited for the storm to pass.

Nevada was not easy to leave. An exceedingly long climb took me to the tip of the plateau that looks out over the Utah flatlands. The smell of wet dust mingled with the tart odor of shrubs. A stack of hay bales deposited in a field smelled like peaches. It was part of the constant pleasure of the desert, the way in which it never fails to offer subtle surprises and rewards. With so much taken away, other things emerge with extra keenness.

Just on the edge of the last ridge one comes to a great change in the world. Ahead and on each side the mountains trail off into the salt flats, the ridged staircase of the mountain spine dwindling away, flattening out with a whispering ridge that finally loses itself in the flats. Immediately about on the last slope down off the rock escarpment is a rock face absolutely barren of green, all gray and brown with what, if it were skin or hide, would be faintly reddish sun stains.

The once immense Salt Lake is not a single dazzling expanse, but rather breaks into great white bands separated by streaks of black. In the distance, depending on the time of day and the light, are all manner of mountains; their colors are grays, blues, browns, silvers and a subdued smokiness. The entire reach of the lake leaves the impression that an immense tide pulled out centuries before. It is an uncompromising vista and a sinister overtone vibrates in the mind of the onlooker who knows that some of the territory viewed to the south is marked on the map as being a weapons test site, unavailable to the public. The sorcery of death is confined to a special locale. It makes one remember, as I ran alone, how mad the world is that we are born into. How can I drift like a mindless leaf, skittering over the roads of the country and not remember the silos and nuclear-bomb testing sites and all the other gear of murder? I have forgotten the cruelty and simplicity of warring peoples. I am surprised not to be dead. It makes the moment seem like a narrow hallway through time. Where are we headed and what are we doing on the face of the earth studying the ways of preparing ourselves for titanic conflicts? It humbles an overblown sense of one's own life. I am reminded again of how massive a self-indulgence I am launched on, devoting myself to something unnecessary. Other people are lucky to earn enough to eat. But there is no reason not to do something just because others cannot. It's impossible to judge the value of the run. It matters to me to do it. That's the only fixed point I have. All the same, I think of my grandfather who sold pencils and candy on the streets of New York as an immigrant child. What would he say if he could see his grandson running over the desert?

Wendover, the border town that straddles the Utah-Nevada state line, cannot help but look surreal in such a setting. The gas or oil storage tanks down at the base of the slope, one of which is painted red-and-white check, the flat tar roofs with all the ordinarily unglimpsed hardware of roof fans, ducts and pipes, and the stable cluster of homes makes it all resemble nothing so much as a launch site on Earth or perhaps a human colony on Mars. Yet at night when the lights glimmer green and white against all that sheer edge of darkness, Wendover might be a tropical beach-front town.

At ten minutes to one in the afternoon I cross into Utah. A large sign advises travelers they are leaving Pacific and entering Mountain Time. It is a fine moment to remember that I am crossing the globe. Even snails can consume continents.

Blitzed by the heat and the old companion, fatigue, we retire to lunch at a Tacoburger joint. Blond, shy, sweet high school girls take our orders. Next to the digital cash registers are copies of the Mormon Bible and brochures about family life.

In the motel room we dive into sleep, shades drawn, falling for the real sucker's midday sleep. Waking up with a charred taste in the mouth and a terrible scrambling feeling coming up the slick sides of the well of consciousness. Terrible thunderclaps had broken overhead and a siren went off nearby. But even on the edge of hell, sleep is more powerful than curiosity. In the motel parking lot are fresh puddles of rain. So I lost nothing by not running. I can't even feel guilty. I think I deserve an extra hour off the road. Black thunderclouds boil up out of the south again.

"Let's scat back out there," I say and Donna zips us back to the starting point.

I thought the rain might skip us, but it didn't. The patter became a drenching downpour. The road was a nice spongy tar, fresh vintage, slightly springier than other varieties. The state truck-inspection site slowly bobbed up as I ran and then the simple equation of the planes of sky and earth and flat road began. Here I was in hell at last, not running over coals, but through a cold shower. The brief novelty of running in the cool rain soon sours. The rain and the wind came slanting in against my left side, darkening the blue tank top I wear, making it cling. On my right side it remains a faded, paler blue, dry as yet for a while. The wind is coming from far places and the chill is cosmic. Soon flashing hail chatters on the road and flays my skin. The pain is too brisk to endure.

I hop in the Toyota and we sit and wait. The car windows flow so heavily with rain that we could see only a wobbly world of gray. Every time a truck passes, the car rocks and the roof thuds from the spray. I read a Nevada newspaper, poor stuff for a *New York Times* addict.

"The hell with it," I say. "I'm going back out."

"Put on a Goretex jacket at least," Donna says.

I jump out of the car, squinting and hunched. The downpour is chilling in weight and coldness. Breath frosts into visibility. The hairs on my hands and thighs are brushed flat by the rain. Donna follows just behind with the headlights on. Step after step.

I feel dizzy and light-headed. My knees ache as if pierced by two-inch nails. My hands stiffen from cold. To my right is what now resembles a giant ditch of water. Overhead is all gray. Below is muddied beige, yellow and white. The only things that are not flat are metal reflector markers that slowly swim past. Step by step. Flat road. Blinding gashes of silver water, as trucks spray east. My toes are now in pockets of water that have collected in the fronts of the shoes. I have a feeling if I do not stop I am going to go over the edge. I can feel Donna's taut watchfulness with each swipe of the car's windshield wipers. You get to know people. I also know I can retire my pride for the day. I climb in and chatter and ache back into normalcy. The world swims for a while and then the gyroscope settles into its accustomed hum.

The black drifting banks of rain had reached the outermost horizons of our world and as we headed back to Wendover for the night, the landscape resembled, eerily enough, nothing so much as a seascape. The mineral beds of the flats absorbed water so slowly that an inch or two of rain lay on its surface, shining in the reflected gaudiness of the hot pinks and violets of a western dusk. The faraway rock escarpments of the mountains looked like the flanks of a Mexican bay. So the desert was, in the glimmering of illusion, a sea again, as it had not been for thousands of years.

Dinner was at State Line Casino. The Utah plates of the cars parked outside, and the number of charter and regular commercial buses, were all indicators of the great flight of refugees from the land of boredom to the palace of delights. An immense neon cowboy blazed outdoors in the desert night, a species of giant cartoon so fizzy and pink-headed in its artistic worthlessness that it had a bizarre charm. Just inside the lobby was the largest slot machine I had yet seen in Nevada. It accepted only paper money and its lever was as long as a small child.

There was a democratically representative set of lotus eaters: Hispanics, middle aged, young couples, rowdy bachelor men. Everywhere the cacophony of jangling money and yammering bells, the good-natured prodding and commiserations of the change-apron-bedecked ladies who patrolled the quarter and half-dollar slots, giving out free half bottles of "Wine?" "Champagne?" to winners announced by a particularly long shrilling of bells. Amid the humbler realms of the elbow-to-elbow nickel, dime and quarter slots, the activity was relentless. Quart-sized containers, used not for soda but for masses of change, were tumbled here and there, the paper liners smeared with nicks of gray from the coinage, which also stained the fingers of the users in the same fashion that nicotine brands its addicts. I pretend to no superior detachment. I would stand by the nickel slots, waiting till someone got weary of tiny payoffs and left. I figured the machine must be getting close again to another big payoff and I would grab the handle, still warm from the stranger's palm, and crank away. All the same, when Donna and I retired for dinner, we were besieged in the dining room by constant reports on the current progress of the ongoing keno game elsewhere. Life inside a light bulb gets your mind off the problems of the road, but soon enough we were out in the parking lot, whipped again from fatigue. As we drove back to the motel I sat quietly on my still-unhatched egg of foreboding. Off in that blankness the flats were still awaiting my attempt to cross them.

We were back out there early the next morning and luckily the chill from the previous day's storms kept the temperature somewhere in the seventies till late morning. After what I had endured in the desert, it seemed delightfully arctic. The colors of the flats were yellow and whitish beige. To the south, not far off the road, ran a parallel set of railroad tracks. To the north was a wide stretch of mineral wastes without a sign of vegetation. At frequent intervals were carefully constructed letters and hearts made from chunks of stone pilfered from the sides of the I-80 roadbed. Frank and Charley—1979. John Loves Judy. Apart from that there was a great deal of sky. The road just went out to the edge of the sky.

For a longish while it didn't seem to matter. I was enjoying the cool weather and determined as I was to get as far as I could that day, I pushed down hard. But, as happened on so many mornings of the trip, I got a bad case of the blues. I think this time I had convinced myself I was going to get panicked by the desolation and endlessness and once I let that train of thought start seeping in, I really did began to panic. It expressed itself in a physical way. I grew dizzy and weak and had to sit in the car for a while, panting for breath, my cheeks and forehead flushed. I was afraid, afraid of being afraid, which is not much fun, although once I was over the dizzy spell, I realized I didn't hurt physically. In a way, the very thing that upset me provided the answer for getting out of it. What was out there to be upset about? It was not the road, but me getting panicky. A heavy fog of mind chatter and commentary had blown in. All I had to do was accept that shimmering streak of tar road. I didn't want to, for a long time. Breathe in the world, breathe out the self, Sasaki Roshi says. Just breathe. Accept the world for what it is. Gradually, my attachment to the fear lessened, the distant mountains in the east grew bigger, which meant somehow, somewhere in time, I would be there.

It was a hard thing feeling a spell of misery every morning more or less like that. I never really understood if it came from a cyclical low point in the body physically and was in a way an attempt to express itself, or if it was a loss of concentration and a corresponding lack of acceptance of what my present situation was. It certainly wasn't expressed just mentally, whatever it was. My limbs felt thick, almost numb, my head would swim a bit, and a general weariness dominated all body sensation. The scale of the trip was always terrifying to think on at such times and mostly I had enough sense not to try to hang myself that way. It would last about a half hour and then fade away. I kept hoping I was done with it for good, but I never was.

On the way out of the flats there is a rest area—it's not even a town—called Knolls. The origin of the name is based, reasonably enough, on the selfsame knolls that crop up in the immediate area. It consisted of some old, disused-looking tourist cabins and a weary restaurant that offered for perusal a browsing copy of a book about Craig Breedlove, who once held the world speed record for cars on the nearby raceway. It was not the first time I had seen photos of him around the area. Obviously, for some, he was one of the local icons. More postcard racks that squealed, and the postcards themselves were of the kind that always look too green or too blue or just too unreal altogether. So we left.

Suddenly, a little way down the road, I ran on into Skull Valley, which, in spite of its fearsome name, was dotted with green sage and had a kind of tilting here and there to the land. By afternoon I was climbing into the mountains and had reached forty-odd miles by four in the afternoon. The mountains were Biblical, stern and somber. The flats were behind me and as I began the long, long run down toward the Great Salt Lake, land of the Mormons, seeing the night lights of a mining operation glowing green and white in the valley below, the sun was just beginning to set. I felt so strong I believed I could run forever. It was just a moment where all the unanswerables don't really seem to matter. Perhaps if I had thought about it, I might have said I was happy. Only now writing this, remembering those ten minutes, do I appreciate how unfettered I was on that downhill slope. All that fuss and fury had been for naught. There was no point in hanging on to expectations anymore about anything at all, so for a while, I did not. As always, even that mood of detachment changed. What didn't? The only guarantees were that always there would be change.

I Take a New Wife

You might as well be married when you have a handler on the run. Of course, I speak only from surmise. Although unmarried myself, I did live with someone for two years and I can hazard a fair guess as to what might be involved. You and your handler get to know each other awfully well, if you didn't before. And I would imagine it makes little difference if you have someone of the same sex as your companion. As a journey runner you are a mixture of various elements: willful child ("Please, can't I run some more miles?"), helpless invalid ("Can you get that sock off for me?"), friend ("Let me tell you what just happened to me"), companion ("What's wrong, you look tired") and cosmic pal (no words necessary). All these elements of your persona are accepted with attention, delight, sadness, anger and humor by your friend. What a friend—what a complete and intense relationship, which they can sustain only by working hard in your behalf. If there is not a good mutual commitment, the relationship is off. There is even more pressure than in a marriage to make it work—no matter what you feel, the work needs to get done. You have to get along. The tiffs Donna and I had were of such simple origin—fatigue—that it was impossible to linger over them. They usually became part of the lore of remember-when stories.

But for all that we had established a happy "marriage" on

the road, a new strain arose. The two weeks were drawing to a close and I was a bit behind schedule. Donna would stay an extra day or two to get me into Salt Lake City proper and then she really wanted to leave. At the end of the following month she would be running for Millrose in the annual London-to-Brighton fifty-four-and-a-half-mile road race, one of the great runs in the ultra world. It was the first year it was open for women officially and Donna, naturally enough, being a thoroughly competitive soul, wanted to do as well as possible. Training in the desert by running broken segments and with all the pressure of being my handler was okay for two weeks, but the prospect of staying any longer gnawed at her. I knew that without being told.

"Well, what will you do?" she asked. "I'd stay if you really couldn't find anyone."

"No, no," I'd say hurriedly and somewhat insincerely, "it's really okay."

It wasn't, but I didn't think I could say it wasn't. On the one hand, I wanted her to shine in her world, and on the other, I was massively committed to my own endeavor. Naturally, I wanted to keep her, but to say so would only make her feel worse about leaving.

Add to that a sudden amendment to the travel plans. My brother, who had said earlier that only Utah and Nevada would require a handler, now moved from a refuse-to-be-committed stance about Wyoming to an it's-risky-as-hell attitude about my trying to make a go of it on my own.

Part of me wanted to get back on my own as a solo, but part of me liked the comfort to which I had adapted. After all, much more of the trip had been without help rather than with help and I was, I think, a bit afraid underneath. What about water? I studied the Wyoming map with a black face. It wasn't just that I had gotten spoiled and lazy, which I had, used as I was now to depending on a handler and hence reluctant to leave warmth for the iciness of solitude, but a sober consideration of the distances between towns and the familiar lack of services in-between meant something very real to me. At home in New York I hadn't known how to read a road map of the West; now I did. If I didn't get a replacement for Donna, I might not be able to finish the trip.

I started making calls.

"Richie, can you come out for a week . . ."

"Sorry, but . . ."

The name changed, but the litany was familiar. How many friends, on a few days notice, could abandon work and family? —no one could. It wasn't really poor planning or miscalculation that had me in such a bind, but all the same I was looking to direct my anger toward somebody. I certainly felt a measure of shame. I didn't like asking friends, didn't like being in such a needy, infantile posture, didn't like the implications of amateurism and didn't like putting even the mildest pressure on anyone else. It was the haste and clumsiness, the compromise of my own standards of self-reliance, that threw me under a dark shadow. When would I ever be free of relying on others?

I blamed my brother: why didn't he tell me earlier that in Wyoming I would need help for sure?

I blamed Donna: well, of course she has to go back, but she said she'd stay as long as was needed.

I blamed others: how can they turn me down?

I blamed myself: you always do it all at the last minute, you acted like this was just something you could pull off as you pleased, instead of really thinking it through.

Like many situations, the comical aspect would have been apparent if it didn't seem so serious. On the one hand, what did it matter in the scale of things whether I ran across the country? But all the same, now it did matter to me. I thought if I didn't finish it was going to haunt me for a long time.

The aggravation was accentuated by the peculiar difficulties of my position. I could hardly ask Donna to make the calls for me. I had to take the time to do them myself. It was no small matter to find a telephone in the desert. I might be near one in the morning and not near another until the evening, both awkward hours for calling—for myself and for others. These calls could easily consume a half hour—several miles of running. Just the sheer mechanics of dime insertions, waiting for the operator to come on, and busy signals on the other end that required further waiting about, in addition to a host of minor, related aggravations, sorely tried my temper.

Everyone had a valid excuse for not coming out, but the repeated denials of my petition, coupled with my native inclination to seize upon the worst possible as the likeliest outcome, worked me into a morbid state.

After several days of this quandary, I reach a point of fatal exasperation. I slammed down the phone and walked over to the car where Donna was once again waiting patiently.

"What did she say?" Donna asked.

"She can't do it. Fuck it! I don't care anymore, I really don't. It's just not meant to happen so I'll do it on my own."

"You *can't* do it on your own."

"I'll just try it and if I get by, fine. If I don't, well, I don't care if I die."

"Look, I'll stay an extra week," Donna blurted.

"I don't want you to. I want you to go."

"I'm not going to let you go off on your own from Salt Lake City."

"Just leave me alone about it, Donna. I'll be fine."

I ended the conversation by just running away. There was no "see-you-in-two-miles" sign-off. Donna eased the car alongside, tapping the horn lightly to get my attention. I knew she wanted to know how far down the road she should meet me. It wasn't fair to punish her, so I stopped and went over to her window.

"It's eight miles to Wells," I said. "Just go on into town. I'll meet you there somewhere."

The afternoon was still violently hot. Even in the coolest part of the morning I would not run more than four miles without water. At this time of day I stopped every mile and a half.

"I'll leave water for you."

"Don't bother," I said. Although I had carefully screened anger out of my voice, the cool desperation of my shoving all prudence to one side deeply bothered her. She was afraid to say any more, knew I would not listen to reason, and could not afford to abandon me. I ran hard and I ran fast and I switched to the other side of I-80 so that when Donna did stop the car and opened the trunk and waited there with a drink, I would not be tempted to do anything other than rebuff her. Although genuinely sorry to trouble her, I was so set on expressing my rage and frustration that I felt just warning her to stay clear was adequate. If I chose to hurt and punish myself, that was my own affair. It was unfortunate she had to be present for seppuku, but I was white hot.

A sorrow of the most cutting simplicity invaded my heart in the midst of all the angry talking I was carrying on with myself. After such devotion to measured restraint in output of body energy and after developing such a respect for quiet, barely audible instincts on how to live out here in the world, it was as if I was now slapping my own delicate child, whose stunned eyes simply faced my ferocious gaze. I was threatening this run. I, myself, who had in the minutest ways threaded my way through all the obstacles between success and failure. I went like a bomb down the road, growing thirstier and thirstier, calming down a bit, but too stubborn in my pride to accept water now. It was a long eight miles, but I made it. I was just okay, dizzy and weakened, but not damaged. The rage was gone, but it was sad to see how I was capable of such lunacy. Clearly, the fatigue left me far too sensitive to my difficult situation. At least I knew that my physical limits for water absence *could* be extended under extreme duress. It was the worst outburst of the whole trip. My fatalism about the hazards of circumstance became genuine later on, an easy part of my skin. It truly didn't matter what happened; the worst events evoked a rueful laugh. Can I seriously write that then I had at last attained mature wisdom? Or deftly imply it? The titanic scale of the endeavor can only be continued if one gets as simple as possible. It's either that or quit. Looking back, I think the incident was a turning point; at the time, after a good meal that evening, I just shook my head over what an ass I had been, especially when my old pal, Melanie, told me over the phone that yes, she could come out after all. So, as usual, exactly when one decides that a situation is incapable of changing for anything but the worse, it shifts to something easier. I had a new wife on the way! The tension bled out of me and I slept well that night.

I have managed to express resistance to the consumer culture by not getting a credit card. I have never had a straight job long enough to pass the credentials test of reliability. Lack of a credit card when it came to renting a car was a near-fatal obstacle. I will pass over the tangle that ensued while Melanie, aided by Innamorato, attempted to straighten out the car rental, all complicated by the fact that Melanie was another subversive who had gotten by without a credit card. Final plans, made by phone, were that rendezvous would take place near I-80 in Grantsville in the morning. Donna would immediately head back for California to turn in *her* rental car before flying home to New York.

The coming separation seemed a little unreal. It was as if Donna and I had been going down the road forever. It was hard to imagine that in an hour or so she would be gone. There is not room for drama in the day's work. I just said nothing and kept running down the road until it was time to drive on a bit and meet Melanie in town.

Nothing is ever simple. Much as Donna wanted to get home and get some rest, she was finding it hard to give up her position. The two cars were parked side by side, both with the trunks open.

"Now the way I've been making lunch for him . . ." Donna began.

I glanced at Melanie's face, but she listened without the slightest flicker. She was, after all, the author of *The Harvard*

Cookbook and had spent a couple of grueling years of nonstop cooking in her apartment to test the menus. Now she was being told how to make sandwiches. Still, Donna's evident sincerity and maternal concern that I not starve with the new baby-sitter could hardly be resented. Soon enough there was nothing left to say. The wildly chaotic interior of Donna's car had been reduced to a chaste cleanliness again. The sun was rising in the sky. Twenty-two miles lay ahead.

As Melanie drove me off, the strangeness of the change was a bit of a shock, saddening.

In ten minutes we were back on I-80. Donna was gone and the day stretched ahead, demanding that it be matched by work. Handlers come and go but the journey runner goes on.

It was a nice day. The smell of the ocean was strong since we were right next to the Great Salt Lake. Sea gulls, light green marsh grass and the dark blue paint of the lake had a strength and simplicity. The oddness of the contrast with the desert that had come before was a lovely thing to savor.

That evening, as Melanie and I lounged in separate twin beds in our Salt Lake City motel room, the phone rang. It was Donna, letting me know she had made it to Winnemucca that night in good time. I felt a twinge similar to what an adulterer would feel.

"How are you doing?" Donna asked. I might have been talking with the ghost of my departed first wife. If I raved about Melanie's abilities as a handler, then I was stabbing Donna. If I lied and said things were bad, that was not fair and impossible to say, especially with Melanie right there. So I struck a pleasantly neutral tone. In any case, Donna's main theme of talk was how unable she was to believe how far I had to go.

"What do you mean?" I asked.

"Maybe it sounds silly," she said, "but I guess doing the route with you so slowly, it didn't sink in how far you've gone. For two weeks it just never really sank in what you were doing. Now that I've driven it and it takes *so long* to drive it, I can't believe you ran all that way. And you're not even a third done. It's incredible."

I was flattered, sardonically amused by her belated discovery, and grabby in the hands, as if someone were yanking me by the neck and forcing me to gaze down a very steep ladder. All the same, Donna's comment about how far it really was stuck to me. It's strange how that happens—one particular comment, out of so much talking, shines up clearly for a long time.

For her part, Melanie handled the transition quietly, attuned to what she surmised might be mixed feelings about the arrival of the new administration. All the same, she wanted it understood she was running things her way. Donna's inveterate passion for saving every plastic bag and juice bottle had amounted to a fair-sized collection. She had tenderly bequeathed these items to Melanie who, at the time, accepted them without comment. At our first arrival at a garbage can, however, Melanie announced:

"Sorry if this offends you, but I am *not* saving every extra bottle and bag."

It was a declaration, not an invitation to debate, and I stood by meekly as these items were unceremoniously dumped.

Attired as she was in shorts and with her zaftig figure, Melanie easily wowed the truckers. Once again the lovelorn wail of horns rent the air from early till late. I wondered what the state police would make of this shift in partners. Perhaps, I reasoned, since we were in Mormon territory, they would simply assume I had a new wife. In any case they never asked, merely zipped past, barracudas in the asphalt stream.

Satisfying as it was to reach Salt Lake City, the first real city on the long haul eastward, it was even more satisfying to leave it behind. I felt as if I had no place in cities anymore and the quickie burger joints, warehouses, low-slung plant buildings, car lots, suburban homes and thick local traffic seemed confining after the roadway through the desert. Besides all that, there were the draining gusts of a hot southerly wind, carrying with it tales of dust and fever.

Just outside of town is a climb of about eight miles up through a steep canyon, the road itself overshadowed by the immense rise of the Rockies. This was relentless slog-along mountain running and it brought me up to chin level with the brief puffs of cloud that simply shone in the clarity of that air.

Melanie's first full day as a handler on the road had a close call that, in retrospect, was amusing, but is a good example of the kind of small thing that can loom so large in the battle against marching quarter-hours. I felt a stab of irritation the first few times I ran up to the car and saw how narrow a margin Melanie had left between the second, inside lane and the breakdown lane where she had parked. Visions of her being sideswiped as she waited there made me edgy.

"Pull the car over more to the side, Mel," I said, as mildly as I could.

The next few times she was over more, but then she forgot again.

"Listen, Mel," I said with considerably more up-front energy, and continued with my spiel.

By this point we had reached a relative sort of plateau about twelve miles outside of Salt Lake City, which was now far behind and below us, hidden by the shoulders of the surrounding timber-covered mountains. Heavy rain from the previous day had drenched the ground. The red-earth shoulder of the road was newly made and graded by highway machines. The utterly smooth finish was deceptive; no sooner did I try running on the dirt part than my sneakers were squelching in the soft mud. Far off down the road I could spot our blue car.

Got to warn Melanie about the shoulder, I thought.

Then as I got closer I noticed the red brake lights were on and then the white backup lights shone. Then red and white again; the pattern repeating itself over and over.

Oh, no! I thought. She's gotten stuck! I was half-ready to be cross, but I knew she probably couldn't feel any worse than she did already. Such zealousness resulting in such a disaster it must have seemed to her then!

Well, I ran up and sure enough, the car was nicely sunken in pretty close to the hubcaps and Melanie looked stricken. Maybe I did, too, but I stayed cheerful. I gathered up some brush and put it under the wheels for traction. With superior masculine calm I mentioned how I had often been in mud-immersed vehicles in Brazil, implying thereby that I would be able to get us out of the mess. I promptly sank us in even deeper.

Ten minutes later a thin rancher pulled over in his pickup. He got his chains out, hitched them up, tugged the car free, exchanged some pleasantries, couldn't abide our thank-yous and was on his way.

Despite cold, rainy weather, Melanie and I plunged on through the world and penetrated a few days later into western Wyoming. We stayed one night in Fort Bridger where the U.S. Army once maintained a post during the early settlement of the West, after having bought it from Jim Bridger, a fabled trapper who was one of the first white men to learn that part of the country. The Fort Motel was housed in one of the original stone buildings and it had more down-home character than almost any other place I stayed. The café itself dated from 1939 and you felt lucky to be in a place like that, as it provided an unglossed look back into the style and simplicity and isolation of a piece of America unaware of how it seemed to others, as yet untainted by the universalist plastic schlock. The red counter stools were made of wood, set low and had a carved-out section for the human rear. On the wall were oil paintings of Jim Bridger and an Indian. Also, a list of eastbound and westbound Greyhound buses for each day (a very short list, written in pencil). Historic belt buckles were for sale, as well as various knickknacks and tubes of toothpaste. There were curios under glass—J. Bridger's shaving brush, ponchos, et cetera, and on a far wall a Mexican hat with a wide brim.

A youngish couple were the newest owners of the café. The new proprietress made real mashed potatoes. I could see her in the back, standing at the stove. It was a hard thing, crossing

America, never finding anyone who respected a potato. I say that with the utmost seriousness. I was willing to settle for simple food, but it was hard to feel *nourished* on frozen, tasteless, deep-fried blah. Few owners or cooks could be bothered to do what I call honest food. In spite of my thanks I don't think she realized quite how sincere I was. She was a shy, very fine person.

Her daughter waited on our counter table. She was young, blond, had long arms. Shy, also. When I asked for a second large milk she nodded and took away my glass, which was a third full, and refilled it! I smiled into my glass as I drank up. The family refused to let me pay for my two platters of breakfast.

Her husband, who had clear, trusting, simple eyes, had asked through his wife for my autograph. Sternly I ignored the request the first time, thinking that he was mistaken to treat me as special. But the second time he asked I wrote a little message and signed it on the back of a green check slip, and when I left the café, I could see him holding it carefully on each edge. He was so pleased. I had never given my autograph like that before to anyone. I had just wanted to be careful. But it mattered to him; such things used to matter to me. He thought he was getting something important. He just didn't understand that what he was asking for he already had.

Wyoming makes you feel you will just step off the edge of the earth or go up into the sky. In the eastern half the tones were frequently buff and grayish. The sun was very bright. Gophers gave a high shrill of warning as I passed, standing up, paws tucked over their chests before diving for cover. Slow rise and fall of plateau land. Odd, eerie erosions of stone, like cryptic and ancient signposts, a set of bright orange ones looking like broken-off columns from an immense temple that stood on the once-fabled tortoise's back that held up the world, the termitelike shavings of eroded rock swooping down away from the base in a clean line. Black Cat fireworks for sale every forty miles in little towns and gas-station outposts. Dogs riding in the back of pickups, snuffling the air.

And the motel rooms with their little paper-wrapped soap bars, plastic drinking cups in sealed plastic bags; paper banners over the toilet lid, announcing the sterility of the seat; Chamber of Commerce brochures regaling the reader with the shopping, recreational and religious aspects of one's temporary new home; the black Gideon Bible in the dresser drawers, and the printed card left by the chambermaid, wishing us a happy stay. In the Desmond Motel in Green River I studied the paper bath mat and here proffer all written and printed visual material to be gleaned from aforesaid item:

"Welcome to Western Vacationland. For you . . . A Personal Bath Mat with Our Compliments. Sanitary. Dispose in Basket. Absorbent. Lund Distributing, Inc., Salt Lake City, Utah." (Plus green and brown ink depicting the following images: pine cones and pine needles, a fisherman in hip boots, a power boat pulling a muscular young man looking at a young woman as they water ski, a man skiing.)

The state was alive, abustle with gas, coal and ore extractions. It was hard to find motel rooms and in the frontier haste to settle in, droves of mobile homes were everywhere, tacked down in towns and floating past on the highways, drawn on toward those who wanted them, the "wide load" banners flapping in the windstream. I often fantasized about seeing a brisk housewife open one of the side doors and shake her mop out onto the highway. Imagine if one were condemned to live in constant motion, an entire family living in a perpetually mobile home. How long could one endure it?

So the days went busily enough, filled with big and little things. Melanie would sit absorbed in her book, sometimes not noticing I was coming till I ran up to the car door. When there was sunshine she sat out in that, hoping to improve her tan. We had short, interesting, intense talks, catching up on different things, since we hadn't seen each other for a while. Part of one day I remember imagining some as yet unborn son of mine running over that same stretch of road or driving over it, looking and wondering if it was still the same as when I had seen it. A blue storm ahead of us filled the great goblet of sky, seeming to gather speed and intensity as it moved eastward, as if it were being compressed into a funnel. The sun shining from behind my back only deepened the cold dark blueness of the storm clouds.

Up over a long, long slope to the crest, to reach the Continental Divide. To the west of that line all the streams and rivers drain into the Pacific; to the east the flow is to the Gulf Coast and the Atlantic. So the trip was half over in a sense, even though I had run only a thousand miles. I could literally see the earth tilt, serene and unencumbered prairie land sloping down toward the Atlantic. Watching a freight train labor up that same slope, I felt a wave of sympathy for its effort; I know how it feels, I thought.

Red Desert. Wamsutter. Places that were chronically weary. Settlements that were spindly, ugly weeds; a dingy gas station, rugged cafés, mobile homes, potholed streets, scruffy, hard-working young men. I stood for a moment outside the motel room where we stayed in Wamsutter, looking at the blinking neon signs. Silhouetted against the green sky were cars and trucks whizzing over I-80. Whither bound? It was cold, too cold to stand there for long, so I closed the door on the delights and dilemmas of the roadway. Sleep was what followed eating, as surely as darkness follows day. So we slept for a while, pretending that this odyssey of loneliness is restricted to the roadway and does not enter even motel rooms where dreamers lie dreaming.

Farewell to the West

There was a certain kind of running I always resented. I called it enforced running because it was forced on me by circumstance. Those were the days when I had to run a certain number of miles—usually a lot of them—to get to a town where there was a motel. Or they were stretches without water or food that simply had to be crossed. Until I got the intervening miles completed I could not relax. I'm not sure why it bothered me so much to feel that I *had* to do a particular stretch of road. After all, I had to run the entire three thousand miles one way or another, so the whole issue of whether it was "voluntary" or not was a specious one. Probably my mental state for accommodating to the task was a bit grumbly and growly and pessimistic and narrow-focused. I never assumed I could run a single mile until I'd done it and I was never sure that I would make it to the end of any given day. Of course, at one level I *was* sure, but at another I wasn't. "Levels" is a funny word—it implies there is a kind of shelving in the brain and yet it doesn't *feel* that way at all. This whole book is an attempt to render the feeling of crossing the country and yet even these feelings of resentment at enforced running were hard to assess—both then and now. I'm not sure if I took them seriously or not—they seemed to come from somewhere and go off to somewhere else, clouds over the moon, and all the while it was as if underneath at bedrock, it didn't matter.

The worst bit of enforced running came after twenty-five consecutive running days, which carried me 1,074 miles from Dillon Beach to the town of Rawlins, Wyoming. The next day was a day off, the first of the trip, since I would drive with Melanie to Laramie where she would turn in the car. Along the way I planned to leave caches of food and water since the last hundred and fifty miles in Wyoming had only three towns and almost no gas stations or restaurants over that entire stretch. Three days of fifty-mile days, fresh to the pack again.

The owner of the motel where we stayed on the edge of Rawlins was, like a lot of westerners, a recent transplant. Tall and thin, with black hair and glasses, he came from Yonkers, New York. After five years out there, would he ever go back?

"Never," he said. "I'm very happy. Why, I know more people here in Rawlins than I ever knew at home."

Behind him on the wall was a framed dollar bill from the Rawlins Chamber of Commerce, congratulating him on opening a new business. May you make many thousands more during your stay here, it enthused.

The final divorce proceedings took place that night in our motel room. Melanie and I divided up our worldly goods, threw a lot of things away, and left a small mountain of food items for the maid the next morning.

The next day, at an early hour, both of us silent and tired for the most part, saw us driving down the road, stopping every ten miles so I could squirrel my Ziploc bags filled with peanuts or trail mix (coconut, raisins, nuts, carob chips), oranges and plastic bottles filled with water. Melanie made cryptic notes in her round handwriting: "MM (mile marker) 227, behind shrubs, water only."

I wasn't happy seeing the road I was going to run over in advance. It seemed to be cheating. Where was the surprise then? We did some errands in Laramie and wandered around a few shops. We were both distracted and overtired so our farewell was quiet, almost accidental.

I rode a Greyhound bus back to Rawlins. Guilt still hung over me. Now I viewed myself as an AWOL soldier, sneaking back to base. A storm front closed in from the west and the windows of the bus were pelted with rain. The world went gray.

A thin man in the seat next to mine was from Philadelphia where he worked in his father's brass-bed factory. He was on his way to Salt Lake City. Although he learned a lot about me, he never volunteered a reason for his own trip. He refused to agree about politics and had his own sharp, cutting observations to make. His face was narrow and squeezed together, some bit of ferret in his face. But he gave a sense of control; there was a keenness and a sharpness to the way he watched your face and never really rested in his seat. He sat on coiled springs of nervous drive.

That night I ate in a restaurant attached to one of the fancier motels in Rawlins.

"Just one?" asked the maitre d', his fat, fast hands grabbing a plastic-coated menu.

"Just one," I said, nettled.

He marched me to a small deuce table, the kind where there is a chair on the outside and a seat on the inside, a long plastic-backed bench you slide into. But it was right next to the kitchen exit. I was alone and in running clothes, a pariah. Exclusion from polite society stung. I smoldered for a while. Why was I so out of sorts? I hated my vacation. That, too, had been another illusion.

The next morning the enforced running began, but in spite of being on the road at an early time, 6:40 A.M., I lost the margin and ended up starting a bit later. These little things that I kept learning all the way through the trip! This time it was that I should not have ended the previous day's run *behind* me, so that I would have to double back there the next day. But I had forgotten that, so spoiled had I become to the presence of a car. These extra twenty minutes here or there meant sacrificing rest breaks later on down the road.

All the way across America people asked if I cheated. It was a curious kind of question and you have to wonder why people asked so often. Either I inspired a kind of disbelief through something in my manner, or it was a way of checking the fact that I *really* went the whole thing. Perhaps it also reflected an attitude on their part about how *they* might do it. I enjoyed the question, the simplicity of such unwitting rudeness—or what would have felt like rudeness if one bothered to care—which was such a complete misreading of my motivation and style that it was just, well, funny. And I was pleased people felt they could ask me, especially the men, with that kind of knowing shrewdness: "And you haven't even taken one little ride?"

I would grin and shrug and say: "Nah."

Who knows what they thought; perhaps a more vehement protest of integrity would have killed the snake.

It wasn't that I didn't think about taking rides or about ways in which I could just ride buses from town to town and call in every couple of days to my friends and tell them I was here or there. Who would ever know? And even the future readers of this book could be deceived. I had been lucky, I was beginning to see, in not having decided to go after a record for the crossing. Oh, some days there would be an hour or so of fantasy math. "If I run sixty miles a day now for two weeks and then seventy miles every other day . . ." Such musings were diversions and I knew it all the time. What was the point of running in the closet of my own ambition all the way across with no time to talk to anyone, continually the victim of a goal? Just finishing was difficult enough. And it hardly made sense to cheat and get such a slow crossing as mine. If you weren't helping yourself illegally to a record then why bother? No one was going to pay attention to a seventy-five- or eighty-five-day crossing or whatever it turned out to be. It doesn't matter how much you suffer or push through your own resistances, because if it isn't a record then the media, the modern-day distributors of glory, will not pay attention. There is an altogether human fascination with the fastest man or woman in any running event; they are by the definition of the sport, the first, the best, different from you and me. And we are dazzled by such uniqueness. Perhaps that is the way it should be. I often thought of others who had run across the country faster than myself. Some seemed completely trustworthy and others less so. I was willing to believe there were men in the world stronger than myself; I was happy for them. I would be happy for myself too if I could just get my carcass back before snow fell.

I willingly suffered from an overdeveloped scrupulousness about covering every inch of the run. Now on this particular morning in Rawlins, I walked up to the exit ramp thinking that I had ended the run at a mile marker. Since the mile marker did not exist, I lost my confidence in being sure that I knew where I had ended the run. I remembered seeing a particular tire tread and a dead shoe warped by the weather, or had I? I was out of control with the business so I tramped an extra quarter mile westward, angrily muttering and looking at my watch. Only the truly tired can sympathize with the bitterness of losing another thimblefull of energy on such foolishness. There are times when you can understand how irrational you are, but it simply doesn't help. But nothing mattered more than being honest. If I said I had done it then I would have to have done it. The transcon was myself, so how could I betray that? All the same, it was a jangling way to start the day. At least running is like sleep; soon enough it was all there was and as I woke up into the world around me a little more clearly, my worries faded.

Not far from Rawlins is a Sinclair refinery and what looked to be a company town nearby. The refinery seemed, as so much does out in the Far West, a reminder not so much of the present as of the past. The blue mountains and low clouds were a backdrop for where early man might have wandered. And before that all this open space had been lush vegetation that had eventually become oil. And now this complicated structure of tubes and storage tanks fulfilled our need to please and sustain ourselves. To do so we tap the stored potentialities of the earth. There was a giant flame burning off some kind of oil by-product. The flame glared and spun, flickering slightly as it danced in the morning air, exemplifying some kind of inevitability of the present moment. What did it mean? Where are we in the world, in the desert, and for what are we headed? The flame was so bright that I looked away finally, although the after-image glowed on for a while, ghostly yet blinding.

At times the day had wildly exuberant parts. The bare rocky slopes, the horizon-to-horizon immensity of the long, stretched-out but still crinkled blanket of earth, steep uphill grades to fight against and in the purity of the blue sky, a sign of change. Fall was coming now. There was a milkiness to the light, some slight dimming and mistiness of effect that seemed different. Near the Elk Mountain turnoff was a wonderful mountain to the south with very smooth brown slopes and a fringe of timber near the top where passing clouds were briefly ensnared. Trees! Even from twenty miles away they looked special.

Just before six in the evening I was holed up in the little town of Elk Mountain. After all the searing clarity of wide open space, it was delightful to be among houses tucked away under shade trees.

Bill, a big pleasant fellow who was doing carpentry work for the woman who owned the place I stayed in, chatted about local affairs as I sat in the doorsill of my cabin and quietly speculated about the origin of his tattoos. His motorcycle was parked nearby; you just knew he had knocked around in his day, not so long past. He was gentle now. His small son cried when he was down near the stream, as if he had taken a fall. Bill dropped his tools and sprinted off through the trees to find out what was the matter.

There was only one place in Elk Mountain to eat. Bill's wife worked there as a waitress. It was an unusually expensive, fancy kind of place, not really in keeping with the simple town. Except that word was that good money could be made nearby in the coal mines. Development and big money were on their way. A gaggle of truckers from the South and the Southwest sat on wooden stools at the bar, knocking back beers and retailing stories about being stuck in snowstorms and which tow-service owner was a bastard and a nincompoop and which ones were good sorts.

In the mountains when the sun goes down, the nights are sharply chilly. The cold seemed different now. The earth was moving around the sun. Winter began to seem not so far off. There was no time now to falter.

The next morning I took a back dirt road to link up again with I-80. To save a few hundred meters, I dodged through some barbed-wire fences and ran over grassy fields while keeping a cautious eye out for some husky-looking cattle nearby.

The first road sign of the day said: MERGE. Good advice, but I couldn't do it! It was a morning of struggle. I tried concentrating on my breath, on a biofeedback technique, on paying attention to my body, but it didn't still the restless jumpy chatter of the small mind. I knew it was a sure sign I was taking it all too seriously. I was worrying about having to get through these long fifty-four-and-a-half miles between Elk Mountain and Laramie, so I paid the price. Not until about thirty miles was there a sudden ah-now-we're-here kind of rush.

All the same, there were always things of the world. Blue shadows from the clouds covered the ground, sweeping along over the folds in the vast yellow blanket. Horses, cattle, deer —all were outdoors as well. There was a nice place for a crap in a drainpipe below I-80. As the cars rushed overhead I squatted in the low drain and admired the serenity of this improvised outhouse. No graffiti marred the concrete walls. There was a rustle as the wind carried the scrap of paper towel away.

The running was all at a seven- to eight-thousand foot altitude and it was a bit hard at times working for air. The hills that had to be surmounted on the way to Laramie were relentless and when some people in a pickup truck hurled an egg at me, I screamed obscenities.

At a rest stop in an all-purpose store and gas station called

All the King's Men, I came in from an afternoon of lightning storms and nearby black rainfall and sat down at a plastic seat with an ice cream shake. There was a ruddy-faced trucker with his wife, both in their early fifties. His sleeves were rolled up to above his elbows and he wore a brim cap. They hated me. I could feel it, but I refused to hurry along and they got up eventually and left. They kept biting me with little glances.

Sitting nearby were two married couples, all of them wearing sunglasses. I tried to read them and their histories the way we all do with each other. They were Europeans, I thought. Something about the way they sat and then every so often *looked* at the interior of All the King's Men. It wasn't the look of someone for whom an environment is home; it was a measuring and a testing, as if to say, so *this* is it, *this* is America. One of the men kept looking over at me. I didn't care exactly. I knew well enough how strange I looked. But he repeated the stare to the point of rudeness. There are tiny contracts we make in the society of our fellows—stand so close and no closer, glance but do not stare—and yet, there he was, staring. It was neither admiring nor hostile, but its meaning was not clear until I walked past on my way out the door.

"Excuse me," the man said. His black balding hair was brushed back along the sides of his stout head. His English was thick. "Excuse me, are you Israeli?"

I laughed and told them my name and what I was doing. They spoke in Hebrew among themselves, but asked little more. Perhaps they thought I was mad. Perhaps I was.

"Shalom," I said.

They smiled and nodded. It would have been nice to talk a little, but I was afraid of night coming, afraid of the miles that lay ahead.

I made good running time coming down into Laramie. A long range of mountains lies in back of the town itself, which is a low smudge of trees and buildings with the white horseshoe shape of the University of Wyoming football stadium gleaming through the vast prairie distance. Although the towns out

West are really relatively small, everything is tight and compact. There is no sprawling suburban fringe. The road-construction crews so prevalent in the West, who get in their repairs before the long winters, were busy laying fresh tar.

Around 7 P.M. I walked off the highway over a bridge that spanned a shabby polluted creek and entered a dingy stretch of town.

Some young guys in a filling station turned to stare and I felt hard again, detached from civilian life, the way a soldier might be. But just when I was ready to decide how people *really* are difficult to get along with, as usual someone would be awfully nice. At the motel that I selected on the far end of town, the very last one before the wide open spaces began again, the woman proprietor said, when I expressed relief at finding a room, "Oh, well, even if we were full we would have found room for you somehow."

Fall is bringing changes. The next morning the first school-bus appears, the first yellow leaf on the tree. The sun is still warm, hot even, but the warning is clear. I waved to a girl waiting for the bus, but she didn't seem to spot the salutation. A moment later the bus swallowed her up. The last bit of fresh ranch-house development fell away.

The mountain range begins quickly, without preface. Up through the pass the road yawns back and forth. A few glances back show the last glimpses of buff prairie land far below. The road has been cut through red rock, the face of which is blocky and rough. At the bottom of the cuts was a litter of red dust like a heavy accumulation on a window sill. Pine trees, black against the rising sun, threw long shadows, but the glare of light was very strong. Plump groundhogs shrilled their warning call as the intruder lumbered up the hill. Yellow-winged grasshoppers crackled and leapt in chattering flights through the air, thousands and thousands of times, repeating their song. (Insects make me nervous.) But my previous distaste vanished at the thought of winter approaching.

"Hurry up, guys," I told them, "your time is running short."

There was no more thought of how far to go that time of day. I vowed a new vow—that I would run without stopping from the bottom of the pass to the summit, a good five and a half miles or so to the 8640-foot level. In the thinner air, the sky seemed both to retreat into a greater spaciousness and draw closer, as the clouds bumped along just out of arm's reach.

Resplendent above the summit's drive-in rest area was a bust of Lincoln, an immense metal casting, slightly tilted, impressive almost in spite of itself. An inscription read: "We must think anew and act anew." Even memorials suffer from bumper-sticker mentality. Did anything need to be said? Would anyone read that line and feel committed to acting anew? Who picked out the line and why? Many puzzles, but all of the nickel variety. A less somber memorial was a rock with a chiseled inscription:

> Telephone Canyon. The first in the West through which a telephone line was run. The first conversation over this line was held in 1882 between Bill Nye at Laramie and Hon. F. E. Warner at Cheyenne.

This was more like it. It was almost odd enough to be humorous and just dull enough to make me wonder if it was worth copying down. It suggested a paucity of eventfulness in the area. And yet one saw how the West was in 1882. What a difference a phone line must have made. It was a day on foot for a trained runner in 1980 to span the two towns and so about as long for a horseback rider to get between the two places. In the town I lived in in Brazil a phone call depended on a couple of big Eveready batteries. A clerk who lounged in the doorway during its erratic office hours waited all day for three calls, the reception of which would provoke a mad dash by some small boy on his important mission. "Oh, So-and-so!" the boy would cry. "The *telephone* is calling you!" And the adult, alert and concentrated suddenly with the gravity of the event, would pull his hat down about his ears and trot over the dusty lanes of the town to the phone line. A small crowd of girls, chewing their nails, one knee bent in a kind of slouchy languor, would eavesdrop with ease on the person yelling into the barely functioning line. And the line itself was but a wire nailed to a series of posts. Could it have been so different after all in these western outposts without paved streets and with no doubt an ample fund of small boys to send scurrying hither and yon? There are worse monuments to remind us that all now is not as it once was.

The top of the pass broadened out into a wide plateau. Unlike most climbing through passes, the reward of a long downhill stretch was postponed for miles since I-80 simply ran along with only the very slightest downward tilt. Up here there were no houses, no walkers, no runners, no humans on foot at all. Neither were there cattle or sheep or insects. Only pine trees and sky. For a while, oddly-shaped rock formations appeared to the north, looking as if they stood on their knuckles. Little stairways of pine trees climbed along the oddly-beveled spines of these hills. The entire scene looked like a fantastical Japanese print. Far away to the south were the more classically serene snow-capped peaks of a distant range. All through Wyoming along I-80 immense multi-tiered snow fences, set at an angle to the road to catch snowdrifts, were set up every quarter mile or so. They were reminders of approaching winter. Already there had been snow in this part of the state a couple of days before and it was only the tag end of August. The locals had spoken of it as well: "Snow up here is just around the corner, another coupla weeks." And they wondered how I would survive the cold all the way back to New York. Clearly the protracted sigh of Indian summer in the East is apparently condensed to one warm afternoon up in the Rockies.

Just west of a dot on the map called Buford was another historical site.

A signboard read: "This tree was growing out of a crevice in the rock when the Union Pacific Railroad built its original main line fifty feet south of this rock in 1868 . . . and supposedly was shifted slightly to avoid destruction of this phenomenon. The fireman of each passing train never failed to drench the tree with a bucket of water." The rock itself is orange-colored and has a cobbled surface on which grows some sort of lichen or moss, presumably encouraged by the extra moisture available to it over the years. A small pine that grows out of a crack in the rock has yielded to the insistences of the prevailing westerlies, since almost all the branches protrude on the eastern side. Some unknown soul tied a yellow ribbon strip of plastic around the tree's girth, a reminder of the Iranian hostages.

Buford itself, which lay a little farther on, is the only real spot to stop at for fifty-odd miles. True to the desolate surroundings and the scanty commercial trade the town (if that is what it is) is comprised of a single store, which also doubles as a post office. They were a friendly bunch in there. One young guy was working there for the summer, home being New Jersey. One of the gas-station attendants had a father who runs in all the marathons in New York. So there were things to chatter about. But in a little while I stood up for the hundredth time, swung the pack up, cinched it tight and ran off.

Afterward came miles and miles of rolling, wild and empty hills. Way down yonder at long last, where the vast downslopes bottomed out, was a smudge of buildings. That was Cheyenne. The long buzz of anxiety faded. There was no New York, no Chicago, no Akron, no future. Such were afternoons. In the mornings, though the goal for the end of the day's run was fixed, uncertainty and despair sometimes snuck in. By the end of the day the great focal point had been achieved. Sometimes it was a little disheartening when there was no obvious place to shoot for. After Cheyenne I thought only of the Nebraska-Wyoming border. After that came a stop with the mother of a friend in Ogallala, Nebraska. After that I had a vague notion of reaching the Mississippi and in a barely conceivable way, the great city whose existence seemed a mere rumor—Chicago. As for the end of the trip, I rarely thought about it.

There *was* a specific fantasy connected with arriving in New

York. I wanted to come into the city over my favorite bridge, the George Washington. Running through a tunnel, even if permission could be obtained, seemed inappropriate, like a rat dodging into a sewer. The question of where to finish was not so easy to decide. City Hall is the traditional beginning and end point for transcon runners, but I thought it a poor choice. Despite its strongly old-fashioned look, the site is a cluttered one. The front steps face onto a parking lot. There is no natural warmth to the place; it remains determinedly anonymous.

As for the very tip of the island of Manhattan, as close to the Atlantic as possible, that too, seemed wrong. There was no obvious terminus unless one sought to eschew all matter of formality by picking any spot out of pure whimsy—say a park bench or a phone booth. The island curves around without a marker or a joggle or a spur or a jutting rock. Besides, if friends came to see me finish they would have to go somewhere where they would not want to linger. So another thought was to run home, just stop at my apartment, which is near the Soldiers and Sailors Monument in Riverside Park on a bluff of land that looks westward out over the Hudson and toward California. That too was wrong. It wasn't open the way a public finish should be. Central Park became the obvious choice. After all the thousands of miles I and my friends had spent running through there, it was a fine site. And since the marathon finish line near Tavern on the Green is marked in blue and is in its own right an obvious terminal point I respected, then that was where it would be.

Once fixed on the idea of where to finish, I felt a sense of relief. There was an absurdity to that, as if I were being shot toward a distant galaxy on an interminably long voyage that would end at such and such a point. All the points of time and space and being that I would burn through to reach a mythical finish point for one infinitely divisible point of completion, so fine that I would never know when I reached it—even setting this kind of sense against the child's simplicity to know where it would end did not disturb me. There was always the danger of not running through a point instead of aiming toward it. If

I ran through the finish line at least there was the chance of actually experiencing something, whereas running toward it would condemn me to living it as a dream. How can you reach something where there is only your idea, your fantasy, your conjuring of it? And I did not expect the run to change my life in any way I could control. There was bound to be a letdown and the more I looked to the future, the rockier the present was ultimately going to be. The expression of these differing attitudes showed themselves in my body. Running toward a point accentuated forward lean and tightening; running without focusing on where I was getting to meant coming back on my heels and staying relaxed. This was no launching of myself toward happiness. Ecstatic deliverance did not await arrival in New York. Certainly, my tendency in the past had been to view long runs or races, in part anyway, as edging up toward a fabulous high. The justification had always been, after all the suffering, at last deliverance. The first one hundred kilometer I ever ran was an all-day affair. The closing six miles with Fat Richie got better and better. My body found a miraculous surge of strength and the sun even shone after a day-long sullen withdrawal. Most ultraraces had that reward. Then there was that training run and walk which took about twenty-four hours. There I had imagined, but did not get, some fine surge as I pounded up the last brutal bit of a Dutchess County hill. It was just—well, it was simply about to end. My primary emotion was the hope of sitting down in a chair. I thought it over later and wondered if I would have done it if I had known there would be so little sugar in the tea. The answer was yes, but the warning from that and many other sources was evident. Beware of greed.

Giving in to exactly what I knew I was doing was all right, I decided, just so long as I didn't deceive myself.

"You want to imagine finishing?" I told myself in the tone one reserves for an overgrown child who still clamors to sit in your lap. "Okay, if you think you'll feel better. Just so long as you realize what an ass you are."

Able at last to be an infant without impediment, I would

lock the door, so to speak, and bind myself up with diapers. Then with thumb stuck firmly in mouth, I would coo to myself over the following drama:

At long last, tanned and lean from the fires of hell, I would round the bottom of the park and then head up the last set of rolling rises that lead north toward the marathon finish line. I would see a knot of people there. Sometimes I imagined them seeing me as well and I felt what I thought *I* would feel on seeing someone finish such a thing—he is, after all, a human figure, just arms and legs moving, a bit of ordinary flesh and yet, he has come *all that way*. It was an almost impersonal admiration I felt. My breathing quickened, heart raced, a surge of incredible strength came on and neither heat nor hill nor boredom could affect me. Perhaps twenty times in all I ran through the finish scene; it was like getting drunk. Afterward I came back to myself a bit guilty and defiant, vowing not to do it again but knowing perhaps I would.

Cheyenne was one of the special arrival points. There were a half-dozen places on the run with which I had a personal connection. For hundreds of miles, previous to arriving—for as much as a week—the vibration of that connection would yield an ever-stronger attraction, much the way the fringes of a planet's gravity delicately draw a passing meteorite in toward the final future impact. I had never been in Nevada before, but knowing that my brother and his family had been there, living nearby, imbued the place with solace, made it real. It was a talisman to touch. It shone like a beacon through four hundred miles of still undifferentiated blankness. I had names of would-be friends or established friends in Nebraska, Iowa and Illinois. The possibility of human warmth sometimes helped, the way a prisoner might hold off for hours or days from the satisfaction of eating an extra cookie.

Many people voiced a fear that by doing this run I was exposing myself to some sinister, not-easily-defined menace. No one would question my running ten miles in my own neighborhood, yet ten miles in a state like Nebraska, which for an East Coast person represents some impossibly foreign region, was where "they" might get me. The film, *Easy Rider,* that came out in the late sixties, protrayed a freewheeling motorcycling hero who aroused the beast in redneck America. Of course, people in Nebraska wondered how I would fare in Ohio, say. For everyone, "out there" is simply not here. We are so tribal in our instincts. We cannot help but change ourselves into "us" and "them." I knew from my own running through upstate New York that what is familiar is a kind of home. Why should I be afraid to run down a pitch black road at 3 A.M. in the Putnam County hills, miles from the nearest town, with only the black rise of dripping forest shutting me in on each side? The cars out at that hour were no more interested in me than in the fleeting, barely glimpsed diving of a bat on the edge of the woods. It was no different anywhere else in the country or in the world.

Of course, if I had run the whole route before, then I would have owned it in a different way. Distance is always shorter the second time; the mind fills with ongoing recognitions. So possession is nine tenths of ordinary comfort. There were the teen-agers in Croton-on-Hudson who tried to tickle three of us one dark night with the edge of their fender. We leapt into the roadside weeds much to the hilarity of the drunken boys and girls. If they try to kill you in your home state, why condemn the unvisited ones unfairly?

There *were* some unpleasant brushes during the transcon. There was a truckdriver in eastern Wyoming who went over a narrow bridge on I-80 the same time I did. The lane on his left was open. I could not get any closer to the bridge stanchions than I was. With that split-second assessment the mind makes every time a vehicle passes from behind, always assuming that potential death comes that way, my nerves screamed "Jump!" No room to jump! The truck barreled through just a hand's width away. He was the only truck driver out of ten thousand to do it so sneeringly. Even the very gurgle of the iron motor had a rawness, a pure hatred that I returned in full measure. I did not yell back, but I drew down on him a curse that would leave him tangled in his own wreckage. So sure was I of the efficacy of such a spell that I withdrew it, worried that even to think in such a manner is to contribute in a way that is never lost in the sky of consciousness we all share. If I could not be helpful, I could at least be silent.

Answering such threats was a sign of my own undevelopment, but I didn't care. So when the people in California threw something out the window at fifty mph that hit me square in the chest, or when the red-headed Wyoming boy delighted his teen-age friends by forcing me to leap for safety, I gave full vent to my outrage. All my weariness and frustration yearned to find a target. I was so angry I was willing to take on any number of attackers. There is a dangerous delusion one develops after enduring so much. You feel you can face down any danger, any threat. You don't run so far, after all, without having some kind of strength and when a flash of anger concentrates it, the rush is not to be believed.

The middle aged and the elderly did not threaten with prankish maneuvers of the automobile. Only young males of the human species felt that instantaneous, instinctive hatred that I remembered so well from boarding-school encounters. Perhaps they did not understand the value of life too clearly. It was always easy to distinguish between the real attackers and the merely inept. Sometimes the old granddads would be peering over the wheel of their older model cars, staring out with a rigid doggedness. Middle-aged women had the same problem of driving stiffly. There was such a sullen, glassy coolness they slunk behind, as if it was everyone else's responsibility to avoid them. These various types piloted their steel craft with undeviating faith in their exclusive rights. I would curse and sigh and leap again and again to safety with a friendly if sour amusement.

Then there was what might be termed the "veer syndrome." Motorists who spot an unusual object farther down the road instinctively swing the wheel slightly toward the point at which they are suddenly looking with surprise. To the weary soul plodding along quietly, this repeated veering of autos toward his poor carcass seems almost synonymous with an aggressive homicidal intent. Clearly, it is not done with such terrible motivation because once it is clear that I am indeed a human and not an apparition, they swing away. Several hundred repetitions of this in a day take a toll.

The truckers themselves were unimpeachable in their road etiquette. The rigs are immense and on narrow two-lane roads through the heartland of Iowa and Nebraska and Ohio I could hardly expect them to always give way to me. And they were at work as I was. So for them I would run over the rough stubble of roadside weeds. Often they waved or beeped.

Many truckers had a plastic hand affixed to the windshield with a rubber suction cup. The hand, which was a flat cutout resembling a palm and set of digits open in greeting, would waggle with the vibrations of the truck's passage. Glancing up for an instant, I was sometimes fooled and waved in reply, only to notice, as the glare on the windshield vanished, that the driver actually had both hands on the wheel. I felt miffed and foolish on such occasions, answering someone who possibly did not care whether I did. It was a curious phenomenon really, another of our remarkable conveniences. Surely a trucker of a misanthropic cast of mind would not bother to purchase such a thing unless motivated by a desire to express a general warmth toward the outside world in the line of: "Hi, there, how are *you?* I'm fine myself, can't speak to you all individually so I'm sending you all the same message—howdy!" Was the little hand that snared such foolish fish as myself there to provoke a derisive smile—"Ha! Fooled that jogger!"—or be instead noted with a warm and sympathetic glow of recognition? And was the hand meant only for people? Undoubtedly, but the hand waved indiscriminately—at desert, at trees, at cloudy skies and clear ones, at dogs and at the scattered carcasses of dead hares, at the road itself. It was a cosmic greeting this quickie item extended. But to give up your own personal commitment to the expression of friendliness, to surrender the effort needed to raise your hand in salutation to a spring and piece of plastic—well, it is a wild world we live in.

The worst incident of harassment took place in Nebraska. I was running through the Platte River valley along State Route 30. The train tracks for the Union Pacific run closely parallel to the road. The summer repair crews were out at frequent intervals. The rails occasionally warp and need to be straightened, ties had to be replaced and new bed laid in. One hot morning as I came around one of the few curves that had appeared for a couple of hundred miles, I noticed the yellow Union Pacific trucks parked at one of the road crossings. Frequent dirt roads, not worthy of inclusion on anything but a county map that connect farms to the main road, provide access for the repair crews. Through the rolling heat waves was visible a knot of dark figures. It was an unusually large gang of men, perhaps twenty all told. They were strung out in twos and threes for about fifty meters.

My mood was sober and not particularly sociable. I wasn't feeling much of anything except an immense desire to just get on with my work. There is a kind of implicit code about encounters in more rural sections of the country. It is not a crowded Manhattan street. There is so much open space, so many fewer people and those who are there are so sure of who they are and who they know, that tipping your social hat is easy, natural, automatic. Now I knew that I fell somewhat outside the normal social pattern. Because of my strangeness, people felt freer to approach me and to ignore me as well. Nearing this group of strange men evoked my resentment. In the Peace Corps, a lot of Brazilians I met assumed I was a C.I.A. spy. I tried to change the mind of every doubter until one day I just decided it didn't matter. I couldn't prove myself to every single person I met. It was okay to be disliked. If they had a problem with me it was theirs, not mine.

In a mocking way I rehearsed the wearisome lines: "Yes, I'm running across the country . . . no, I left on the thirty-first of

July." I would have to ask for directions to give them a chance to paw at me and decide I was okay. It was none of their damn business who I was. I wasn't interfering with anyone; the road was public and free. I didn't need directions. Let them say what they wanted.

As usual, words are not needed to carry thoughts, and the mutual hostility of both parties crackled as they were exchanged. I had almost gotten by without difficulty, due to the tall weeds that prevented my being clearly seen, but lulls in the manful chatter warned me to stay alert. I stared fixedly at the road. Then the grass near the shoulder began to rustle as the first stones were thrown. It was hard to believe such nonsense and it took a number of similar pitches before it was clear that it really was not an illusion.

"Stay cool," I told myself.

Another rock chunked into the ground a foot away. Then someone whistled. That did it. I wheeled around and walked back toward the men, who variously nudged one another, bent to their tools again or stood waiting.

A few younger men, just into their twenties, sassy looking, were the ones who had done it. You just sense these things.

"Somebody throwing rocks?" I asked with elaborate sarcasm. I took my hat off. I was adrip with sweat, could smell the brine from my armpits.

The three young men giggled and looked at each other.

"Somebody got a loose hand with rocks?" My voice got louder. All down the line everyone was leaning on their tools and listening.

No one answered.

"I've been running sixteen hundred miles and I don't need any more trouble than I've got."

A few questions came. Surprised that they recognized me as human, I answered straight. I still wanted an apology, but this game wasn't worth the time. I turned away. More cracks, bursts of laughter. Angry, but understanding how easy it is to hate those who are different from you, I could hardly blame them.

The long run down the tremendous slope of land into Cheyenne was the end of the prairie and the special solitude that went with it. One more day's running would carry me to Nebraska. Boundaries are not quite as arbitrary as I once believed. State lines exist only because we all agree to it. And yet often the *vicinity* of the boundary is where a change ought to come. The time zones always came when darkness arrived much earlier than eight hundred miles west of there, even allowing for the shortening days. And the lay of the land changed within a few miles of state boundaries. Now the prairie was turning into something less thrilling but more tranquil.

Cheyenne itself was a disappointment. Where were the proud main streets with brick fronts and some older, pure sense of an earlier generation of homebuilders? The motel strip is not astonishingly vulgar—Cape Cod is worse—but fast-food joints, convenience stores, auto dealerships and all the trashy western reality reduced to symbolic logos and names are—cowboys, cattle and desert. To resent vulgarity is a luxury; at least a city existed here. Cheyenne is a town whose being is not totally servile to the dictates of the interstate. Some smaller places in Wyoming, Nevada and Utah are like semirotten melons split in half by the whack of the knife's edge where I-80 cuts through. The proud four-lane transcontinental highway beggars down into a two-lane rutted road. Trucks jounce along like donkey carts in a Brazilian market town. Especially at night with the low one-story bars and stores casting fluorescent patches of light on the ground, one might be in some seedy Mexican town. Dust spun by the wheels of the rigs clouds the air. Dark figures tramp over the rocky street, a hot jalopy driven by some local kids burbles with loud exhaust pipes. What do you do in the desert—pump gas, drive umpteen miles to work in a mining or chemical plant, fry hamburgers in a café? These towns exist for the traffic of travelers and strangers. Cheyenne

had its own dignity, but the beauty of the West did not seem
to find expression in the physical expression of mortar and
brick. The mystery and the magic is in the sky and the earth;
the cattle and the crops. Space, literal space in all that miraculous abundance, is the source of the dignity of that region.

As much as I could regret leaving an area I had struggled so
hard to get through, I was sorry it was ending. I thought of the
West now as a good friend. The road toll was expensive, but
the rest of the trip was going to become tamer, more socialized,
more humane. That was wonderful, but so is the wildness of
those desolate plains and mountains.

Plowed fields appear soon after leaving Cheyenne, alternating bands of open earth and autumn stubble. Herefore cattle
grazed in the pastures, as stolid as animated oak tables. They
turned their muzzles toward me in the hot hazy sunshine,
displaying that comical patch of matted white curls between
their horns. Metal windmills signaled the presence of water.

At the end of the day a set of low rocky bluffs with scattered
pine trees appeared. The town, named appropriately Pine
Bluffs, is a short run from the Nebraska border. I stumped
straight off I-80, our nine hundred miles together over at last.
I was too tired to acknowledge the end of the drama. I was
beat. Many days were to come when I could pay homage. I
limped along, hampered by a muscle problem in my right calf,
just in back of the knee. It had been brooding and speaking to
me for days, off and on. I had had to throw myself into bouts
of intense stretching and, as tonight, hunted up Epsom salts.
Many motels do not have tubs. That blissful release of a good
soak was the nearest I could get to a massage. With a 1 percent
margin of safety, having a tub made a lot of difference. The
leg was so bad I did not see how it was possible to get up the
next morning and run forty to fifty miles on it. Under no
circumstances in my previous life would I have violated all the
instincts that warn you to lay off. What could I do? It didn't
feel like a one-day rest would help—it needed at least a week.
Sleep was the cure. Go to sleep and wake up and get out of bed

putting your weight down slowly. Newspapers and phone calls and the prattle of your children and the hope of success in your job that morning do not exist in the world of the journey runner. The world has gone about its business of daily mayhem and earthquakes, but all that matters in that empty motel room, empty except for yourself, is how that muscle will speak.

It was better, it told me. Not great, not terrible. Willing to try. Another day is here and carefully, running and walking like an old fellow, I pick my way to the state line.

Oh, Nebraska!

Time is as long as you make it. But it also is as long as it is; a long time does take longer than a short time. Which is all a way of introducing the simple but neglected truism that some states are wider than others. Nebraska is one of the widest— four hundred and fifty miles. Distance, after all, is one of the basic ways in which a transcon runner judges upcoming real estate.

Entry into Nebraska is a somber occasion. To get from the western border to the eastern border is going to take some doing. After about 1260 miles of heartbreaking effort, there is still somewhat more than halfway to go—1740 miles. So for all the expenditure of energy, I have gotten far enough along only to begin to truly understand just how hard and long the rest is going to be.

In part, misconceptions about Nebraska contribute to a sense of foreboding.

"Nebraska!" people said. "I've driven through there. It's so flat and so boring."

It was lovely to hear such statements, just what I needed to look forward to—two weeks of flatness. It was the Salt Lake syndrome all over again.

My last night in Wyoming, just in case I had forgotten to think about how far I had to go, the paper placemat in the

coffee shop shows a map of the United States. I use my knife
to measure how much behind and how much ahead. Once I
come out on the other side of Nebraska, I will be on the
downward half of the journey.

At the Nebraska border the road sign reads: "Welcome to
Nebraska . . . the good life." The first piece of welcome is a
relentless twenty-five-mile-an-hour headwind. One of the
disadvantages of running in the direction opposite to my own
is that you buck the prevailing westerlies. Going east, the winds
push you. That's the theory. Winds turn out to be as inconsis-
tent as people. They blow every which way whenever they feel
like it. Only about 60 percent of the time were they helpful.
On days like this I was relieved to know that headwinds were
infrequent; nothing seems worse. There is no way to avoid
wind. In the Panhandle, trees are as rare as skyscrapers and the
wind has been whistling over oceans of counties before collid-
ing with one's frame. The pressure totally envelops every parti-
cle. The zip-up jacket I wore fluttered madly against my chest
and my eyelids curled up so far that my eyes felt like peeled
onions. Even birds and hawks hung motionless overhead.
Sometimes I turned my head to break out of the envelope of
humming sound, but there was really nothing to do except
submit.

Part of my occasional mental homework was to review what
I was carrying in my pack to decide which items no longer
seemed necessary. I was obsessed with ounces, but it was hard
work giving up certain possessions. Perhaps I would need them
later, I thought. All the same, my first day in Nebraska the
wind encourages me to discard a set of blue sweat pants. I fold
them up neatly and kiss them good-by. They had been with me
a long time, but it is now time for them to find a new life. I
hope they will be owned and not merely rot. The same day I
also discard a turtleneck, an extra kerchief and a pair of socks.
Each discard of ballast means a momentary lift.

Ah, that feels *good!* I think, reaching a hand behind to
joggle the pack from beneath to test its weight.

What ecstasy such small pleasures and preoccupations carried. Discarding a pair of socks could buy a half hour of pure pleasure. There is so little variation in what I do. Sometimes, with a kind of distant observership, I take my hat off my head during a rest and pluck out the fine curly hairs that had become ensnared by invisible irregularities in the fabric. Simply to engage in fine motor movements and to see something in detail up close that was not moving—oh, it is remarkable.

Most of the time all I do is breathe while my arms and legs move. Sometimes my head moves when I look at something of interest. But how can I describe what running all day is as a sensation or as an experience? It simply does not *feel* like much. Apart from frequent aches and pains, there is no local sense or spot where it is the running. The running comes from the entire body.

Sometimes fatigue becomes local. The upper arms talk of weariness, the soles of the feet sometimes are sore, the chest seems to bristle from breathlessness. There were several distinct running minds. One was a high-pitched yammering of endless babble: "Where are we going what are we doing how does this feel why did you fall in love with her when are we getting home how are you going to write the book why is he such a bastard I wonder how strong I'm getting . . ." And so on.

Another voice was deeper, more philosophical. Perceptions, strong waves of emotion, reaffirmations of commitments to and relationships with life and death. Why I was out there, how I really felt about certain people, what different things meant. They were strong moments and since they were honest ones, even the harder truths brought peace. They were explicit acknowledgments of limitations and definitions. Expressing them bought whole quiet pieces of the day. I felt more or less then that things were okay as they were. This voice sounded like my own voice, the way it would be out loud.

As for the third . . . once it occurred to me that I was expressing the will of the earth the way a cloud expresses the will of the sky. Not that I was some remarkable poetic monster of special sensibilities. It was as if, at such times, it wasn't work. Everything expresses itself—rocks, trees, dreams, roadway, cars. What I was about was, without my being able to decide anything about it, the same as what everything else was about.

I talked a lot about the run to this person and that person, but it was all ultimately not it. So that after a half hour of talk, suddenly I wanted to push back my chair and stand up and fling my arms wide and spit to get rid of the taste because I know it won't add up. It just never adds up to what it really is. It's not running a hundred-mile race and hanging on until it's over. This is not a temporary episode you're involved in, it's your life. In a rational way you know that it just goes on for two and a half months, but in the middle there is nothing else. Past life is gone, future life will never come, so there is only the doing. I could talk for ten thousand years, but it would not carry me an inch closer. If I said it hurt, the next morning it would be easy; if I said I was a hero, by noon I would be humbled. Even the expression of this book is in a way very much not the "itness" of that kind of doing. There was so much time spent in motion that the dream was to be off the road, at rest, sitting down. Especially then because fatigue blurred the edge. No matter how tired you are, you are awake when you run, in the cleanest, clearest physical sense of it. Nothing mattered too seriously, serious as it was. Fussing and fuming came and went. So did elation. Fear of falling, fear of not finishing, fear of getting even more tired—didn't matter. Somehow there was always a way. Even at night it was possible to see.

As if I were a rock. Immense rocks litter the slopes of Mt. Baldy near the Zen Center buildings. When the sun came out and there was a sleepy hour between lunch and the afternoon's work, I would lie down on the flat face of a boulder, savoring the warmth as if it were a dog's chest. But a rock is alive, too. It changes. Rocks speak with their own voices. Some days a rock materialized in my gut. I felt I could tumble wildly all over the desert, popping up, a self-righting inflatable clown ready for any kick. No up, no down. Compass and watch dial alike scattered like straw for all one could use them as crutches. Everything was fine as it was. Complete, Sasaki Roshi would say. Every moment is complete as it is. It's just easy sometimes to feel it isn't so. Then for a while there would be suffering.

Take Nebraska. I had just decided that I didn't like it, didn't like the concrete roadway, the weedy shoulder, the speedy traffic and the look of Nebraska. But it was no good trying to dislike entire subsets of humanity. Between Dix and Potter the driver of a battered station wagon shot me a quizzical look. Not too much later the car passed me again and came to a stop.

"Howdy," the driver said. "Where you headed?"

"New York."

"Well, I can give you a lift to the next town?"

I stopped, glad to rest. The driver got out as if this road were his backyard. There was no danger of being run over unexpectedly. You could see for miles around.

His name was Dusty. He wore an old Army fatigue jacket and worked for a nearby farmer. Dusty had an open, intelligent face, blue eyes, several days of beard, sandy hair and a stocky frame. He informed me proudly he had picked up his car for $250. It looked it.

"You want some water?" he asked.

"I've got some, thanks."

"Yeah, but it's warm, right? Right! Come on, I'll give you some. It's *icy.*" He pronounced the last word in a way that made it clear he felt I would have to capitulate.

Dusty slid in behind the wheel and reached down amid the clutter on the passenger's side on the floor. He emerged triumphant with his portable cooler. He blew the grit off it with the same pride a woman runs a towel over a table before setting it for dinner. I took ahold of the thermos and held one of my water bottles below the spigot. The little twist of water spattered unevenly against the lip of the water bottle so that some spattered on the ground.

"Did you grow up in a city?" Dusty asked, standing back a few feet, both work boots set firmly on the ground. He asked it so mildly, with the truly loving condescension of an older brother, that it did not hit me at first what he was really saying. I was so dim that I answered that I was raised in New York.

Dusty smiled, stepped forward and took both cooler and bottle from me and demonstrated that by bringing the spout to the mouth, it was no problem for a country boy.

"All right, be careful now," he said, "if you drink too rapidly you'll get cramps. Put a lemon slice in your water and that'll cut your thirst."

It was a good trick using the lemon, as I discovered the next day. Even flat tap water went further and tasted worlds better. But his tone made me smile privately. He acted as if I was too simple to make five miles on my own; maybe I really was.

"You hungry?" he asked next.

"Uh, no."

"Okay, well, if you run out of food here's whatcha do." He mimed the act of trimming a stalk of a certain variety of cactus so that the succulent inner meat would be exposed.

"Are there cactus in the Panhandle?" I asked, not having seen any for a while.

"Are there!" he said with a tremendous, completely impersonal scorn. I was to be taken care of.

"Now if you run out of water," Dusty continued, "here's what you do."

He snatched up a green roadside stalk with a seed cluster at its pinnacle. He cut the bottom neatly with his clasp knife, slit it slightly and told me to suck on it for the protein.

"Don't eat the seeds," he cautioned.

I avowed that I would not.

People like Dusty are full of useful information. There was the matter of those oddly shaped cranes in farmers' fields that looked like birds dipping for grain. Their purpose was to pump oil, which farmers then sold to refineries. The "poppopping" ones were powered by gas engines and the "hummers" were run by electrical power. He pointed out the wheat and alfalfa. In two weeks they would be planting winter wheat. It was also missile country. Somewhere in the warm earth were all those poised nuclear blowaways—which explained the military uniforms and vehicles that occasionally zipped past.

Nebraska was a wonderful state for meeting people. There were just more of them around the farther east I went. There and in Iowa were the warmest and friendliest receptions of the trip. Scratch in any direction and a conversation was underway. It got so interesting that I had to remind myself to break off and get moving. It was frustrating in a way not ever having time to get to know anyone really well, but you read people very deep and fast and the energy from even a brief encounter made the days pass more easily.

All that flatness was not so bad. In fact, it was just fine. For one thing, there were not always mile markers on the road the way there were on I-80. There you could see the mileage stakes long before getting to them. Here they were often missing and the sequence began afresh in each county so the cumulative mileage for crossing the state was not constantly in my mind. There were no road signs saying: OMAHA 475 MILES. I thought it would kill me off if I thought about how wide the heartlands were.

It wasn't that numerology didn't have an incredible pull. Other men drink to ease the sense of pressure; I did mental sums. I could spend a couple of hours at a shot murmuring about how many miles in how many days and how far today yet to go, and so forth. Time flew then. It was a way of checking myself and my position on a linear scale. It's just that if I didn't throttle it off, it always ended by getting to be a depressing enterprise, because, ultimately, no matter where I was, so long as it was not over, it was not going to change anything. Plus it tended to inflame a greediness for going faster, which always led to a dissatisfaction with the current pace. Some amusements need a short leash; otherwise they devour the owner.

The really fine surprise was the beauty of Nebraska towns. From far off the white towers of the grain elevators shine like cathedrals. The shape of the elevators is classical and serene—immense cylinders whose simple shape is in utter harmony with their function. Drawn in close around their protective strength like moss at the base of a tree trunk were low white homes and green shade trees. Even the houses, many of them looking to have been built around 1900 to 1920, had a simple beauty. Their white clapboard siding was like a line in one of Elizabeth Bishop's poems about houses in Nova Scotia whose siding called to mind the ridges of a clam shell. All that fine abundance of light makes those simple structures special. The sense of work, order and thoroughness permeates the air. It is a quiet and massive section of the earth, an appropriate site for one of the earth's principal granaries. And then looking back at one of the towns—Dix, Bushnell, Kimball, wherever—as they ever so slowly reduce in scale as you run on over the curve of the earth. And there ahead jutting up, pure and undefeated, are the white elevators of the next town on the horizon.

The proximity of the towns afforded a luxurious sense of relief. Towns were a mere twelve miles apart. Why, in a day I would go through four or five. Food, water and shelter—all were to be close at hand again. Inspired by all this, I would gaze benignly at the old couples who drove in their carefully tended 1962 Chevrolets and Pontiacs. The women had curly white hair (I could picture them fresh from their weekly visit to the local beauty salon) and were pleasingly stout. The men wore brim caps and had roast-beef faces. Couples with children and grandchildren. Conservative and ordered. Very simple.

The Platte River, which runs across the middle of the state flowing from west to east, is accompanied by Route 30. This was the major east-west road before I-80 was built in the last ten years or so. Sometimes off through the trees I-80 would appear and I would gaze fondly at the toy-sized trucks and cars speeding along. Train tracks also ran along next to 30 and it seemed that every hour enormous freight trains of eighty to a hundred cars would rumble past.

The headlamp of an oncoming train, when it first comes into view, glares like a daytime star, some indeterminate but long distance down the track. For a while the headlamp seems hardly to move and then suddenly a black plume streaks the sky. A strong low pressure fills your ears until at last the demon strength of the three diesels coupled together at the front adds up to a growling, chunking sound. The train does not just pass through; it splits the air, scatters birds sitting on telephone wires, dust and straw flaring from beneath the wheels. The engineer rests one pink-skinned elbow on the cab window sill. Sometimes they give me a few wailing toots; I am as proud as a five-year-old.

I have been running, if backward, over many of the same roads the pioneers followed. They arose even earlier than I do, up a couple of hours before dawn. Only oldsters and children rode on those rough buckboard wagons. Everyone else walked. A few wagons appear at wayside museums in Nebraska, rare relics, historical driftwood, the timbers now unpainted, the grain of the wood grooved by the erosion of age, the canvas that once must have been pulled taut against these pedestrian clipper ships now long-since rotted away like flesh off a skeleton. The fabled covered wagons. And yet when I examined them up close and saw the single wooden plank for those who sat guiding the oxen or donkeys, and how narrow a space there was for all of a family's bodies and the possessions needed for a new life, only then did an inkling of the rigors sink in. Often enough in Utah and Wyoming I looked behind at the sunsets and imagined the early pioneers who, only eighty years ago, had studied that same vista. California! they must have thought. What fabulous dreams it must have evoked. That magic zone which would end only when the ocean begins, so clearly established in one's mind as being somewhere ahead, in the region where the sun makes its flaming bed. When I heard in Wyoming about the trappers who used to sleep out wrapped only in a buffalo hide, I could only acknowledge that I was a spoiled child of 1980.

And after all the effort needed to go on foot or horseback

with all the penalties carrying weight brings in its train, what a marvel the trains must have been, a species of genie. A train was more than a yawning commute. A train carried you immense distances in one smooth steady leap, brought plows and news and family and new settlers and mail from distant parts. Standing next to a parked freight train, I could see just how much bigger than a person a hopper car is. I would put my palms against it and the cool metal, dense and heavy beyond reckoning, spoke of its own life. How many men would it take to haul even a single car a single mile? I was living so unindustrial a life, as a trained species of animal that survived on its own strength only. So great was that distance, that leap between raw humanwork, humanpower instead of horsepower, the gulf between my own individual vigor, when set up against all that machinehood! Carry eight pounds on your back for eighteen hundred miles and win every inch by effort and you, too, will feel that you understand the miracle of such things as trains and planes as never before.

In Ogallala I took my second voluntary day of rest. A friend, Tim Storer, told me to look his mother up in Ogallala and she would put me up. It meant a chance to talk with someone who did not serve my food or rent me a room, or be otherwise bound to me by the politeness with which we oil our commercial transactions.

In *Wind, Sand and Stars,* Saint-Exupéry, the French pilot, wrote of how when the early aviators returned to the earth, they would savor domestic humdrum. The isolated pilot in his frail craft drew intense comfort from the lights of small towns in the Pyrenees far below. The details of life we brush over with a surface inattention. Sometimes what we love most truly and deeply can only be understood through its loss. We act as if we are free, able to go our own way, but even the fiercest solitary needs ground to walk on, sounds to enter his ears, sights to enter his eyes.

Thus the very name Ogallala, which I once might have

viewed with a mildly snobbish disdain as some utterly rhubarb
midwestern town with zero interest to someone like myself—
that coupling of fat vowels and lilting consonants adding to the
comic effect—now seemed a wonderful name to evoke. For
three days I had run toward the name.

Ogallala is a somewhat larger town than the ordinary Nebraska variety, an important commercial center for Keith
County. The strength of achievement in the farmlands is not
measured by the dense pile of stone and glass the way it is in
Manhattan, where the very height is a measure of human
interests and importance. Out here it is the very openness of
the space that allows the fields to be tended and the cattle and
hogs to graze. But after all the productive stillness of the
surrounding fields, I looked about with respect and interest at
hardware stores, supermarkets, even stoplights, all indicative of
Ogallala's position in the world.

On the side streets the houses had porches and lawns. There
was the sound of children playing, some small boys pedaling
furiously on bicycles, a dog trotting on its business somewhere,
the steady *wisssh* of vehicles bearing moms on their way home
with groceries. Utterly prosaic, but after all the glaring sun and
singed brain from the effort on the roadways, I could appreciate such domesticity. The very confinement of rest, its inescap-
able brevity, is what makes it so special. It is hard to think on
that. Hard because when I looked at these comfortable, well-
fed people who had no idea of what I was doing, whose own
lives did not entail such struggle, then I thought: well, I could
have been living here, raising a family and this late summer
evening would not have been pierced by such fatigue. It could
have been just another August without any challenge more
difficult than the one of just getting through one's life. Yet I
didn't want that; whatever the price, I would rather have done
August the hard way. Free time is never so good as it sounds;
time without the purpose of work is a killer. The price for
committed time is that the rest is never so long as it seems it
ought to be; the reward is that it allows one to extract the

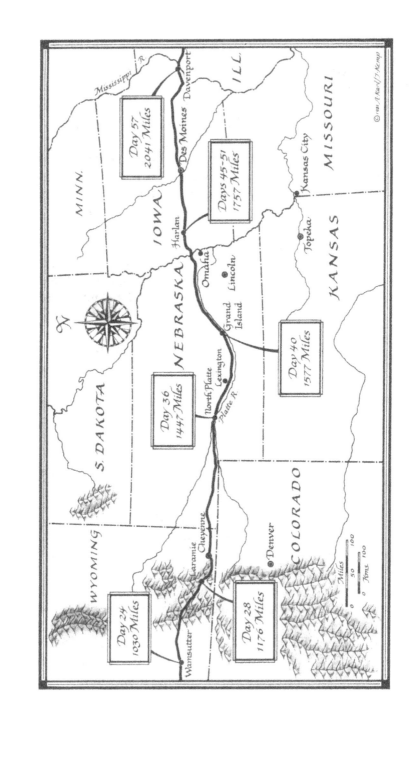

© 1991 A Karl / J. Kemp

Day 57
2041 Miles

Days 45-51
1757 Miles

Day 40
1577 Miles

Day 36
1447 Miles

Day 28
1176 Miles

Day 24
1030 Miles

MINN.

ILL.

MISSOURI

KANSAS

S. DAKOTA

NEBRASKA

IOWA

COLORADO

WYOMING

Mississippi R.

Davenport

Des Moines

Kansas City

Topeka

Harlan

Omaha

Lincoln

Grand Island

Lexington

North Platte

Platte R.

Cheyenne

Laramie

Denver

Wamsutter

Miles
0   50   100
0   50   100
Kms.

sweetest nectar from such dry stuff as trees, human voices and the sunlight broken up by tree branches in a quiet street of homes.

Gwen Storer, a white-haired woman with a strong, open, cheerful face, was one of those people whose simplicity is of the kind that allows you to feel as if you can walk about their home with the same ease as you would in your own. Mrs. Storer, whose husband was a pharmacist until his death a few years ago, had lived for years in a smallish frame house visible from the third story of the "apartment building" where she now lives, a small development of recent vintage. She had told me over the telephone that she lived in a "tall apartment building." By New York standards it was the height of a brownstone —I had expected to see a twenty-story creation. But even so, it was the only apartment-style building I had seen for hundreds of miles. This was a land of individual homes, even if they were just trailer homes.

Not wishing to take on fifty-odd miles to North Platte the next day, I rambled along for a mere nine miles the next afternoon to take the edge off the mileage. My legs felt thick, almost numb at the start, overwhelmed as they had been by the rest. Complete days of rest are never as helpful as they sound; it's easier to do a little than nothing at all.

We drove back into town for dinner at the Elks Club. I felt a little shy as I had only my running suit to wear, but amid the tieless and jacketless informality, it hardly mattered. We sat in the dining room while plump, well-to-do men and their plump, well-to-do wives ate dinner. I was introduced to a fair number of folk with the obligatory explanation of how I had arrived in Ogallala. It was embarrassing in a way; these men were golfers and tennis players. They were rooting for the Cornhuskers, Nebraska State University's team. These selfsame gents would be yelling "Go Big Red!" in front of their TVs. I didn't expect them to be interested or to know how to ask about it. It was irrelevant, what I was doing, but of course it was completely natural to have a placard hung around my neck.

Mrs. Storer told stories about growing up in town. Her great-grandmother was a full-blooded Indian with a Scotch husband. Her grandmother, whom she loved very much, died when Mrs. Storer was three. She remembered the old lady had been ailing and when a bird flew into her house one day she said, "Death came in the window for me." Soon after she died.

It's a funny life meeting people you could be friends with if you stayed, but you don't. You just get up early the next morning, back to the gypsy life. Some days I squat over dusty soil for a crap; other days I get to rest my ass on a comfortable toilet seat. Some nights I wash my clothing out by hand and everything turns gray and stained; other times a washing machine and dryer produce clothing that has that special mommy smell, fresh and mildly fragrant with the soap and bleach.

Mrs. Storer drove me down to Route 30 where I left off the night before near a tiny building called the Roscoe Hunt and Gun Club. We shook hands and on I went. She turned her car around and sped away.

Another hot day and a rugged time without enough water until I hit Sutherland, Nebraska. I found a small grassy park with picnic tables right next to the train tracks. I sat down and carefully consumed three pounds of watermelon, a quart of milk and a half gallon of orange juice in twenty minutes. It was hard dozing, what with ants, thorns, flies, twigs and the hot sun. As usual, bouts of dehydration seemed to summon a greater frailty in the muscles, so that whatever weak area was ready to speak would come up more quickly. Suddenly, near the end of the day I just bore down, hard and ruthless against the subvoices of complaints. I was banging out the miles and getting irritable. As I rounded a curve heading into the outskirts of North Platte, there was an old couple sitting out on their porch. I cursed them for their vegetable stolidity and flat-faced back country curiosity. Whatever they were, I cursed them for it. The faded billboards extolling the wonders of Buffalo Bill's original ranch house awoke another crackle of anger. The commercial vulgarity of modern-day merchants sucking the past dry was no worse than usual. Such a mood simply came from being overtired. This was the warning to rest. But I did not rest and the cost was to be immense.

There was one nice moment going over the railroad viaduct into town. The sun was just about set, a rolling incandescent ball of yellow shimmering down upon the sinuous tracks. The tracks glowed with a clarity and purity of line one sees in microscopic photography where the trueness of the lines of crystal structures and cell formations have a coded yet clear mystery about them. That drab rail yard looked like paradise. Unexpected moments in unexpected places. I thought how it was not yet sunset in California. That same sun we were losing now was still above the horizon to the west. I had been running around the curve of the earth, 1,441 miles worth.

My right leg was damaged now. I knew it. In my gut I felt grim and unsure about what to do. You get to know the boundary lines of abuse and the only time doubt comes up is when you try to pretend to yourself. I tried all the stretches and the hot tub. But every fractional movement of the leg awoke such a steady vibration of tornness and sharp pain! Even worse was the swollen, thick quality deep inside as if the membrane of the muscle groups was bleeding. Whether true or not, that was the mental image that flickered into my mind. And then the endless testing of the leg action as if every five minutes the injury was supposed to heal.

When things go wrong it's hard sometimes not to just give in to disorder. I strewed things wearily around the motel room, knowing all the while that it just meant more cleanup time required the next day. I called my sister and talked for close to an hour—one of those just-have-to-talk-to-you-for-five-minutes calls. Suddenly, it was late in the evening when I hung up. A late dinner, one of the worst-cooked of the entire trip, a late night getting to sleep, a late awakening and a late start the next morning. I knew it was foolish to push on, but I thought I could not tolerate another hour in North Platte. There was no place open for breakfast within easy walking distance and the places

that were accessible for lunch and dinner were ghastly. And
sometimes physical problems just disappear if you bull your way
ahead. It hadn't failed yet.

The sun was up, uncluttered by clouds, and the main street
heading east on Route 30 was a shining asphalt way lacquered
by great patches of reflection. It was one of those summer
mornings when the blood sings in your ears at 9 A.M. and the
glazed somnolence of the world promises a blistering afternoon.

I set off walking. Every attempt to run was a stump-legged
performance. The back of my knee felt even more immense
and swollen.

At the edge of town, desperately hungry, I stopped in a
superette. Two young, good-looking women were working behind the register. One was blond with a wide, sassy bright face.
Some construction workers, who looked to be just a few years
out of high school, were buying cigarettes and coffee. The men
were like the way men can be, like a different tribe than the
women, and the humor and the slight electricity in the flirta-
tious banter was even more interesting than the copy of the
Omaha World Herald I was reading as I waited my turn.
When the men went out the two women talked about the
tallest one, a fellow about six three, blond, good looking.

"Why, he's already twenty-five," said the blond. "I'm
younger than he is."

"I thought he was just a kid in high school," said her friend.

"Oh, he's got a wife and two kids! She was here with them
the other day."

The friend nodded. I tried to listen discreetly, waiting with
my cluster of purchases, letting my eyes rest on a smeared
plastic jar filled with cellophane-wrapped sticks of beef jerky.
They went on talking about flirting with men.

"This all?" asked the livelier woman.

I nodded, a little shy of such pulchritude.

"You walking far today?"

I explained. They were nice, really nice, I thought. Beneath the painted nails and tight jeans and standard American beauty look currently in fashion in the mags, with the hair swept back on the sides, they were not really affected by the sassy, glitter look they wore. Their enthusiasm and admiration tasted sweet.

Then when I started out the door, the flashy one said: "Good luck!"

Her friend added: "God bless you!"

Such sincerity. Such genuine maternal personal caring, as if I were leaving the sanctuary of that store for the rigors of a lonely pilgrimage. Such unsolicited love in their voices. All that sexy stuff was just feathers small girls had stuck in their hair before the mirror, just the instinctive preening of the unmarried. I sewed the precious stone away in my threadbare traveling garments.

But the empty haunted feeling I had talking to the women about what I was doing, when all the while I was worrying if I could last another mile on that leg, as if they were admiring and curious about something I could no longer do, turned out to be an accurate guess at my fall from grace. It took three hours to go six miles. At that rate, further effort was absurd. It was hard to just cut it and get back to town. I walked, limping fiercely. Then with both hands balled into fists against the pain, I would attempt to stump along at a run. The pain was ferocious so I backed off. I was ashamed when cars passed and saw me walking. Walking! Only the weak would walk. So all along I had been proud, attached to the image I had in the minds of motorists who were strangers. Down, down, down through the layers of ego, and still hanging on. Stung as I was by rediscovering that, the worst was having to decide what to do. As it was, I had fallen smack in the crack between two poor options. If I went on, trying to run, I was destroying the leg. If I went back, I was not getting anywhere. So here I was, hopping and hobbling along like Long John Silver with his peg leg, not forcing it to the extreme, but not resting. And my watch read noon.

A long internal debate took place finally. I reached way back to a conversation with Melanie earlier in the trip. I had been resisting taking that day off in Wyoming.

"You don't need to prove that you can go on or that you're disciplined," she said. "You don't know how *not* to go on. It's harder for you to rest than to work. You know that's something you need to learn. I really hope that later on in the trip you can be relaxed enough and mature enough to do that."

"You've just got to go back," I said to myself. "I'm sorry."

The phrase I used a lot was "busting." It was crude and harsh in its sound and I slapped myself with it in moments of more extreme discomfort.

"You've never busted yet," I'd say. "Don't start now." It scarcely needs to be said that everything I owned I had put into the hungry firebox of my locomotive. Burned everything to keep going. Shutting down for any reason was a bitter moment. I turned around at the six-mile point, blinded by tears as I hobbled back toward North Platte. It was the first time I had voluntarily given up on the transcon and that made me cry even harder.

Tears dry fast enough in the hot sun and by the time I was picked up by a rancher, I was able to chatter away merrily enough. I carefully explained what had happened, defending myself against accusations that only I imagined.

Every motel was booked or unresponsive. At one place I waited for twenty minutes in the office, occasionally pressing the electric buzzer, but without anyone coming. Funny how moments come up like that in life where you just hang around some place where you never expected to be, a particular stretch of roadway where the tire blows. There were framed color photographs of children and the children's husbands and the grandchildren. All round-faced and freckled. It was one of those tedious days where nothing really went right.

I paid a visit to a podiatrist, who nodded sagely when he felt the fatty pad behind my second and third toes and elicited from me a choked grunt of pain.

"It looks like you've inflamed the periosteum of the sesamoid bones," he said. "They're a couple of small bones just in back of the metatarsals and the lining of tissue around the bone is aggravated, probably from overuse. Under normal conditions it would take four to six weeks to heal up. With what you're doing, I just don't know what to tell you. What should you do? Well, just do what you can. Rest would be the best, but . . ."

A whirlpool bath, ultrasound and some felt padding were his treatment. He was a nice man and charged very little. I felt better, but still limped like a madman. Fifteen minutes later I was in a modern chiropractor's office. One of those painted cadavers for a secretary, with a head of hair that resembled a topiary achievement, instructed me to sit down on a chair. The room had a bright, clean, fluorescent-lit, wall-to-wall, tight-ass decor. My last chiropractor's visit had been in Elko, Nevada, in a shabby house. That chiropractor was a red-headed, affable guy whose energetic tongue was matched by the drive and vigor in his hands. The massage on my right leg had been hard to sit still under, but I knew that it had saved me from imminent damage.

"How did you get this far on a leg like that?" he asked.

And now, humbled again by the vulnerable right side of my body, I was back in the hands of that profession once more. The padded leather and aluminum rig you lie down on was now familiar to me. It resembles a clever S & M contraption and in fact the usual neck crack and spine crackling maneuvers took place for the fabled realignment. If I sound a bit mocking, it is not for any lack of respect for chiropractors as opposed to any other branch of medicine. Sports medicine, for all its vaunted leaps forward, has large holes left through which the injured fall. We runners resemble rats scurrying back and forth in a darkened tunnel, squeaking and chattering as we stream through various offices laying down money in a search for the right touch, the final cure, the one perceptive comment or utterly right placement of the electrode or the heat pack that will dissolve the dreadful and disabling knot of musculo-skeletal misery. In North Platte I had scanned the Yellow Pages for any kind of specialist I could find. Try 'em all, I thought.

This chiropractor had a cruel, digging touch. His hands were big and his fingers were studded with turquoise rings. Each toe was snapped as he quizzed me.

"Who's sponsoring you?"

"No one."

"No one! Come on. You ought to have been able to have drummed up some good support and p.r."

There was a pause as he grimaced and gave an extra-hard tug on a small toe that stubbornly refused to give a crack and acknowledge itself as defeated. I braced, waiting for the reluctant joint to cough. Crack!

"Well," the man said reflectively, moving on to the next poor digit, "you know, you can always write a book about it. Everyone else is."

There was envy and practicality in his voice. Perhaps he yearned to have a book or more glory. I just laughed and said nothing. I didn't want to give him the satisfaction of feeling he'd made a shrewd shot. As if my self-proclaimed indifference to the media would be exposed for a fraud if I said I was a writer. I didn't want to see a knowing look of oh-so-you're-just-like-all-the-others.

Finally, I was free to find a motel. I collapsed into sleep and forced myself awake hours later. It was already dark as I hobbled along the sidewalks on Fourth Street, gazing at the city park where a black locomotive retired from the rails was now the object of schoolboy attentions. Chugging lawn sprinklers puttered away in the darkness under the big shade trees, slick stretches of concrete sidewalk glistening with wet and the reflected blobs of street lamps. At the Merrick Café the waitress was young and breathtakingly sincere. Her side of the flirtation was unblinkingly open.

"Have a nice evening," she said when she laid her check face down. In the large open penmanship of a woman was the formulaic blessing so familiar now: "Thank you! Vicki (or Suzi or Carol or Joan)." Sometimes a flower, usually a daisy with the petals perched on top of a curved flower stem. Less often, a smiling face of the kind in such common use during the late sixties and early seventies. Out here, west of Manhattan, the tips for waitresses are stern and sparse. I left a big tip and at the cash register when we parted at last, she said again:

"Have a nice evening."

How nicely she said it, too, as if she had never uttered it before. She was as trusting as a child. I mumbled something and slipped away.

All this melodrama subsided quickly the next day. I slunk past the superette where God's blessing had been called down on my head, wondering if they saw me what they would say ("What's that fake doing here again? Why, he's just an old liar."). I hitched back out to where I had left off, driven by a fellow who was doing an aerial survey for uranium deposits. Walking, a little running, more walking, more running and finally by noon, suddenly just running again. Then after an afternoon stop under a shade tree, unable to run again. I took aspirin and then was able to run the last few hours of the day. It was poor mileage—twenty-eight miles to Gothenburg. But it was better than having stayed put.

After that day the leg was once again able to resume its share of work in spite of intermittent bouts of painfulness.

After all the stark days in the desert without human society, Nebraska was, relatively, a regular party.

There was, for example, the Harvest Days parade in Cozad. No one seemed to know the origin or meaning of the celebration. It didn't matter. Banners hung from the windows of shops and homes declaring: "Welcome!" A red-and-white hot-air balloon bobbled invitingly over the rooftops, rising and falling with a periodic rhythm. A local bank had sponsored free rides on it. A long line of excited children and adults waited for their chance to rise in the straw gondola fifty feet above the dusty vacant lot. A proud-looking young man turned the hot-air torch on full blast for a few seconds with a great and casual authority.

The balloon rose and then sank again, held in check by tow lines manned by a muscular youth of lesser dignity than the pilot.

The midmorning sun was 95 degrees, but the crowds for the parade clustered thickly through the several-blocks-long parade route. The marchers were various. To wit:

—the lieutenant governor of Nebraska, borne in an automobile. Weak applause.

—various bands, including the Marching Swedes from Gothenburg. Some troupes looked brisk and well-fitted. Others were hopelessly awkward, with sleeves that drooped on scarecrow frames and shakos that sank down about the glinting eyeglasses. Big, ripe athletic girls pranced at the head of their entourages.

—a passle of four- and five-year-olds wearing Danskins and Indian loincloths. They wandered hither and yon much to the amusement of the crowd.

—a fire truck crept past with the cardboard legend: "This cost $50,000." "Who cares?" said the village skeptic behind me. He had a sour comment for everything.

—variations on the *Sesame Street* theme with Cookie Monsters, green, sap-headed dinosaurs and a raft of Miss Piggies. In keeping with the importance of porcine production in the Midwest, there was a "Pork Is Beautiful" float. "Miss Piggie for President" followed next, her snout set in a fixed smile as two supporters (human) marched behind carrying placards emblazoned: "More Room at the Public Trough" and "Pig Power."

—Miss Teen-age Somebody or other.

—a pack of Shriners wearing fezes piloting miniature Tin Lizzies with their knees up about their ears as they did a snake line across the road.

—various antique autos.

—registered Belgian horses pulling stagecoaches, their great hairy legs and manes all brown and blond while the male drivers wrapped their stained leather gloves tightly around the reins.

I saw enough finally and left. On a side street awaiting their chance to troop past the public eye were horsemen and horse-women in pink shirts and blue jeans. An old white-haired grandma with a pink face and tight cluster of white curls around her head was taking pictures of her granddaughter, a young teen-age woman who stood next to her horse, very straight and totally innocent, presuming that is the way things are. That, of course, in your own tightly secure life your boring granny takes a picture of you as if it mattered, as if the picture itself would not vanish into dust or be pitched out someday. I looked at them as if I were two hundred years further along than they were. That young woman did not yet know how things blast apart, how loss infects our history more and more. Grandma knew about death. She had made her peace with it, I guessed. What else is there to do in this world but love other people? Behind my sunglasses I was weeping. I had cried more in a month on this trip than in the previous umpteen strew of months.

As if all this excitement were not enough for the day, one of the great meetings of the trip took place in Lexington, the next town down the road. I stopped in Tom Paris' Café where I nursed along a midafternoon bowl of vegetable soup and crackers.

A tall old man came over to my table and asked if I knew So-and-so. I said, no, I didn't. We got to talking and soon in his whispery voice the old man began to talk about the early days. His name was Jim Sarr. He had a narrow countenance with the line of his jaw much narrower than the rest of his face. He wore a grayish-blue working man's shirt and pants, the kind you purchase in an army-navy store, suspenders over that, had glasses, a mustache and an old greenish brim hat. His hands looked good; vigorous ones that had done hard work in his life. The nails were longish, cut square across if a little unevenly, and there was dirt under them. He was a tall fellow, had a kind of singing, loose, what you might call musical stance to the way he stood in the world, a good deal of humor twinkling in his eyes.

He beamed down at me as we were talking after a few minutes, hardly knowing each other, and then suddenly with great tenderness, the way a dad would do with his five-year-old son, pinched both my cheeks. What love!

Jim Sarr had a hard time understanding what I was doing; he kept thinking I was walking across America. I kept correcting him once in a while and he'd just look at me and shake his head doubtfully as if I were repeating a grammatical mistake.

"I was born in 1900," he said, "so now I'm eighty years old. I'm forty-six years older than you. And I'm older than that old lady who you spoke to on her way out. I was born in Iowa. I moved to Lexington with my family when I was six.

"When I was thirteen I ran away from home. A friend and I went down to the station to visit the train. We got up inside one of the passenger cars and when it began to move my friend said, 'Come on, Jim, we got to get off.' But I said I couldn't. I went on down to Omaha where I knew a fella. I went straight to his hotel and rapped at the door. 'Who's there?' he called. 'It's me, Jim.' I just walked in.

"Well, I had some different jobs down there in Omaha until one day walking down the street with a young fella a little older than me the police questioned us. I wouldn't give them my name so they held me in jail. Finally I got around to telling them who I was so they sent me back home. The police chief in Lexington woke my dad up at 3 A.M. to tell him the news. Oh, was he mad! He whipped me with a buggy whip until I had big welts on my rear. I couldn't sit down to eat. But I didn't run away again."

In Jim Sarr's early days there were no motor-driven tractors, the threshers being pulled by horses, but he was not a farmer himself. He sewed flour sacks shut at the local mill all his life, an old-fashioned hand process that apparently went on into the 1950s.

"Be careful," Jim Sarr said to me when I was getting ready to go.

"Oh, there's no danger."

He looked at me square on.

"Don't let anyone *pick* on you." The way he stressed that
word was so special, the kind of concerned capitulation of a
good-tempered man to the realization that the world had some
bad in it. I left a good-sized tip and he kept saying, "That's too
much money."

"It's all right," I said.

I thought no more of it and went into the back to talk with
the cook, who kindly let me fill my water bottles from one of
the taps. It was a small-town sort of place. Some of the other
customers had glanced over while Jim Sarr went on in his
whispery way, talking about life in 1910 and 1920. They looked
pleased at seeing the two of us talk, the way one is when a
member of your family is appreciated by a newcomer. You've
heard the stories yourself maybe and maybe you're critical
when you want to be, but all the same you love to see that
person appreciated. Something like that was going on. So I felt
at home.

The owner came in the back and said quietly: "Here's your
money. Jim paid your bill for you."

I protested, but then the woman who was the cook said:
"Jim has no family of his own."

So all I could do was shake that bony hand again and try to
remember his mischievous ten-year-old boy quality at having
outfoxed me and promise that next time I came through Lexington, Nebraska, I was going to buy *him* a cup of coffee. We
just kept shaking hands for a while. Earlier when I'd asked him
for his name he tried to give me a blank check with his name
and address printed on it. I was appalled, I am ashamed to say,
by such trustworthiness. When I went back on the road for my
twenty-mile stint before I could rest, I thought of the brutality
of the roadway and the spontaneous love of strangers who were
really not strangers at all.

Lexington was also the site of mile marker 238, what I
calculated to be 1500 miles, the halfway point. It was just an
anonymous spot next to some mill whose exudations had sifted

down over the street in a fine white powder. The sun beat down and it was nice to think about it, but it didn't affect me much. Somehow earlier I had thought it through and been excited then. The actual moment was dry. Max Beerbohm once wrote an essay on such a theme. He conjured up out of his fantasy a man who was a professional leavetaker at trains, a consummately skilled actor who could carry on the suitcases, rush to the train platform, clasp the young woman's hand as she leaned out of the train window just beginning to move, and weep at exactly the right moment. What grace! What feeling! And, best of all, what timing! It spared the clients who hired his services the dreadful necessity of having to perform at the formal moments of their lives as if their emotions were activated like jack-in-the-boxes.

By this point in the run when I look back over my notes, the endless changes of the trip had moved me to a point of relative serenity with my lot in life. I was a road hog who both suffered and enjoyed things. Every day seemed to be a roller coaster ride, but I knew better than to struggle against the hard times. I can't even dignify it with the term wisdom; it was just common sense anyone would *have* to use to get through.

The longest day of the entire trip was the forty-second. I left Central City feeling physically spacey. My right leg was still stiff, although able to get to work immediately. Between twelve and sixteen miles, one of the first frequent dizzy spells hit me. I think they came from sleepiness and fatigue. Sitting in a chair, I could have gone to sleep in an instant; running, most of the body is so engaged in effort that sleepiness has no way to express itself. So these stabs of vertigo where I would start to fall for a half second would hit once in a while. The mind has gone off on its numerology kick so I had to ask: "Rattling the bars of your cage this morning?" It was a new line and got a fresh laugh.

That day I retired to a cornfield for a quiet crap. When I emerged and went a little way down the road I realized I had left my sunglasses back in the corn. There is a rhythmic sim-

plicity and sameness to such pure space in the plantings—none
of the individual, endlessly subtle quirks of the ground you see
in an upstate New York farm. Every row stared back blankly,
defying me not to be confounded by the mirror image of
sameness. I plunged down one row after another, searching
vainly for the obvious clue as to where I had just been. A half
hour of casting about left me no wiser and I had to go on
without sunglasses. By the end of the day my eyes were blood-
shot and weary. So much light falling upon the open ocean of
terrain. Not that I did not appreciate such strength, but I
yearned for change. Change for its own sake. And change that
would bring back a more eastern scenery, for that would prove
as nothing else that I was getting somewhere. And so many
days of scorching summer heat with nowhere to hide. I was an
infinitely small white speck crawling over the rooftop of the
world with no awning to crawl under. Shade had become as
precious as water. The shape of a tree was as heartening as a
face. Now in eastern Nebraska for the first time were spontaneous growths of trees. Just like that, a brief stand of them by a
creek meandering through a field. No one had planted them;
no one tended them. So their own line and stance, the gait of
their own presence in the great field of consciousness was as
pure and unrehearsed and as settling as the mountains and
rocks and sage had been before.

Coincident with the ever-increasing numbers of trees was
the fact that thirty-eight days after entering the Sierra Nevada
mountains, the sky was high and remote again, the way it is in
the East. Slowly, slowly I was sinking down closer to sea level.
After climbing up the California mountains, the run across
Nevada, Utah and Wyoming had ranged from five to nine
thousand feet in elevation. After crossing the Continental Divide about halfway across Wyoming, the earth literally tilts, on
the average, down toward the sea, so that by the time I reached
Manhattan I would be, practically speaking, as close to zero
elevation as I had been when I started. Nebraska was at about
twenty-five hundred feet in the east. Iowa was a roly-poly kind

of terrain and there were still the Appalachians to come in Pennsylvania, so the ascent and descent of the folds in the earth still meant a lot of work. It was not precisely an uninterrupted downhill slope from Wyoming to New York City.

As for the longest day of the trip, the dizzy spell eventually passed and at a decent midafternoon hour I had logged forty-two miles. Well content with my progress, I entertained notions of a good meal, possibly the movies, just cheerful solo social chatter going on in my mind. Unfortunately for my plans, the town of Columbus was seized by its annual fling with parimutuel racing. Although it was a good-sized place with lots of motels, every single room in town was booked. The owner of the Keen Korner motel, a fellow with one arm, tucked the phone under his chin and with his free hand, dialed a slew of motels to find out if they had a single bed.

"Every fancier of horseflesh from Missouri, the Dakotas, Iowa, all over, they all come here," he said sympathetically. "We're booked solid for days ahead. The only thing I can tell you is to ask the police if you can sleep in the jail."

My thanks for his forty minutes of endeavor on my part simply embarrassed him. Having a handler and a support team is very nice, but the chance to learn from the willingness of others can slip by that way. This guy didn't look like anything special. You wouldn't look at him ahead of you in line at the supermarket checkout and say, "Oh, what a generous man!" But he was. It was hard to just quit judging people.

Well, the well was dry. There was a Greyhound bus due in a few hours, but the idea of giving in to circumstances disgusted me. All that wasted time today and the next day to get back again. With a mildness of heart that was startling even to myself, I just set off down the road. When you feel as if there is no choice, then things are always easier.

Some miles later the road tucks around a sharp curve and then drops down into a wonderful flatland. Now I had really entered the Midwest. The West was forever behind me. Natural-looking swaths of green. Grazing cows. Farm horses. Endless traffic. The northern sky was a long band of dark storm cloud threatening rain, but filtering the light to a soft peach that suffused and irradiated the entire world. Immense feed plants with grain towers. Hopper trucks bearing freshly stripped corn kernels from all the fields swept past, leaving in their wake a warm and sweetish smell. The flyaway motes of chaff tumbled in the air. Corn kernels, puckered by dryness, littered the asphalt road. Many of the cars had Iowa plates and that anticipatory leap ahead gave me greater strength. Oh, Iowa! What love one can feel for the face of the new state that is to become your lover!

The Korean Zen Master Seung Sahn talks about "the back-seat driver," the part of yourself that is always checking and analyzing and verbalizing instead of just letting you drive on through the world without hindrance. I remember that day well because I kept slapping down all the excitement in the back seat. There was a time earlier in the run when the notion of running close to sixty in a day would have had me at a fever pitch. I would have run myself back and forth across the country several times in the course of an hour, not to mention making much of my own strength. Well, I knew now that what I did today had nothing to do with tomorrow. Besides, even spilling emotional energy in the dust was a risk. I didn't shove down on the emotional gas pedal. I remember laughing at each mile marker about how fresh they smelled. "Easy, easy," I kept saying aloud. Just go nice and easy. And then at last, feeling reasonably tired but very proud of myself, I jogged into town. Fifty-eight miles that day, 1658 all told. With what a fine old swagger, I strolled over to Johnnie's Steakhouse that night. But the body was only and could only have been more tired than before. Within forty-eight hours I would be reflecting ruefully on the fact, well known to cats and dogs, that after much scampering must come rest.

The Road Show Closes

On a stinkingly hot and humid day, the kind where even your eyelashes bead with sweat, I ran over a bridge that spans the Missouri River. Dodging traffic left no time to consider the sweetness of leaving Nebraska behind at last. Now I was in Iowa, officially in the Midwest, not impossibly far from Des Moines and Chicago. I was rolling all right, rolling for trouble, although I did not realize it. More long grinds without water had left me badly tuckered out, but what was new in that? A sore right foot and a throbbing left shin, but nothing worse than any previous problems. That day I did forty-two and a half miles and holed up for the night in a small town called Logan.

I was overtired, but shrugged it off. Another night of edgy sleep seemed in store, but Des Moines was just a hundred and twenty miles down the road. One thousand, seven hundred and thirty-one miles behind me. If I just held my breath for one more week, I would be two thirds through this madness.

During the trip I had this recurring image.

What does it feel like to do this? asks an imaginary interrogator.

And I answer that at the start it feels as if I have been strapped inside a tank of water filled to just below my lower eyelids. I cannot speak or even breathe. If I panic and strain against my bindings, I may lose my self-control and breathe in the water. This is what it is like to have three thousand miles to go. It *is* possible if I just concentrate mightily that the water will sink below my nose so that I can breathe. That is the twenty-seven hundred mile mark. A careful series of gradations correspond to precise points on my body as the water level lowers. I forget about this image for a week at a time and then recall it. The water level in Iowa is near the top of my legs. I assume, as before, that all will work out if I simply continue.

At midnight I am awake. I never awake and wonder where I am. I know I am in a stuffy room on a hot night in Logan, Iowa. There is a sharp needling pain, red hot, in my right ankle bone, the one that juts out on the inside side, smack dab in the center. My eyes are open and I feel totally awake. I move my foot carefully, but the pain does not go away. There is a relentless itch about it so specific that I switch on the light. A very faint red dot glows like an ember below the skin. It merits a shrug. Insect bite. I turn the light off.

I don't believe my diagnosis. I want to, but it's not right. I'm not interested in having problems, so I go back to sleep. The rest of the night is broken up by wakeful fits every forty minutes or so. The pain is remarkable. It is not that the level of it is so intense; it is the clarity of the pain, as if a tiny channel to release a molten flow has been drilled through rock. That kind of pain does not go away quickly. The very bone is wide awake; the bone has not slept for an instant.

I have a lot of practice in ignoring damage, so I wake up in the morning and scratch the ankle. A rash has been troubling me for weeks, probably from dirty socks and feet that have been sweaty and dusty and unexposed to sunlight for six weeks. Perhaps it's the rash, I think, but I don't believe that either. The first few steps of the morning are hard to accept. Even walking is going to be a bore today. All the same, I have no desire to stay in Logan. It is not a pretty town. It does not satisfy my aesthetic standards. After breakfast I tramp to the northern edge of Logan. That takes three minutes. The road plunges down a steep hill and beyond are trees and rolling farmland. I hesitate uneasily.

Don't think, go, I say, as I always do on the trip. But the

body is like the fabled mules they talk about in Brazil, the ones that balk at night at a point in the road they have been over many times before. And then the owner, in a fury, dismounts, to discover there is a freshly dug pit a foot in front of the beast. Abashed and repentant, he scratches his head. "Now how did you know that?" he asks aloud. Donkeys are not interested in conversation with their owners, so they look as sour as before. Body doesn't want to go. Owner wants to. Owner wins out.

A quarter mile out of town, I think, be reasonable. Take care of it now. So I turn around and head back. At a local garage a lounging gas jockey in a chair and his stretched-out German Shepherd both raise their heads. Word is that there *is* a doctor in town. The hitch is that he lives elsewhere and his office hours do not begin until ten. Small town Saturday morning waiting rooms—the thumbed copies of magazines from last year and the early arrivals! Now is not the time to hesitate. Otherwise it'll be midafternoon by the time I am done. And for what? All it is is pain. Does it prevent you from walking? No. Stomp your foot—hah! Did you feel anything? Just a little. Just a little, you big baby. Go to the next town and if it's still bad, see a doctor there. Just go go go go!

There is no one around to ask. I see a pay phone. Should I call someone thirteen hundred miles away and ask him what to do? The phone rests in its cradle. I have used a phone many times before. I am sure I could pick it up and put myself into contact with someone, but how can I learn to be independent if I am looking to someone else to get me off this hook? No matter what they say I will ignore it or resent it, because I want both to stop and go ahead. It's funny how easy it is to blur your instinct, make difficulties, and all the while time is going by. I should have been six miles down the road by now. What a precious piece of distance. Some days each step, each alternating motion of the leading leg seems to flash out over the shining chasm of infinity. So I made the wrong decision. Nameless fears, images of this and that, dreams. Sand in the waking eye. I run down the road. It's easier than outsiders might imagine to cast away responsibility by taking on too much pain. Chogyam Trungpa said once that everyone is like a loaf of bread. You have to know what temperature to bake yourself at.

The initial part of the morning, once launched, was wonderful countryside. I had chewed over this choice of roads so thoroughly and at last accepted the fact that the most direct way home was sometimes going to be roundabout. Only in the Far West are pedestrians allowed on I-80 because no other alternate routes are available.

Elsewhere, I had to strike a parallel road to the north or south of I-80. In any case, it was time for a change. Running on more rural roads would mean more encounters with people and towns. Steadily quizzing passing cyclists, farmers and waitresses, the choice of State Route 44 emerged as the best. I may have been out of Wyoming, but there were more grueling hauls of twenty to thirty miles between towns with motels. As usual, all one can hope for is that the informants had forgotten or overlooked cabin-style places. Most motorists are not in the habit of memorizing such things. But what is the good of worrying over sleepless nights in a field when the sun is shining on the rolling cornland and the trees and undulating hills that are like waves to run over? Down in the trough the flat knee of the roadway makes a smart line with the sky and puffy clouds. Up the road and I clamber, traveling together, clouds moving, the leaves on the trees moving, the flashing of brown thighs appearing, until up on top of the world another house appears and then another rolling hill covered with green rows of corn as neatly scored as the tine marks of a straight rake in gravel. The gagging stench of pig manure reeks in the fresh air. The steady clanging of the tin chute-covers as the pigs snout their way into the feeders for their grain and then withdraw for a good chew has a comic intensity about it. Such eagerness! Such single-minded hunger! *Clang! Clang!* Future sides of bacon in the supermarket, gray soldiers of type in the hog-futures listing in the newspapers, the lives of the families in these neat houses—all this rides on the sun shining and the steady banging of these hungry fellows. Pigs are good runners, too. When they spot me, they don't like it, and they streak around to a far corner of their pens, bathtubs of flesh propelled by four smart feet.

Everything one could ever want in a landscape is here in Harlan County. This is mythic America. This is what I hoped to see, at least for one county's worth. This would be worth running through forever. It evokes images of an America that we have never really had, but that we accept as the national median, the stuff that commercial illustrators love to conjure up for civics textbooks or pamphlets distributed by the government in overseas information libraries. Green rolling land and white pure houses. Sunshine. Freckled, mischievous little boys and cunningly coy little girls of Norman Rockwell, interpreter *par excellence* of our own version of Socialist Realism that one sees in Russian and Chinese exhortatory poster art where fine citizens shine with a sincerity that tugs ever so slightly even in the hearts of the cynical. Such people do not nag or wipe their asses or get unduly cruel. Marine Corps! Landlocked Iowa! This is no European duchy already crisscrossed by immigrants and border wars with half-a-dozen different neighbors a few hours drive in every direction. It is at least a thousand miles by every point of the compass to reach the sea. This is all there is, America and nothing else.

But all that was just paper, just dreams. It was its own self quite freely and there is no way to recall it too specifically even now. I just remember the feeling of peace and labor, the integration between the rolling earth and the red barns and white houses that were studded like pastry sugar on the earth. Grass, the way grass grows at home, right up to the edges of the tar. How was there time to appreciate each blade? How could there be a purpose in running across so much territory, when to learn about the world all one needs is a campstool and a few feet of earth? Like the character in the Tolstoy story who is allowed to keep as much land as he can plow in a day. He and his beast who pulls the plow strain mightily, but the exertion bursts the heart of the greedy seeker and he dies at sunset. And all he needed at the end was the earth it took to swallow him.

Once in Nevada I glanced over a highway bridge. There was a characteristic set of lines to the molds for the concrete that made up its sloping support sides. They were trapezoid shapes and I noticed suddenly a giant weed that had burst through the opening left by the not-completely-flush concrete seams into an exuberant flourish of green cloud. Just a weed. It didn't ask anyone else's permission to be there. It didn't mind living in such unfashionable surroundings. This was no florist's display window on Madison Avenue. It wasn't even a decent field. An access road for some distant farm family passed underneath I-80 at that point. As for motorists hurtling along overhead, not a one of them would see it. Yet the weed for all one could tell was not sulking, not lonely, not waiting for me to spot it, not sorry nor glad about my arrival or departure. It just lived. It would live anywhere. And everything there is is in that plant, living and dying. Where did it come from? Where is it going?

I could have ended the run there. I wasn't going to see anything better than that, but how could I explain such a thing, even to myself? "I saw this weed and I went home. I mean, I realized the weeds on Route 9 in New York are just the same. Different but the same." For that matter, why run at all? Running is not good for seeing weeds up close. They swim past beneath, seaweed at the bottom of the ocean of air. A single blade might be good. A whole weed would take too long to swallow.

As for Iowa, the morning was an odd one. I could run while I ran but when I stopped I was not sure if I could start again. The pain in the ankle had spread. Over and over I pulled down the sock and tried to scratch the fiery itch that eluded my nails. There is a particular kind of weed in the Midwest that has a sticky burr with hooks at the end of each tiny quill. Every time I jumped in the weeds to avoid oncoming vehicles my socks would get layered with burrs. They sometimes broke the skin and to get them out required a bit of a tug. There was an art to seizing the burrs hard enough so that your grip was secure, but not so hard that they imbedded themselves in your fingers. In Brazil there was exactly the same kind of burr and simply breaking the skin in a tropical climate, which is such a prime medium for potent bacteria, had led me to a couple of cases of infection so severe I could no longer walk. Now as I ran I wondered if the slight puffiness and increasingly angry look to the ankle bone area wasn't the same thing. Gray wool socks that I hadn't washed for several days, road grime along the shins, no sunlight getting through the sock, a moist film of sweat—an ideal microclimate. I cursed my laziness for not having washed my socks.

Slowly the day changed in character. Harlan had once been marked as a mere pass-through place, twenty-six miles down the road. I wouldn't even know the number of times I had run twenty-six miles in a race or in a day of training. And now not only did the marathon distance begin to seem very long, it seemed impossible to rely on as something achievable. The ankle got worse and worse. The poor foot tried to wince away from impact. There was just no way a foot can avoid hitting the ground. A mad thought of hopping fourteen more miles flashed through, but was absurd. What else to do but continue? Like holding a piece of your flesh against flame when every instinct begs not to endure it, sometimes resolve weakens. Then I would limp, spit, laugh and curse and shake my head in the middle of this rural country. How did I get here? How is this happening? Why now?

Bruce Tulloh figured four million footsteps to cross the country—I never checked his math but he's a very precise fellow. Two and a half million down, one and a half million to go. Not that the previous two and a half million had ever seemed exactly facile, but in comparison with what each footstep cost now, I had been living in a paradise. I looked back on my earlier days and the confidence that it would always be possible to go on. Now I wondered about getting to Harlan. New York was not a concern. Only Harlan survived.

Run nine miles more. How about that? Come on, this is the last time I'll ever ask you, I swear to God.

You always say that!

No, no. I promise. *This* time you have to!

I won't, I can hitch into Harlan.

No, you have to do it running. Just get there. You always get there. You never bust!

But I did bust in North Platte.

Once. Don't get into bad habits.

But I can't do nine miles.

Silence as I went step-wince, step-wince, down the road. I was grinding my teeth and balling my hands into fists. I recognized that to a degree I was feeling sorry for myself, fighting the pain. Accept it, accept it, I thought. But the wince was getting bad, the flash of light every time the weight of impact jarred through made the roof of my head crackle. I was impressed. Wow, this *is* bad. Let's walk. We walk. I am the parent holding the hand of my willful child. Okay, now can we run again? Not four, just two miles. No. One mile? I shrugged and started up again, bobbing up and down crazily, weight all wrong, the thigh on the bad side binding up from the wacky stresses hitting it from the wrong angles. Then it would ease for a while, inexplicably, then return. I measured the road in quarter-mile sections. To that big tree down there without stopping. To the top of the next rise. Slog, slog along. The scissors close, demon jaw on the ankle is going to bite off the foot. Okay, try cracks in the road, follow cracks. Remember Mavis Hutchison when she ran across and she did that. Now me, too. The scissors close. Even one-step-at-a-time philosophy is dead. This is bad space, haven't been in bad space since the twenty-four-hour run. When my mother died when I was fifteen and I didn't expect it, I remember the image coming to me of a steady beam of pain right between the eyes. You can turn your head side to side, but you're strapped down.

Then it zaps you. If you can breathe you can live, however. Zazen pain when I wanted to faint to get an excuse to get off the cushion and get away from the pain in my bent legs and the pain of tying myself up in my head. But breath was like a crack, an indivisible slit through which I could breathe. Or the other image that has haunted me since I was a small boy and saw *Bridge On the River Kwai* where you lie under water and the enemy are looking for you so you breathe through a reed. I would practice that with soda straws, pinching my nose shut, trying not to panic. One hour—six hours—how long would *I* last?

And there are the Nazis coming. I would dream about getting a suitcase ready. I was eleven years old, reading William Shirer's *The Rise and Fall of the Third Reich*. My own family were being led before the table where they decided left or right. Left if you went to the showers to be gassed. Right if you were to work and live. I always wanted to live so I would think about how skinny I was as a little boy and how unlikely it was that, standing naked before the Gestapo, they would want me. I used to love forgery, however, and would spend hours imitating signatures. I would tell the officer that I was a skilled forger and they would put me to work at a table heaped high with documents. Later, when I began running and I felt strong as I had never felt in my entire life and began to penetrate further and further into longer and longer distances, the fear began to surface again. As I ran I could see thousands of us lined up in Van Cortland Park. Only those who ran fastest and longest would survive. But it wasn't just being allowed to live, because as I grew stronger I began to become aware of how I was learning streets and alleys and dodges across vacant lots, gritty paths under the railroad bridges and elevated highways of upper Manhattan so that when partisan warfare came or the nuclear holocaust arrived, I would be able to slip through the ruins of Boston or Manhattan or upstate New York and live like a coyote. I ran paths not just for their own sake, but in order to survive. To be Jewish and to be physically strong was a change from the age of twelve when I considered becoming a rabbinical wizard like the one who prepared me for bar mitzvah; his white indoors skin and glowing eyes were washed in a daily bath of Hebrew characters and Talmudic references. His shoulders were stooped from so much learning. At the age of thirty-two what mattered was not to be taken alive, not to be led before the table. To become a dagger you must live like a dagger.

What is the final generality to draw from all this that is solid? I can't say. Those things once mattered. Somehow they no longer seem to. The terrain of self no longer seemed to be thoughts or images or opinions about why I was doing it. But they all came up again, all had led me to this place on the road. None of that mattered in Iowa right then. When you cannot run, then you can't. Nothing special. Perhaps there really were limits, finite physical limits. When you can only hobble, then that's all that's left. Perhaps someday it would all end and the pain would be over. I thought to myself, well, the run may be botched now, if it's a chipped bone or ruptured tendon, something really bad. I'd spend a week in Harlan and then I might as well go home to recover. I'd just have to come out again in a few months. Finish in winter.

In five minutes I had reviewed my options, selected the worst, explained to everyone and gone home. For all I knew this was the end of the trip for good. Did it bother me? It came as a relief in a way. If I was hurt then I was no longer responsible. I was worn thin. It was the only possible way to find rest and, of course, I wanted that. I do not in the slightest believe that I was secretly egging myself on to a crisis, but there had certainly been times earlier in the trip when I had said to myself I wished I would get a broken leg so I could go home. But so what? What does a thought like that once in a while mean? Were they really connected to some deep disgust about doing it at all—I knew they weren't. I have a personality so swift to manufacture guilt that even an infinitely small trace of genuine shirking would have plunged me into spasms of remorse. I wasn't afraid of every single thought I had—there were too many that came up to evaluate each one. They just came and went away. It is true that much earlier, before the trip began, I was deeply engrossed in other projects and themes in my life in New York. The ups and downs of finding a publisher for an account of this transcon gave me a chance to see how much I wanted to do it. Motivations are always complicated and they rely on guesswork, instincts that emerge and that then will not appear again in any tormented attempt to be "rational." Mostly I had wanted to do the run, but I had had my doubts about just how much. Sometimes the twenty-mile-a-day runs and the thirty-to-forty-mile stuff through June and July could be boring. What did so much running prove? I didn't need running to make me happy, whatever the devil that much-abused word really signifies. It wasn't that it didn't; it's just that at base I felt I could drop it. Of course, if I couldn't finish, it would leave a terrible sense of incompletion, but there are worse things to live with. This was not the most important event in American history or even necessarily in my own. Maybe not finishing could teach something, too. But when your foot is on fire and the last reasonable goal in your life, the only one, is to get off it, choices are easy. There was nothing to debate. At the time I wasn't particularly shocked or upset the way I had been in North Platte. Actually, what I thought of was how boring it would have to be to explain why I didn't finish. "Well, my son, once I ran partway across America." He looks up at me, eyes shining with curiosity at this latest marvel from his Dad's life. "Partway, Daddy?" "Yes, from California to Iowa. You see . . ."

Anyway, the last few miles dragged on and on. Running was out of the question the last eight, so I walked all that. You know that distance will eventually go by, but it doesn't come easy.

I stumped up the hill into the edge of town and down the main street, hoping to hell some motorist would get me to the hospital, since it was two blocks away. I didn't want to have to crawl there, which I was literally considering. I had nerved myself to get *to* Harlan, not *through* it. A car pulled over. A young man gave me a somber look and opened the passenger door.

"Where can I take you?"

"Hospital, please."

Without a word he drove me to the emergency room entrance. I sat in the front seat, panting in relief. When we got to the hospital, I hopped on one foot to the door and buzzed. The Good Samaritan waved and left.

Changes are seamless. One moment, roadway and sky. The next, I was lying on a table, inhaling the astringent odors of a hospital, while my eyes examined the plastic grid over the fluorescent lamp bulbs. In the morning, whole; in the afternoon, crippled.

Eventually, the cherub-cheeked Dr. Robert Donlin arrived. After my explanations, he said: "Let's see that ankle."

I hadn't looked at it for a while. It was impressive, a thoroughly grotesque distortion of its once simply bony lines. The whole area was puffy with a sort of rotten red coloring, verging at times on violet. The pain, under Dr. Donlin's inquisitive touch, was the kind that makes the eyes sit up.

"I don't know exactly what you did to get it this way," he said. "It's apparently not soft tissue affected—no damage to ligaments or tendons. There are no signs of bone chips or stress fractures in the x-rays. Very likely it's some kind of infection, of the kind you suggested, from a scratch or a burr. I want you to take antibiotics and wait a while to see what happens. Meantime stay off it. In fact, stay flat as much as you can and keep your feet elevated."

If I had to be told advice exactly the opposite to what I had been trying to do—that is, stay upright and use it—that was it. It was rather comical to wonder at such nonsense. But there was no choice. Even the weight of dangling the foot over the edge of the table was too much to take.

"Where are you staying?" Dr. Donlin asked.

I shrugged.

"The nearest motel."

But when I got up I couldn't take a single step. The nurses helped me into a wheelchair and rolled me to the door. Dr. Donlin came with us and had me loaded into his car. There was a motel about a block away he drove me over to.

"Any bookstores in town?" I asked.

"No, there aren't. Just some paperback books at the supermarket."

I nodded. Television shows in the morning would be boring, but that was that. I hopped over to bed and lay down. A while later there was a knock. Pat Pedersen, the black-haired pharmacist's wife, had driven over with the antibiotics and a pair of crutches. Any New Yorker knows one tips those who deliver.

"Oh, no," said Mrs. Pedersen with such emphasis that I didn't dare press the point.

"If you'd like to come for dinner tomorrow night, we'd love to have you," she said. "We'll come by and pick you up."

The next morning there was another knock. Dr. Donlin had stopped by on his way to work with an armful of books. He told the hospital staff to rip up the bill. A reporter came to do an interview with the land bird that had flown into the rigging until its wing healed. One of the local lawyers issued an invitation to the country club where, over two beers, I got to shake hands with two-dozen genial men who happened to wander past our table. Dave and Pat Pedersen had me over for dinner several times, offered to put me up in their home, but not wanting to be weight, I declined. Along with them and their two daughters, we watched the nightly performance of *Shōgun.* While poor Dave dozed off after a long day at work, the rest of us consumed a large bowl of popcorn.

Mostly I was on my own, but time went quickly. I had little incentive to get off the bed the first three days. Hopping to the bathroom was about as much adventure as I wanted, especially when there was the daily expedition to the local supermarket. It is hard work being crippled, even for a strong person. It was a big push just to do the eighth of a mile to the store. Pushing the shopping cart ahead was easy enough by giving it occasional shoves, but in the final moments by the cash register, the ankle was under ruthless pressure. And how do you carry a bag full of groceries when both hands are occupied with grasping the two crutches? It provides insight into the situation of those who endure them all the time. Like fat people running—their agony is greater than for the skinny wraith who floats along. Old folks on walkers must navigate fifty yards with all their strength. Motion without restriction; who thinks of it till it's lost?

So I spent the hours reading, dozing, eating, watching TV, going to the Pedersen's in the evening. Road life was forgotten. I let people at home know, some of the small boy pleased by the concerned reaction. "Oh, I cut my knee." "Oh, my God!" "Oh, it's nothing. It's just bleeding a lot." There was nothing to say, nothing to do, but wait. I certainly needed the rest, so I slept away great gobs of time. Mostly what I felt was relief that it happened during the *Shōgun* series.

The first three days the foot showed very little sign of improvement. The fourth day I was able to walk short periods of time without the crutches until the old pain came back. I went down to Omaha one day to see a specialist in orthopedics. He thought perhaps a predisposition to gout had triggered the attack. I was pleased at that notion—at least it would absolve me of the obsessive charge, while still proving that I had run to my limit and hence could not accuse myself of laziness. Unfortunately, it turned out that I was perfectly normal. So what caused it, what was it? I never found out. The fifth day came and I returned the crutches to the Pedersens. Dr. Donlin thought the foot still not ready for the road and wanted me to see him before I left. I wasn't about to risk a "no," so I decided to leave without telling him. The Pedersens, true to their wonderful hospitality, gave me a present of a T-shirt from the local football squad: the Cyclones. My name was printed in red on the back. They had included me in their blessings before meals. Meeting people like that in Harlan was very special. I arrived a stranger, but did not leave feeling that way.

All the same, on the nineteenth of September at 5:30 A.M. I was getting dressed in my motel room, lacing the shoes with double knots again. Time to head for home. It was dark outside as I went down to Mickel's restaurant where I had breakfast among the farmers and truckers for the last time. A little before seven I was facing east, walking along on the great route homeward, watching a fat orange sun come up over the next roll of earth. I didn't feel anything special about being on the road again; just underway once more. A lazy part of me said it wanted still one more day of rest. The original, sincere and serious plan was just to travel fifteen to twenty-five miles and call it quits. I could hardly risk another breakdown. Certainly, running was impossible at the start since the skin over the bone was too sharply painful when I tried to start up. The pack was crammed with all kinds of unnecessary goodies civilian life had corrupted me into thinking I needed, mostly food and books.

Slowly a rhythm for progression began to emerge. Run one mile, walk two. Then run two, walk one. Then run two and a half and walk a quarter mile. Slowly the needle flickered up to four and a half to five mph. Ah, speed!

It was a windy, hot and humid day, flowing through the rolling cornfields, listening to the gusts hum against the telephone wires. Long stretches, at one point twenty-one miles, without water again. Although farmhouses now came every half mile, gas stations and cafés were rarely found outside of towns. There was nothing for it but just to get thirsty and hang with it hour after hour. It's funny the things you never take for granted anymore out here. To taste water sometimes could almost make you cry.

Starting to run forty-five-mile days again after a five-day layoff was, in a mild degree, like starting the run all over again. I couldn't sleep as well at night. Hour after hour the body pumps out the juices that keep you active and awake. A few hours later you're lying in bed expecting that the body will shut off like a car motor. Even with eyes closed, you feel just an inch away from getting up and running down the road again. Bring it on, for Christ's sake! I'll run a hundred miles tonight! Wild surges of exultant defiance, an overpowering desire to hurl myself into the cauldron of intense work—more and more and more—has to be resisted. Carefully, night after night, I simply smack the pillow down and try to forget such things. The more awake you get, the more you want to stay awake.

Also, my feet were sore and aching again. In such a short time they lost that ability to heal themselves from the shock. My gait was still way off. I ran with a built-in wince. The first day the right foot slapped the concrete face of the road like a dead fish nailed to a broomstick—*thwack! thwack! thwack!* The next few days crossing Iowa took a tremendous toll of nervous energy. I was running on a bum foot and I knew it. Ted Corbitt had spoken once about injuries that you can suppress almost through force of will. They stay submerged and you do what you must do; you can hold them at bay for months, but they are not healing. They are simply waiting for the chance to express themselves. I would never be able to encourage someone to do what I did. I understand it when they do it and I respect it and I make room for myself to do such things, but deliberate abuse of the body is a serious business. I was a tired man and this kind of enterprise was tough. It was the toughest thing of my life I had ever let myself in for. But this was my problem now and I was going on with a fool's game. Cost doesn't matter in this kind of struggle. You get in too far. How could I ever have imagined that I wanted to quit? Words. I was tired of words. I was just an animal, running on forever. Never mind.

Outside of Des Moines diarrhea left my ass hurting from the acid of caked-up shit that couldn't get cleaned off till nightfall. Who would imagine that your asshole could burn so much? It was ridiculous how there was always something to contend with. I was nearing two thousand miles now. Richie Innamorato had said on the phone: "The first thousand is easy but the second thousand will be the hardest. The third thou-

sand will be easy because you're heading for home." I hated
him for saying that. I was getting superstitious about such
things. And he had only run eighteen hundred himself; how
did he know the third thousand would be easy? I didn't see any
signs that some mighty wave of strength was coming. It was
work now all the way to home. As I began to think about the
Mississippi River approaching, I kept shrugging off all the
battle weariness. But I was entering the ozone level without
knowing it, heading for the outer spaces of fatigue, a new phase
where the price of the effort would demand the highest payment yet. That was all to come. I felt then that the worst was
over. I had passed through the fever point by breaking down
in Iowa.

Sometime around then I read a magazine article in *The
Runner* about Jay Birmingham, who had just finished a completely solo transcon a month earlier. He said that almost every
day he had gone through some kind of crisis about going on
with it. I read it standing up in a supermarket aisle. I don't
know who else in America could sympathize with that statement the way I could. Okay, I thought, I know what you mean,
wondering how I could ever have let myself feel competitive
with someone like that, a fellow traveler. But I had been. The
five-day rest had scotched forever all chance of beating anybody. So now I could really forget the calendar for the last time
and forget worrying about other transcon runners, past or present. I just wanted to finish. I was going as fast as seemed right.
Anyone else who wanted to make himself immortal on the
highways—I was willing to shake his hand. Just get to two
thousand miles, I thought—then we'll talk. What I was going
to talk about with myself, I didn't know. Probably about Chicago.

On the Map It
Says "Chicago"

A journey runner loves maps. They tell you where you are in this world. They tell you where you are on the map itself. It sounds strange, perhaps, but maps themselves can become the journey. Two more inches and we reach that fold. The letter for that grid is H across and the number is 7 down. The Indiana border is at o across and 7 down. So just seven more letters to cross to reach it. At the rate of three letters a day, we will be there on the third morning from today. That means something familiar, the idea that mornings will come and go. All you have to do is just work for three more days, and you will get to Indiana. Then what does that mean? Well, the truth is it means that three more mornings must follow before reaching Ohio. "But surely," one of the thoughtful voices inside says, "surely, reaching Ohio is different from merely reaching Nevada." A hum of approval sweeps the higher chambers of the mental parliament in session.

"Granted," I say, from the lower chamber, "but is a thousand miles to go or seven hundred miles to go really less than twenty-seven hundred? It is time, more time, more future time. No matter what you do you will never catch up with yourself. I mean ultimately catch up with the dream of getting somewhere. Because that dream itself depends on your not being in that wonderful future. Best not to try to lean on it or your hand will go poking vainly through space."

"Listen," says the first speaker, thoroughly irritated by this line of thought, "it's true that your idea that being on the path is only being on the path means we'll never get *somewhere* but, in fact, there is an external reality to this run. I mean New York City is not the same as the desert. And then it *will* be over, you *will* be doing other things again in your life. Just look at the map as a chance to express movement, freedom, eternal hopefulness. Don't be such a prig. We don't really disagree, let's just get on to the next pole star."

Vigorous cheering from the less spiritual members of the assembly. I was a bit disheartened over such discussions, but I was voted down again. Chicago was, in fact, the next great goal toward which the troops mustered all their loud strength. I looked down at my once-young thighs as they ceaselessly flashed back and forth, second after second, as one waking hour changed into the next. The word "Chicago" sang in my veins. Dark from the sun and drunk with desire, we rolled on toward the next stop, heedless of the bitter hangover anticlimax brings.

All the same, map reading is one of the great blends of dreaming and pragmatism. Travel is always based on hope and assumptions. Death could always intervene in the next instant. You can't ever be completely sure you will get there, but what a strange and indefinable joy it was to sit on the side of the road eating a candy bar, shoes and socks off, as I reclined on a cut through the crest of a hill, my map spread out over my knees. I folded and refolded state maps so often that the lines softened and the paper fibers emerged puffy and bleary from fatigue. Sometimes the names of towns or mileage totals got obscured by the chafing of paper against pack. How I noticed such things with the fretfulness of a god who has seen an earthslide obscure one of his favorite villages! The wind would be blowing from the southwest, cars would speed past as I studied the tiny puckering curves that were to be my experience for the next three hours. I would measure my thumb against distance covered and distance to go, constantly checking the mysterious equation that work equals movement.

Where I was on this piece of paper will change. I will devour a county, ten towns, half a state, a region, a desert and eventually, a continent! To run across a continent! My ears rang when I muttered such a thing. It was a whole lifetime to do such a thing. Much time. It is not a two-hour run. It's a whole piece of your life, you slide across the counter to be able to purchase the achievement. It's a scary little club to belong to. What simple, but what arduous membership rules—just do it. It wasn't me really doing it, was it now? I just worked in here. No glamour. Nothing but work. Anybody can work, all you have to be is simple-minded and not forget what you are doing. Read the map and go east. Women hold up cosmetic mirrors for many reasons; some of them were mine, too. Checking where I was, checking what I looked like. It was a magic mirror, a map. You could see your past, your present and your future, all at once.

All the same, maps have their limitations. They themselves are not reality, just a set of choices of certain kinds of information that most people want. A road hog needs to adapt the information to a particular use. Take the question of color. The fat red roads signified much traffic; thinner yellow or pale rose lines evoked images of two-lane blacktop. The thickness of the circle, the height of the typeface for population centers gave off a particular odor of density of services—laundromats, restaurants, motels. But what I needed to know I often had to surmise. Was the road concrete or asphalt; was it a heavily used way out of a city or a quiet back exit? Was the shoulder nicely trimmed by the road crews or was it a bushy growth, or was it altogether different, say chunk gravel strewn over a forty-five degree pitch? Which road saved miles on the way east; where were the short cuts only the locals knew about? So I had constantly to guess and ask. Intersections with other roads often suggested restaurants and gas stations. Hilly states like Pennsylvania could be read almost as clearly as topographical maps by studying the way the roads adapted to the reality of mountain ranges.

And what imprecision infects the maps! Texaco, Mobil, Exxon, state highway departments—all have different mileages for the same routes. Do they round their fractions up or down? Whom do they turn to for their figures? And why are these figures usually different from what one sees on road signs? And what is the basis for any of those numbers? Do the little red arrows on a map point to the middle of Akron or to the city limit? —and the answer means whether or not I get in before dark. If that space is worth two miles, why is that one which looks wider, worth only a half mile? Often to rectify inconsistencies I would check the distances by using the scale of the map as a guide so that a matchbook cover from edge to first fold might be equivalent to thirty-one land miles. Three and a half times the matchbook equals so many days of running. I could spend twenty minutes on such a task. Small stuff, one might say, except that for a journey runner mileage is a sacred beast. How can one be imprecise about the very standard of one's universe? Does a cook cut with a dull blade, or a carpenter approximate fits to the half inch?

There were the rare days when the road signs announced MEASURED MILES. The same emotion that stirs others when they stand on the sill of a church gripped me as I set my digital watch to time a "real" mile. What relief precision is in a world of dreams. It gets bred into you in a remarkable fashion. Often on roads where markers were put at each bridge or underpass that were accurate to the hundredth of a mile (107.11, for example) I could spot the stake as much as three quarters of a mile away. Then I would guess the reading in advance and usually come within three hundredths of a mile. Or I would see a bend or a city or a tree way far off and would guess twenty-one minutes to get there. The same pace, arrival and another glance at the watch: twenty-one minutes! At noon I would look at the map and say: "Twenty-two miles to go." A look at the sky, a brief muse on the weather, a sagacious frown at the direction the wind came from and then the announcement for the benefit of one: "Looks like the outskirts of Joliet by a little after 5:30." At 5:35 P.M. I would be looking at my watch and smiling at the signboard saying: JOLIET. Distance is the stuff of one's craft. Distance is realness divided by effort and body mood.

Anyone who suggests to you that they know exactly how far they ran across the United States is a liar. Well-meaning, of course, but guilty of misrepresentation. The maps are off, car odometers are not very accurate, and who has the money or inclination to hire a surveyor to check? For those who do not blink at whether you cover 3026 miles or 3019 miles, the answer is they are right to be indifferent. It makes no differ-ence. All the same, I cared for myself. I was frustrated. I would agonize over entries in my log for the day's mileage, especially if I had to estimate exactly how far I went. The only safe thing to do was to underestimate the distance. So when I reached the 500, 1000, 1500, 2000, 2500 and 3000 mile points, it was like celebrating approximate birthdays. Well, somewhere around here is that point. But the feeling of anticipation was just as good as if the point itself had been marked by a fat stripe. I may have been obsessive, but I was not completely insane on the topic.

Which leads in a backward kind of way to the issue of records. Most journey runners who cross the country take a different route from anyone else, in the neighborhood of twenty-eight to thirty-one hundred miles. Then, if they are lucky (and assuming they are reliable characters), they claim the fastest crossing. In a way, the only thing that matters is getting from one coast to another in the least amount of time. But the term "record" implies that there is a standard basis of comparison. In road racing, different records are kept, for ex-ample, for fifty miles on the track and fifty miles on the road. Racing fifty miles over a bunch of hills while dodging traffic is very different from circling a track two hundred times. And even then there are plenty of variables. The weather, the alti-tude, the wind, the track or road surface, the number of com-petitors, the amount of traffic, the time of day, the time of year

—it's wild to compare any two runs, although it's certainly, in a sense, fair to do so. The same issue of comparability plagues any look at records for a journey run that do not follow the same route. Who has the nerve to say that the Mojave Desert in June is twice as bad as the Salt Lake Flats in August, or vice versa? I am not trying to legislate a ban on having a record for crossing the United States. I may feel competitive with those who ran faster than I did, but I appreciate the strength they had to meet that cost. What I am suggesting is that there be a softer use of the word "record." That comes from recognizing the whole slew of differences that make each transcon so different from any other. It is a kind of record, an unofficial, unsanctioned sort of event. Maybe as I get along I am getting more tired of the fastest anything in running. I don't begrudge records—I owned one myself, but so what? Is everyone else supposed to cringe? Quantification is worth noting and enjoying and wrestling against with all your might, but some days, most days, what does it have to do with anything, with the sound of the wind or the color of the rain clouds blowing down from the North? It is better to get ourselves back on the roadway.

As for the maps I studied so carefully, they were never discarded in a trash can. It would be easier to throw away a book than a map I had used. So I would mail them home in long business-size envelopes, formally buried in white rectangular graves, bound for a dignified final rest in a shoe box on the West Side of Manhattan.

Sometimes there is an odd sense of justice about the timing of things. When I reached the two-thousand-mile point, it was the end of the day. The sun had been going down over the fields, wide fields themselves drenched in the fragrant weariness of September sunlight. It is not yet autumn, but the vigor of summer light is confused and lets spill an extravagant warmth and far-flung golden haze. The sun's presence had been unbelievably demanding for weeks, full of raw heat till sunset. Now the nights, even at the lower elevations, are cooler.

The vegetation, reminiscent of subtropical climes, and the subvoices of winter combined in a haunting way. The shrilling of insects surged out of the ever-darkening green grasses with a full choral voice, an intensity made more urgent by their impending death. Insects are emotional creatures, but you must live with them for two thousand miles to understand their heart. They had been alive with that sound weeks earlier in Nebraska, making an individual tree burn with the rattling death cry that warns of the end of summer. They talk to you before leaves color, before frost comes, before birds leave, although birds too were now beginning to band together and chatter madly at rest stops, great black crowds of them overrunning a strip of trees that follows a line of a fence.

Along here now the houses were mounted on stilts because of flood waters. Dead box turtles lay in stiffened postures, shells cracked by auto tires. Big snakes with ribbed white underbellies gleaming against the dark tar of the road. You can smell the big river coming. It has been working on the land from thousands of years back. Geographical history is lively again somehow. Long before we mashed through here with high schools and shopping centers and all our comings and goings that stain the air with footprints of exhaust, there was other business afoot, the Mississippi before it had a name, scrubbing the harsh face of the land, softening the lines, raking it down finer and finer, like a relentless gardener. I went aloft on a reckless, soaring feeling, not minding the painful foot. Somehow I would make it last.

There it was—2,000 miles at milepost 67 on Route 22 heading east, 5 miles west of Muscatine, 286 miles across Iowa. A barn building, a stretch of field, and a sports car pulling over. That was Rick Bowers, my contact for a night's rest, the brother of a friend. A big well-set fellow with long fair hair, a golden mustache and the dapper clothes of a city professional got out. I told him what the milepost meant and he was a quick appreciator, had a positive knack for it. I was within five minutes of the time I had told him I would get there and he was within forty-five seconds of my running up to it.

It was a little hard, what happened next, because Rick drove down through the town of Muscatine on his way home, which meant that I first saw the Mississippi from a speeding car rather than on foot. It was dark when we reached his home. We were greeted by a barking dog outdoors, and indoors by Ginny, his wife; India, their little girl, who was four; and Eric, who was twelve. Kasha, the cat, had a bronchial cough that she hacked away at with periodic intensity, a kind of miniature live-in ailing relative who ceaselessly reminds you of her presence. I was guided upstairs to a bathroom with plants and there in a *long* tub that for once was not made from a mold of plastic that resembled an oversized fish tank was able to soak at leisure with a lit taper on the edge of the tub. It was an old easy kind of house, which seemed immensely comfortable and domestic. After a while I had, without knowing it, begun to miss the assumptions and pleasures that come with a home. It was possible to walk up- and downstairs, to be in a place at rest without hearing a stranger's cough cut through the plaster-board or the infantile cadence of TV voices tug at your energy. All was silent upstairs except for crickets coming in the windows. There were kitchen cabinets with various goodies to rummage through. People to talk to. So the dry old mouth that hadn't said much lately was suddenly awash with words. I realized as I talked with relentless intensity to a patient Ginny for an hour about the run that the loneliness was cutting deeper. Phone calls home or to friends were wonderful, but more wonderful was to be together with people.

And the truth is that sometimes already established relationships were a burden. I had worked myself into a funny state of mind about some people. I reviewed past love affairs, deciding that this person was really wonderful and that person was really not so nice. There was a degree of agitation and intensity about such ruminations that is not entirely easy to account for. Perhaps they surfaced again in lieu of present involvement. Old canker sores throbbed anew. Once in a while I made a new kind of peace or accommodation with the past, but, more often, a surliness boiled and fermented. Perhaps I was angry at my ghosts for my loneliness. I never used that word once during the entire trip, never said to myself, I'm lonely. It was like talking about quitting; it was just better not to let certain words come into circulation. All the same, you go on to express loneliness or your reaction to it. I didn't always like being so alone, so I would think about other people. Unfortunately, the physical and emotional stresses did not always foster a serene or forgiving state of mind. So I had plenty of angry thoughts and to a degree that made me uncomfortable. There was an obsessive repetition about it that seemed to have nothing to do with granting a new perception space or discharging some irritation, but reflected instead a discomfort about my immediate situation.

On the other hand, even good friends at home, even my own family members, represented at times an obligation that I didn't want to accept. I knew people were loving when they worried about me, but it was the very isolation of my situation, the escape from being available, that I enjoyed. Five years earlier I was riding in a bus in the back seat over a pitted road through the Colombian Andes. The jouncing on the old springs was so tumultuous that I could not sleep, but it didn't matter. The bus ride had been going on for hours and hours. Hot sunlight poured in the windows. Green mountains and blue sky were printed on the glass. I had never been in that part of the world before, knew not for where I was headed or where I would get off. No one who knew me in the entire world knew where I was. I felt unreachable, free. How many times in your life do you escape from the telephone and the mail and the sounds of voices you love? No matter how lonely travel can be, there is always the other side to it, the chance to become something fresh and unheard of, completely new. Of course, eventually change for the sake of change pales and when the newspaper in Spanish at the thousandth café table turns to ashes, then it is time to go home, but that comes later. So as

I lay there on that seat and gave in to the thudding jolts that winded me, I remember just laughing aloud.

For the transcon I had donned emotional blinders. Perhaps I did it with an internal ruthlessness that was not necessary, but perhaps it was the best way. It did matter to talk to people at home, and God knows I made a slew of calls, but it was hard to have the energy to share it with everyone who was concerned. So there were times I resented the forty-five-minute gap shot in the evening, that precious margin of time that I wanted to use for something mindless like watching TV or walking a little more slowly to the restaurant in town. And it seemed as if this would go on forever. The past was irrevocably gone. What was there in my immediate surroundings on a county highway to suggest the face of a friend in New York? So there was not much sense of future either. I kept getting ready to die, so when folks rapped on the coffin, it was an effort to yell back. It was easier to love those whom I immediately met, than to love ghosts. But there is a danger in these musings if they are not set in the full context of many hours. Sometimes I felt distant and angry and sometimes not. The more the weariness took ahold, the easier it was to give in to demon chasing.

It is lonely work. Who else in the entire country lives in the way you do, a homeless runner, constantly in motion? There is no one who understands it, no one who shares it. Bruce Tulloh said of his own crossing that you are alone with your own ambitions most of the day. A paraphrase for me might be you are alone with the nature of a solo enterprise. To do it solo is to be solo. And yet that was what I wanted. I did not want to rely on anyone any more than I had to. So when I began to hear the question around this time: When do you expect to get back? a kind of fabulous caution closely related to anger would rise up. Who could say? Who was I to dare to assume a single mile as done until done? I was grateful to reach the end of the day. The end of the trip—that was an illusion.

It was impossible, as it turned out, not to set myself up as a sucker as I headed toward Chicago. Bart Rocca, one of my oldest friends, who dates back to the faraway epoch called the "late sixties," was living in the Chicago area with his wife, Catherine. I was anxious to see them and their children. Unlike New York, Chicago was a possibility—less than a week's hard running from the Mississippi. I felt as if getting to Chicago meant the rest of the way would just goof on by. How could I not have known better? Well, I probably did, but the need at this point to sustain myself with a reward was so strong that I was willing to ignore the hazard of setting up a goal to reach. I had decided to take a day's vacation in Chicago, another wonderful dream! A subtle excitement flowed through every artery, vein and capillary as I considered the blissful chance just to rest. I would not go anywhere. I might go up and down the stairs in their house a few times, but otherwise I would simply stay put.

As usual, there was a lot of territory coming up. I had prepared for the Iowa-Illinois border by buying Mark Twain's *Life on the Mississippi* in a Laramie bookstore. It seemed obscene to keep ripping out the pages as I finished them, but about weight there could be no sentimentality. Twain evoked the bygone days of his youth when the paddle-wheel boats navigated the ever-changing, frequently perilous face of a moody river whose hidden tree snags, sandbars and changing water levels required the utmost finesse and concentration in a riverboat pilot, especially at night. Gradually, the work of the Army Corps of Engineers tamed the fickle waters that in the past had so often played havoc with state boundaries. A calmer era on the river ensued as evidenced by the present day barges being snouted upriver by tugs. So it was another kind of roadway that ran north and south instead of east and west the way I-80 does. The Mississippi was about travel and history and it was easy enough when gazing at the low, tropical-looking density of green trees on the Illinois side of the river to people it with the boats and houses of the past. The town of Muscatine proudly notes in a historical marker that Twain wrote how the sunsets around there were the loveliest on the river.

A friendly but intensely unyielding toll collector on the Muscatine bridge refused to let me cross.

"Sorry, it's federal regulations," he said. It was another in the distressingly antihuman regulatory clauses and attitudes that made pedestrians so unwelcome in America. Throughout Illinois and Indiana a fair number of towns were almost impossible to run through safely in the business districts since they were designed only for motorists. Littered as they are with fast-burger joints, Pizza Huts, acres of tar parking lots, one-story professional buildings housing doctors, dentists and lawyers, and through it all, no sidewalk to run on. The determined foot runner is forced to jump up and then down off curbings, dodge past vehicular inlets and outlets before drivers, unused to the presence of humans on two feet, run him over. The squashy feel of grass turf laid down by the square yard and never designed for walking is the nearest one comes to a decent running surface. The sense of literal exclusion and indifferent neglect is compounded by the ruthless laying down of vehicular by-laws. Granted, without cars, a transcon runner would be at an immense disadvantage, but to keep one off a bridge? What driver can appreciate a bridge the way someone on foot does? Usually the narrowness of the lanes, plus the high speed, reveals nothing more than a fleeting glimpse of water. I wanted to lumber over this sweet green bridge in peace, savoring the significance of the crossing, which was more mystical and emotional than anything else, but who can deny the power of such rituals and formalities in a run? Joy can be found in the explicit shape of the world.

As it was, I was forced to run along a road parallel to the east-west bend in the Mississippi down to the Quad Cities (Davenport and Bettendorf lie in Iowa whilst on the Illinois side of the waters are Moline and Rock Island). The day was bright and sunshiny and through the heavily wooded banks on the Iowa side I got occasional slices of views of the muddy, choppy swath of water glittering in the light. Apart from the

Hudson, there is no other river between the two coasts as
impressive. Crossing the Big M over I-80 on another vehicular
bridge was possibly courting an interrogation by the highway
patrol, but the possible illegality of the venture gave great zest
to the actual sprint over a long, thoroughly handsome and
satisfactory steel bridge painted blue and gold.

Out by the airport I suddenly found myself thick in the
embrace of another kind of America. I stopped for a light
afternoon meal in the Holiday Inn. I pushed in through the
swinging doors and my ears were enveloped in that kind of high
open chattering noise one associates with immense airline ter-
minals, public library reading rooms in major cities, and great
hotels. Phones ringing, voices chattering, the scuffle of luggage
being stacked and hauled, the smells of tobacco and perfume
and air-conditioned air, the press of flesh, this time a delegation
of women wearing fezes. Some of them had legends they wore
describing them as Daughters of Mokanna. It seemed mad
because they looked so settled, so fleshy, so self-satisfied, so
impenetrable, so forever such adults, and yet they were in the
guise of children using make-believe. The old defensive and
angry instincts from antiwar days surged up. I felt I would die
in their homes, die in their embrace, that all the quintessential
American Kulture of television shows, game shows, talk shows,
fast cars, paperback novels in supermarket shelves, all the
stuffing that America makes you feel you are going to die in,
immense butts on golf carts, bowling for dollars, something
dark and airless, dry farts in a closet, God how I bristled with
distaste! Being hungry didn't help nor did the languid, interminable disappearances of my waitress while I studied with increasing rage the pseudotropical decor (green motif) and
watched with bitterness as the white ceiling fans turned overhead so that the whole simpering loathsome place might seem
so *nice!* It did me good to be uncharitable and I was quite
prepared to be despised in return by anyone who chose to react
to me. The waitresses hated their jobs; I knew it but I was an
innocent sufferer.

I spent a second night in Muscatine and the next morning Rick drove me out again to where I had left off in Illinois. Like his father, he had become an insurance salesman, a job that he genuinely loved.

"At graduate school I had a Mexican shirt and a beard," he said. "I was older than some of the other students and I was a bit of a guru for some of them, but I can tell you I lost a lot of credibility going back to sell insurance in Iowa! You learn a lot about people in this job. I know more about my clients' lives sometimes than their wives. I have to know what they own and whom it should go to, so I learn about their mistresses, their hopes, everything. Money brings out a lot of emotion in Americans."

Rick had a real sense for perverse mind tricks. He was the only person I met who thought to ask how it felt to wonder about running the whole thing again. It was one of those deviling obsessive fears I had sometimes. I would imagine someone saying: "You can't finish the run unless you run through Nevada again!" "Okay," I'd answer, and would actually begin to prepare myself to do it. I would have to slap myself a bit to say, hey, wait, you *don't* have to run a single step again. But the hold of such wanderings was as intense as that sick feeling when you wake up in the morning feeling guilty for having murdered someone in your dream. Rick mentioned, just before dropping me off at the mailbox that was where the previous day's run had ended, how he had heard an ex-POW in Vietnam address a convention of insurance salespeople who belonged to a certain club, I think, where to renew your membership each year, you had to have sold a million dollars' worth of life insurance. The ex-POW said "the body can endure anything" and that what sustained him was an ever-stronger faith. He had been in solitary confinement under horrendous conditions for years. As I set off running toward the town of Geneseo through the green countryside, I felt ashamed. I now had less than a thousand miles to go. What was that compared with what the POW had been through? The body can endure anything. Now that was something to derive faith from!

Illinois went quickly. There were swift, indelible reminders that life was becoming more domesticated and more eastern. Further west the farming towns had been simpler and those who lived there seemed to have a cleaner, closer life to the earth around them. In Harlan everyone spoke business—the pizza-place owner, the pharmacist, the commodities broker, the life-insurance salesman, the motel keeper, the newspaper reporter—everyone I met knew corn and bean prices and how much farmers paid for their metal silos and what the banks were doing in terms of loans. As agriculture prospered and suffered so did their own fortunes and those of their friends. In Illinois the towns along the Fox River often resembled mill towns in Massachusetts or factory towns along the Mohawk River. Places like Peru, La Salle, Marseilles, had old brick manufacturing plants, big stacks and a firmly entrenched underclass of blue-collar workers. The closer to Chicago, the deeper and denser and more industrial the state became.

It's hard to know how much one's own mood affects a judgment of a place, but however fair or unfair it is to say it, Illinois was not a comfortable place. There was some strange, dark undercurrent to the state, some sense of bad business that had been kept secret. It wasn't that the general reserve was cool —it was the reserve of tightness, of fear and of some weary moroseness. It's not to say that individuals weren't as warm and open as they had been elsewhere, because there was the fat Australian guy who bubbled on merrily when he stopped to offer a ride, the couple who ran the fresh-baked donut shop who wanted to stuff me with free samples, the runner near Chicago who slowed in his car and on learning what I was about, gave a wonderful smile of encouragement just when I needed it most, or the owner of Walter's Men's Shop in Geneseo who plugged me with questions, called me a pioneer and in general gazed at me with such intense and genial well-meaning that I felt like looking over my shoulder to see if he was addressing the right person. There were the children in La

Salle who were finishing up a twelve-mile walk for charity, their noses and cheeks red from the cold; they addressed me with the fearless innocence of children who do not live in large cities. They were as trusting as the small boys in Nebraska towns who piped "Hello" when I walked by on the street.

But it doesn't change the down-blue tones of those towns. In Marseilles I sat eating some rotten breakfast in a smoke-filled workingmen's café. It was the kind of coffee shop you would normally associate with a YMCA in a medium-sized town in the 1960s. The plastic display covers for the Danish pastries were scratched from interminable summers and winters of service and if you removed the paint from the yellowing hamburger menus that were hanging on the wall, you might find them originally costing seventy-five cents. At the dog leg in the counter on my right, two guys sit side by side with that frozen early-morning look the shift-weary have, as if they are breaking ice in their cups when they stir the java with their spoons. They inhale smoke as if it is an old friend and they blow it out with a kind of disregard for its hazards that no middle-class simp like myself would dare to question. I would no sooner have asked them to blow the smoke in another direction than I would have put my finger in the way of a moving fan blade. One is young and the other is old. The first one is eating a jelly donut and the other a Danish. That's their breakfast. Ten minutes go by.

"Got real cold last night," the young guy says.

There is a longish pause.

"Yeah," says the older one.

The silence sets in again. I thought of the Nebraska café, clean and scrubbed, where the local farmers sit, whooping it up like hearty old peasant women at their shoved-together tables. Those were men who work in isolation on their farms all the time. To see their own kind is special. And one of them had his young daughter with him and it was just fine. It was a land of families and diapers and cows and chickens; one would as soon see a child in this Marseilles diner as a live stripper in a morgue.

In La Salle I looked in the yellow pages for a masseur, hoping to ease some of the recurrent cramping in my right foot. In the middle of downtown was a sign offering massage services, special rates. There were colored light bulbs, I think, in the front window of the converted storefront. Heavy drapes blocked the view into the inside. Delighted, I pushed open the door, which jangled with sleigh bells announcing my arrival. A young woman, about twenty at the most, blond, cool, confident, vulnerable as well, with a look about her thin, experienced lips that was a cultural kind of innocence, the innocence of a TV watcher and comic-book reader, the innocence of someone who was the third out of four children, who had somehow tight and bitter conversations with her family, vulnerable in the way teen-agers look when their very insistence on distance bespeaks such neediness and such reliance on the opinions of others, all this was clear to see, accurate or not as my impression may have been. It was immediately clear she was in a whore's business, especially when she said:

"What do you want?"

It is the oldest of the feints from the city-wise who are just keeping one step away from an explicit statement; those who have been entrapped offer nothing that you can drop into a glassine envelope as evidence.

She looked nice and it would have been nice to have sex with a woman like that, although not under circumstances like this dreary little sitting room and with all the attendant train of circumstances, but even that was just a flicker. I yearned to solve more fundamental concerns. Sex would exist in the afterlife, when the run was over. For now I needed work on my feet. And I was embarrassed even to hint that I knew the real purpose of her question.

We got entangled in an odd conversation, one somewhat at cross purposes.

Yes, I had money, but I wanted a real massage. How good were the girls?

After all, $40 for a bit of lotion and some bored ineffectual strokes on my metatarsal heads would be a terrible disappointment. As for my pretty interlocutor, the queerness of my garb, my mission in life and the real drift of my questions were baffling and mysterious. She did not smile or flourish in any particular human way, simply repeated the price with a kind of managerial confidence in the employees' technical abilities. Perhaps she was a hooker, herself, not just a manageress. I thanked her and retreated, glaring a bit defiantly around as I exited from the little shop of pleasures, challenging anyone to assume that I had been in there for any other reason than the best. Middle America has yet to learn what real massage is all about.

Although the towns were changing, the space between them was still farmland. The earth had flattened out and was now colored a rich black. Miles of yellowed corn and soybean plantings were just beginning to be harvested. Big combines were at work early till late, their metal dividers trembling slightly from the powerful motor as the beast lumbered down the rows. It was a steady kind of magic the way the plants were there to be seen one instant and then were gone the next, leaving behind the neat brushstrokes of stubble. Unlike the West, it had been quite rainy in parts of Illinois this summer and some of the small brooks were gushing with water. Big soft mosquitoes would settle as gently as moths on my arms and legs every time I stopped.

It was a somewhat dislocated sensation to reach the town of Ottawa. Until six months earlier, my brother and his family had been living there. Just nine months earlier I had been in Ottawa, going over topographical maps of the U.S. with my brother to plot the basic route. I remember being a bit bored by it as if the map part were just a hindrance and the real thing was just to get out there and do it. How strange and how wonderful to have talked about it, not knowing if it would really happen and now to be well through a good chunk of it. A dream comes and then will chases after it in its own kind of dream. Things change quickly. Once I would have been so excited to run through Ottawa with my family there to greet

me and now as I ran past Terra Cotta Road and looked up
toward the wooded ridge that prevented me from seeing the
flat-topped stretch of achingly wide farmland where they once
lived, I realized the fantasy that my sister-in-law was making
dinner for me would have to be shelved. So now I had run to
a part of the U.S. I had actually run through before. Well, even
if I walked the last eight hundred miles, I could be home in
three weeks. The pessimistic mind, the sad old shopkeeper
always ready to declare bankruptcy, was still in business.

An odd thing happened in Ottawa. I was walking down one
of the main streets in town heading for one of the motels, pack
on my back, jacket on because of the chill, but in shorts, clearly
a wanderer. A car slowed and a man leaned out while the heads
of his family could be seen through the closed window turned
my way.

"Is that you, Jim?"

I thought I recognized the face.

"Hey, yeah! Hi!" I called, but the car kept moving and the
heads looked ahead again. It was baffling and amusing, crazy
almost. My brother and his family had been gone for months.
Did they think I was living on as a ghostly caretaker in the
unsold house? Or that I just happened to be going through
town on a casual stroll from the brink of the earth? It seemed
so odd, so repressed, so strange.

Later that night I walked past a bingo game being held in
some local building. There was a cluster of funny types outside
on the steps, some teen-age girls wearing nylon zip-ups with the
name of the high school printed on the back, immense stocky
girls with shoulders, backs and chests as round and undifferentiated as oaks; a thirteen-year-old boy, the perennial twerp type
with snub nose, sharp features and a loud voice. There were
one or two adults there, sitting with that same tight, we-are-
equal stance of the undeveloped when older people are keyed
without discrimination into the same behavior as younger ones.

It was 1965 again in the summer as I was walking down a
street in Central Falls, Rhode Island, in a working-class district

where one did not wear jackets and ties. I slung the jacket over
my shoulder and rolled my tie up to put it in a pocket, but the
slumming look did not pass. Some of the pretty if sour-hearted
girls in the neighborhood a little younger than myself were
quick to do public readings on my walk and manner while
continuing to graze hips with mine in that most insolent of
sexual ways— pretending interest, but full of spite. This Ottawa tribe knew I was different, not from there, and I knew it,
too. There were comments and cackles and the sense that you
are being memorized so that later if the police came, all of
them would have an absolutely clear recollection. Being in-
furiated by those pickled in provinciality is a waste of energy.
All the same I gave them a quick stab or two in my imagination. Sometimes sneers came on the trip when I was involved
in self-preening and self-admiration. Then it was easier to take,
as if I had invited such a bring down. But when I was a
half-lonely soul who was attached to the idea of finding friendliness and when I looked at them from the deep devout space
of effort that it had taken me to get me to that town, then I
was grateful for the perpetual traveler's blessing—that not only
the enjoyable but the unenjoyable will not endure and that
shortly movement will swallow all. So after a night in an expensive but weary motel, the kind where traveling salesmen and
grumpy families have worn the carpet thin and the massive box
spring speaks of a tight, malodorous sexuality and the single
paper-wrapped bar of soap seems such a weary bit of concession
to your being another, yet another ghost traveling through,
small wonder that before six the next morning, under a dark
blue sky, I flew down the road, consuming the fifty miles
between Ottawa and Joliet in one tremendous push.

There were always other people easier to get to know. At a
motel restaurant one night that week I fell into conversation
with a short, balding farmer and his wife, both in their early
sixties. Soon I was seated at a table with them, their son and
two grandsons; we were waited on by the son's wife.

"Yes, I know New York," he said. "I was there during the

Second World War. We were on leave before we got shipped overseas to Europe—I was in the Army—and our idea of a real bang-up time, you know, was to go get a good dinner at a fine steakhouse. We were walking down this neighborhood where there's a lot of theaters and so on."

"Times Square?"

"Yes, yes. I think that must have been it. Anyways we were walking down the street and on our right-hand side like this was a big place where we got a very good steak."

"Did it have fish tanks in the window? It might have been Jack Dempsey's place."

"Oh, yes, I think so."

There was such a wonderful, simple charm about this man, a farm boy in uniform in the big city still recalling as freshly as if it were happening again the steady-headed (and so innocent!) excitement that he and his friends sought along the Great White Way. The simplicity with which he had described the particular side of the street it was on, as if out of all the continent of streets in New York it might still be there, the way things stay in small towns in Illinois, so that even if one store is replaced by another, why everyone knows it. It didn't matter if we had guessed right about Dempsey's, it gave us a mutual connection.

He went on to talk about his poor dad after a long day of work getting up from the dinner table and going back out into the night with a lantern to keep on harvesting. The amount of hand work was tremendous just a few years ago. Husking corn was a tedious hand job that went on well into November. You tied a kind of hook into the palm of one hand, made a few swift cuts to loosen the dry husks, and ripped them free with the other. He had figures to recite that I've forgotten, about how many bushels of corn a man would husk in a day.

Meeting men like that changed my crabby notion of farmers out in the Midwest being the spoiled recipients of a lot of government money for plowing land under, much the way non–New Yorkers view residents of the city. You know a little bit and you get cartoon-intellect notions in your mind. From what I could see, some farmers were certainly worth a lot of money. Some were millionaires, if one assessed all their holdings. But a lot of them were finding that as independent small farmers, they simply could not survive any longer. Flush harvests bring low prices. Bad weather drives prices up, which is fine if your own harvest survives. Increasing costs in fuel and machinery have been rocketing upward. Estate taxes make it very difficult for children to inherit the land and over and over you hear that it's just about not possible anymore for a young person, starting out on his own, to raise the amount of capital needed to buy land. A brand of silo, called Harvestore, a blue metal storage vat with white lettering so familiar through parts of the Midwest, offers one of its biggest silos for sale at a cost of $100,000. That takes a lifetime to pay off. Land prices were commonly cited between $1500 and $2500 an acre. Wealthy city people, foreign investors and big corporate interests were putting a lot of money into land and for an ever-larger number of farmers, they were renters who no longer owned the land they tilled. "I hate losing that basic freedom to work my ass off year round and all the same do it for myself," one farmer said. There are a lot of nice farm buildings in these middle states, big white barns with the name of the founding family painted on the side, along with the date. Occasionally a state sign will proclaim that this is a century farmstead or some such title, meaning the same family has been running this farm for a hundred years or more. That all seems to be changing and one wonders at the hidden costs of the severance between ownership and work. Some unsettling gray anonymous fog that infests the world where we all work for hidden, subtle interests, crucified between the ledger sheets of accountants who themselves are not responsible to anything but the endlessly receding caves of faraway ownership that no one can bound anymore with a signature, or their own body, or their own gaze. The age is forever different than it was.

At Joliet an immense electrical power plant loomed up out

of the ground, took possession of the sky. When you live in a
city all your life an industrial beast like that means nothing. But
when you come out of the desert, come out of the great western
desert and midwestern farmland where mile after mile is unbroken by the expression of this kind of focused, actual industrial strength, the shock and exhilaration is tremendous. The
stacks ran up into the sky, defying anyone to conceive of the
work and muscle involved in their creation. The great pyramids
of coal—I had seen the places in the earth where that was
mined and all the hopper cars raising dust from the rail beds
as they were hauled over the bedsheet wrinkles of Wyoming
on their way east. Men and women in the four corners, all
dancing together in the industrial dance. And from this plant
came the ability to run lights in the bedroom, heat homes,
dance to records. This was our god. This had a power and
brutality to match the Mayan temples at Tikal, even the ones
with the steepest steps where the living hearts were ripped out
of the human sacrifices. No one can live in the immediate
precincts of such highways and access roads and buzzing high-
tension lines except for rats and flies. Through this graveyard
of glass and rusted metal, not another living human soul had
ever walked. Brown and green shards of glass crunching underfoot, flashing up at me as I ran steadily on. Who is to say this
is not as much to be loved as the gilded treasure in art museums?

    Joliet was funky, industrial, crowded, bisected by a river
afloat with serious-sized barges. I stopped in a gas station in a
poor black neighborhood, confused by where the local motels
were to be found. A few young guys were there. I went through
my explanations and turned down an offer to buy some sticks
of Mary Jane.

    "Tell you what," said one guy, a fairly plump, slightly be-
draggled man in his early twenties. "You buy me some gas and
I'll drive you back over the bridge to where you need to get to
go."

    I bought two dollars of gas and jumped into the rickety old

car. The exhaust pipes jabbered mightily, my new friend working the loose gear shift into a delicately balanced state that
allowed it to engage, and we flared off onto the highway. He
was up from the South five years earlier, laid off a year ago and
completely unable to find work. He tugged at his knit cap, ran
his eyes restlessly, mournfully over the speeding metal beasts
on our stretch of I-80. The windows were smeared, the floor
littered with this and that, and he was a stuck human being.
Couldn't find work, wanted to and couldn't. What do you say
except to listen?

"Here you go," he said and pulled over to the shoulder near
a thrifty motel. We shook hands, exchanged wishes of good
luck and he rattled off, bound as surely to the problems of a
troubled industrial time as anyone could be.

Joliet was a grim place. Running through the dark streets
before dawn the next morning over the concrete sidewalks,
past all the wooden homes that might have been Dorchester
or Salem or Swampscott or Mattapan, all towns in Massachusetts, all working class, all with lights on in the bedroom or the
kitchen as people struggled awake, running past the downtown
and the nailed-up windows, and the rusting-out frames and the
lurking uncivility of rust and soot and that absently soiled
scratching of a gray city brow—all sobering. It seemed a dark
village, peopled by the salaried of the earth. The jollity and
relative freedom of the farmers had vanished. I was running on
the fringes of that great sprawling beast of the multitudes
known as Chicago. So even the joy of holding the *Chicago
Tribune* in my hands as I waited for my home fries and eggs
was a subdued one. The world is an immense place with many
problems. I did not feel cocky on the thirtieth of September,
1980, with 2,216 miles behind me. I was not conquering anyone or anything by arriving. I was just lucky to share space in
this mad fashion.

I ran a little way south of Chicago on Route 30. I could not
see or smell Lake Michigan or even glimpse the towers of the
not-too-distant city. But all the peripheral satellites held in

place by the gravitational pull of Chicago were there—the Ford stamping plant, the barrage of traffic, a trillion souls let loose upon the world, the posh shopping malls of Frankfort, the poor ghetto world of Chicago Heights with all the night clubs and private social clubs, heavy gratings over grocery stores, paint peeling on door jambs, a call from a very sharp-looking black man out drinking in the afternoon, holding a paper bag, standing by his long white car: "Where ya heading?" "New York," I yelled back. And suddenly it just seemed like it might be true. He smiled and clenched a fist in greeting. He believed me. Maybe it was all true.

I had hoped that Bart would be at the Indiana state line to greet me. I tried to run with a bunch of attitudes about how I was going to look something or other. I still didn't know what suffering it would take to burn off ever yet more vanity. Bart wasn't at the state line, however, so I simmered down and got a big freeze at the Dairy Queen to celebrate. I sat in the warm sun. Chicago. That sounded nice. Now what happened?

How Long Is Forever?

Everything changed again after Chicago. Things always change, there is no surprise in that, but sometimes, all in a rush, deeper, more fundamental themes change. There was the bitterness of the anticlimax of rediscovering that for all I had done, there was much left to be done. Chicago was just another way station. The dream had been to be away from the road for a day; life only seemed real again when I buckled the chest strap of the pack and shuffled off, a companion of buildings, winds, cars, clouds and the ever-present road that always stretched ahead, always receded to a point in the distance that I never caught up with.

Body weariness was a tremendously difficult problem. There are times when you have to eat yourself, consume your own flesh to keep going. Those are the knock-down black hours of extreme stress in the one hundred-milers or longer. You can get through, but you know, deep inside you know, that you are asking for things that cannot be given without cost. For me it was my thighs. They took the hard edge. Through Indiana and Ohio they began to go dead some afternoons. I lost that connection to their deep strength and buoyancy. Looking down at them earlier in the run I had almost admired them as being different from myself, like horses that I did not own, but simply had attached reins to. Brown and powerful, they ceaselessly pumped forward and back in alternate rhythm. In the engine room of a freighter the pistons are immense and complete expressions of an energy so vast and relentless that even the constant tugging and dipping beneath your feet that signals the resistance of the water to the impetus of the boat only adds to the profound respect a watcher feels. The pistons go on, un-affected. Somewhere along the way I no longer could look down at my body and feel pride in it. With an instinct that came long before my conscious mind understood it, I had to look away from the illness of endeavor. It broke my heart to know what I was doing, to see the thinness setting in as if my flesh were melting away like the torso of a snowman in the March sunshine. I was no hungrier than before; I ate as much as seemed reasonable, but perhaps there was no way to catch up. Perhaps what I had reached to do required an overdraft and the minus would be greater than the plus. So I no longer looked at my legs, no longer felt I was a rugged-looking man of the hardened runner variety. It was the final humbling and in a way, it matched a broader mood.

For even this sadness of physical decay was absorbed in the broad current of acceptance that carried me along. I started running frequent fifty-mile days, but it no longer meant too much. It was time now to finish, to bring it all home and end it without any more stops. I no longer glanced frequently at my watch. I no longer stopped every forty-five minutes to spend five minutes on the maps, solacing myself with the quarter inches of progress that once seemed so important.

It no longer seemed an issue of happiness or unhappiness, proving something or failing, achieving or not achieving. I had considered having Donna come out to Indiana or Ohio, since she had a little spare time again and I had to remind myself with a shake, ah, yes, I was supposed to do it solo, so I guess I should keep it solo until I'm a few days out of New York. But to care whether I finished with a handler or not was just a joke now as far as I was concerned. I had already been alone, been unhappy, been afraid, been sick and broken-down, been in rebellion against the run, and I had gotten through all that. I didn't have to prove anything to anyone else. The ghosts and demon voices who had ridden on my shoulders for so long, mocking me, defying my moments of weakness, goading me constantly into proving over and over that I would not stop, that I would never give in simply because that would be nice, they were still there, but in a different way. There had been plenty of times when I felt too dry to sit down by the side of the road and cry out of some stinking weariness, and I hadn't done it. Nobody congratulated me. Nobody cared. Not right then and even later talking about it when it's over or hinting at it, what can anyone say? So I wasn't interested in proving anything. I knew I was human and had my own funny ways. Sometimes weakness, sometimes strength. If I had learned anything at this point I had learned that you have to nurse yourself along, take it as far as you can, but not to kill yourself, not to cut it so hard that you can't keep going over the mountain into infinity. I know that much of what I have written sounds far beyond the pale for ordinary physical endeavor and perhaps it was and certainly I was exacting a steep price. But the point is I was willing to pay it. It had to be paid now. It had no relation to earning merit in the eyes of others or even in my own eyes. It was just dedication to effort for its own sake.

In Bowling Green, Ohio, a community relations rep for McDonald's, a very attractive woman in her late thirties, fell into conversation with me at a Dutch Pantry restaurant. We both were sitting on the plush banquette side of our deuce tables. She began grilling me about why I was doing it and partially out of vanity, partially out of a desire to flirt and partially out of a dispassionate interest in seeing what I had to say, I responded with a good deal of care and candor. But it was useless; she didn't seem to get it and I couldn't get it either. At the time I thought you wouldn't ask someone why they married whom they did. And the why of it was . . . well, maybe there was no why. You just make up reasons. I could never explain adequately to myself, even, why I was doing it. Words

were inadequate. Of course, I could say that it had qualities
that appealed to me. It involved running and involved a great
deal of difficulty. But it didn't really matter to me why. It was
more what it involved—it involved doing. The only net that
can snare doing is doing.

The weariness was the most troublesome thing I had to
contend with. Sometimes I would get a stabbing pain that
would seem to flare out of my stomach and through my penis,
just a shockingly sharp flash. There were flash seizures, too,
deep in my groin, in the muscles of the butt, in the attachments of tendon and ligament around the head of the femur
bones, so sharp and startling that I would literally gasp and leap
crookedly into the air as if to try to fly out of the grasp of the
whitened knuckles of a giant fist. I would stop running and take
baby, tottering steps and then very gently shuffle into motion
again as if I might set off another attack by greediness. The
cutting edge was never far away. So I would back off and not
fight such things all the time the way I had early in the trip.

There were cycles in life, cycles in the body's mood. The
entire basis for physical endeavor, which I had so unwittingly
molded around inappropriate ideas, had been shattered. Always I had felt more is better, longer is better, the more you
do somehow the more you get. The entire notion that had
hypnotized me at the beginning of the transcon that I would
get stronger and stronger and hence go ever farther was an
absurdity. You cannot have strength without weakness; cannot
have effort without rest; cannot give without ever taking in. It
was always different. Every hour, every morning, every afternoon was a different world and a different self that sought to
run through it.

The sweetest sleeps of the trip took part around this time.
I would buy food in supermarkets and then with my paper bag
full of this and that, would go out along the cozy strip of grass
on the sides of supermarkets, have lunch, read the local paper
and then with my cap pulled over my eyes and my pack for a
pillow, would snooze away. Under gray clouds and sunny skies

alike, I would nap in a patch of deserted woods, in culverts by
the side of a road, on steep fallaway banks at the sides of
highways, in city parks—wherever there was a bit of earth and
grass and a little shelter so that, like a dog nesting in high grass,
I could have a sense of being tucked away. The sound of
passing cars and trucks was a soothing lullaby, a kind of reassur-
ance that the cosmic American roadlife was awake. Through
the pinholes in the hat, I would study prismatic bursts of light,
or if it was a larger, brad-secured opening for one of the small
vents, there was a little telescope into the universe, a piece of
cloud floating overhead. Insects ticked in the grass. It was the
half hour of healing, that sweet hammock of doziness tied
between two great stretches of work—the morning and the
afternoon. I slept in fields with no name, no rental fee, no other
humans. The lull in this massive endeavor was a piece of
complete freedom. I slept with a sweetness I have never experienced before. And then, as if floating on my back in a pond
rather than on my back on the ground, sensation would carry
me up again so that I could feel a twig pressing against my
shoulder or a patch of cold that had put its chilly fingers around
the exposed skin between the top of my sock and the pulled-up
cuff of my running pants, things to remind me that I was
human and that I had a name and a piece of business to attend
to. Waking up in the middle of a day is like coming into
another day altogether. Towns I had been through that morning were a blur. The names of counties that once had thrilled
me to run through were forgotten. I could hardly remember
anything much. It would take a few minutes sometimes to
remember the name of the place I had slept in the night
before. Once I had thought I would remember every footstep.
Now there was such abundance of impression that I couldn't
try anymore. Some I would remember, some I would forget.

The last and worst mental crisis came about midway through
Ohio. The name of the state had always conjured up an image
of a green and pleasant land. The rolling *o*'s suggested serenity

and roundness, hilliness, greenness, kind of an eastern Iowa. The land was pleasant enough, but it was really pretty flat. The weather had changed and for all that I had imagined I only wanted some cool weather again, the flat grayness was harder to take with my own cloudy mood. It's never external weather that matters, just the internal kind. I had to contend with the problem that I could never see my goal. No matter how far I ran I could not reach a vista or mountaintop high enough to see the distant smudge of New York City on the skyline. Only those cursed numbers "proved" that I was only about six hundred miles from home. Twenty percent of the run. I would get out my mileage log and see how many days at the start of the trip it had taken to run the first six hundred miles. Less than two weeks. Just fourteen days and I'll be home, I thought, but it was a thought that led to other thoughts that all had to do with how long and how difficult it was. Every runner knows that in a race, even as the distance left to go shrinks, the effort needed to get through it continues to remain far higher than in the opening stages. I don't remember anymore exactly how or when I railed against my lot, but I recall distinctly that it was a bad dream, a regular nightmare for a day or two, off and on. And then I just decided to stop making such a fuss and really get down to work for a change. Running fifty-mile days was costly, but it certainly made the trip go by quickly. A hundred miles in two days, three hundred miles in six days— that kind of mileage will eat up even plump states with a satisfactory degree of speed.

A large portion of my life as a schoolboy was spent studying the various clocks in the various schoolrooms I spent most of my waking hours confined in. Or drawing up a list of the days left to go till vacation. Thinking about time is the surest way to become its victim; only concentration on the moment makes it fall away. There was a kind of balance to all this. If I got too fuzzy about what I was about I lost just enough tension and impetus to keep the day as full of movement as was needed. Chats with storekeepers would go on too long, lunches would extend to three rather than two specials, et cetera. So it was helpful not to run in some mystical fog, but to pick a place to reach at the end of the day. Just sticking to what is possible on a given day is the most anyone can do and is so obvious a piece of common sense that it is easy to wonder how many days during the trip I had to relearn it. But it is easier, I had discovered, to think that way when you are two thousand miles from New York than when you are two hundred miles from the end. Far away it is so obvious how far away it is that imagination cannot do much and simply sulks silently. Once close, then it is possible to get distracted more easily. So even at this late stage in the crossing, distraction was potentially fatal. I was going to fall off the ladder. So you go down inside yourself and summon up what has to be summoned. Nothing special. Just do it.

I had an image I scribbled down in Ohio that came to me sometimes. Running, one is like a lit stick of incense. Breath is the smoke. One's life is the smoke. The graveyards I passed are when we are completely done, completely turned to ash. But before then there is no end, whether we are asleep or awake, because we are always consuming ourselves. The past is the ash, the present is the burning point, the future is the part of the green joss stick yet to be burned. Where does the joss stick come from and where does the smoke go?

When that image came up the run was easier.

One other element undoubtedly contributed to the overall calming of my mood (apart from just getting closer to home!), which was that the wild drama and relentlessness of the weather and terrain of the West and parts of the Midwest had completely changed in character. Although there were still days coming up in Pennsylvania when twenty or thirty miles without food or water had to be endured, it was basically a run through a more densely populated, older, calmer, more industrial, far more familiar part of the country. I was in the East. I was in home territory. The trees, the brand names, the look of the rock formations, the quality of the light, the sound of crows—each tiny happening was another thread binding up the Gulliver of Restlessness.

A wonderful thing happened in Wellington, Ohio. It had been one of those interesting days where you plod on through the sunshine meeting interesting kinds of people at each stop. All morning dogs had been leaping up from naps on the ground to curse and howl with frustrated rage as they ran to the full limit of their chains. There was the fellow in the garage who had a terrible stutter and, in his attempt to explain a short cut on some county roads, spent fifteen minutes of his morning drawing a map. There was the proprietress of Trail's End Motel whose office smelled of dogs. She was a plump, older lady who also offered careful directions. She had a card on her wall with a nail scotch-taped to it and a poem printed underneath with a message reminding the reader what He endured for us. There was a reproduction of the Ten Commandments and a contribution sticker for a county animal humane society.

Anyway, I walked through Wellington, which had a very strange-looking sort of city hall, somewhat Russian, I think, with onion roofs, but altogether a wacky potpourri of styles. As I walked along the main street heading east, I pondered where to kill my thirst. A little soda shop caught my eye, looked like it had been on the same spot for umpteen years, quite homey, but a peep in through the glass of the door seemed to indicate it was not one of those fearsomely stale dens of bad cooking. So I went in and sat down gratefully on a round counter stool and got a strawberry ice cream soda.

The white-haired woman who worked behind the counter was talking to a farmer about somebody's property and who was going to inherit what. I was clearly a stranger so they paid me no mind and talked on freely enough. Gradually, the place began to fill up with midafternoon coffee drinkers. I just kept sitting, not saying a word. There was no need to announce my plans for the three-thousandth time, but when I took out the Ohio road map, it provided the obvious way for someone to ask where I was headed, which they did. The dozen or so people in the café all fell quiet and then an old man a few stools down, dressed in olive coveralls like a factory laborer, piped up with a question.

"Did you ever hear of a man called Edward Payson Weston?" he asked.

I was electrified.

"Oh, sure!" I cried. "Edward Weston was the greatest walker America ever had. He crossed this country a few times on foot early in this century. His first walk was from Boston to Washington, D.C., to attend Lincoln's inauguration. He walked tremendous distances even when he was in his seventies."

The old man had a certain smile with a certain knowledge behind it, and then it flashed on me.

"Did you ever see Weston?" I asked.

"Yes, I did," the man said, who introduced himself as Harold Lee, age eighty-two, proprietor of the town's Cadillac agency. "Now I don't know if he was one of the greatest walkers, but he was a great self-publicist. We read about his coming through on his way from New York to California in the local newspaper. I was about eight or nine years old, this was back about 1910, and I lived with my family a little ways out of town here. So I and a few of the other small boys went out to meet him.

"It was a baking hot day. Weston came walking up, a fairly short man, medium build and he was carrying a pack just like you are. I remember he had extra shoes hanging from his side, flopping against him as he walked. We went with him for about one mile and we had to run to keep up with his walk. He smiled at us and maybe said a few words, but he didn't stop. This highway you're running over used to be called the Yellowstone Way. It was just slag and sand that was packed down with a steamroller, watered and then left alone. Very few automobiles came through in those days."

After I had squeezed Mr. Lee dry of every detail he could recall about his meeting seventy years earlier with America's

first transcon crosser, I went back to my own crossing in an
ecstatic frame of mind. It was as if I had stumbled on a direct
transmission from the founder of the transcon guild down to
myself. How strange and marvelous are the workings of circumstance and fate! I would not have missed that brief encounter
for anything. And when I thought of the odds against having
picked this road to cross Ohio, and of all the little stops and
confusions and pressings on and all the other variables that had
led *in toto* to my picking that particular afternoon to stop in
that little soda joint. I kept reviewing the way I had looked at
this restaurant and then another, almost deciding to go into
them, and yet had not. So the five days off in Harlan and the
day off in Chicago had meant that I could have this experience.
So who can presume to guess at the results of anything that
happens?

Seventy years earlier, Weston had come over that same road
on his way to becoming a national folk hero. Now who remembered him except for a few people in the ultrarunning community? He was the originator of a very specialized tradition and
there had only been a few who have followed since. No one
keeps accounts of who crosses the United States on foot, especially when they are not setting records. Except for the great
burst of activity in 1928 and 1929 when two transcontinental
races were held with fields of a few score men each year, all the
walking and running crossings had been individual in nature.
As far as I know, no one ran across the States in the thirties,
the forties or the fifties. I owed a debt myself, both to those
whom I had never met like Don Shepherd, the South African
coal miner who crossed the U.S. alone in 1964, solo, *completely*
solo, and to those I had met—Bruce Tulloh of England and
Mavis Hutchison of South Africa. Tulloh, now a schoolmaster,
was initially cool as I began to pelt him with questions, but soon
enough his eyes shone as he discussed his 1969 crossing for a
record time of sixty-four-plus days. Hutchison was tremendously intense from the moment she began to recall what
happened on her crossing at the age of fifty-three, a grand-

mother of seven, who is the only woman to have run across the country. She did it in sixty-nine-plus days.

Now it is true that Weston was not a runner on those crossings so much as a walker, but he was still the true patriarch of the event. But he seemed very close on that warm October afternoon. My mind buzzed with speculations. Motels and Coke machines did not exist in 1910 in the abundance they do now, so did he carry water, where did he spend the night, what did he eat, how much did his pack weigh, what did he think about when he looked at that same stretch of farmland I myself was looking at now, plowed probably by the sons of the small farmer's boys who had dogged his heels as he went California-bound? I looked over my shoulder repeatedly to see the vista the way he would have been likely to have seen it himself. And I wondered if seventy years after my own crossing, because of someone meeting me or reading the book about it, in 2020 say, there would be some similar transmission of energy. Whatever you do affects others, no matter what you choose to do. I hoped that out of the hundreds of millions of Americans yet to live, there would always be a few who would continue to try.

I often thought about things they had said and wondered what they had felt. Stan Cottrell of Georgia had crossed the country earlier in 1980 for a short-lived record that was to be taken away by Frank Giannino of upstate New York. In fact, when a newspaper reporter interviewed me in Akron, he said, "You know, there's someone hot on your heels." It was Frank Giannino. Although Frank left about a month after I did, he finished a day earlier on the Brooklyn Bridge, for his second crossing, with a time of forty-six-plus days. He was traveling with a support van manned by his mother and father. I felt a bit ashamed for a while at traveling so slowly and being such a tired guy, but I shook it off. It wasn't even the validity of the many reasons that make a solo, pack-carrying venture so different from an assisted run, but simply the unadorned fact that this *was* the best I could do, so what did it matter? If I could have maintained such a philosophical attitude had I been literally passed on the road I'm not sure, but I like to think so! I did actually yearn at times to meet a transcon runner coming the opposite way or catching up with me—what an interesting conversation we would have had.

But they were all out there with me. I had met men who had themselves been handlers or runners or friends of runners in the 1928–29 series, so I thought a lot about the heavy shoes they wore and the things they thought about and the way they were up against the edge all the time when racing and about the muddy roads and the concrete highways.

I had written to one, Peter Gavuzzi, an Englishman who was in his early twenties when he ran in both races with fellow countryman Arthur Newton. Although the two were among the very, very best ultrarunners in the world at that time, a series of flukes and apparent bad judgment deprived them of victory each year. Newton, an eminently shy, proud, fastidious, former farmer turned runner who wrote a series of droll, dry-humored, out-of-print classics about ultrarunning in the 1920s and 1930s, was hit the first year by a parson driving a wayward auto and the second year was forced out by an aggravated Achilles tendon. His partner was Gavuzzi, who fifty years later recalled in an English retirement cottage just how it had been, between sucks on his eternal pipe and sips from his teacup. A coal fire blazed on the hearth as he peppered his recollections with Cockney "blimeys" and "bloodys." Even then when I was interviewing him for a book about ultramarathoning, I had this itchy, almost embarrassed feeling at wanting to know if he thought *I* could do such a thing and how to go about training for it. That was what lay behind the intensity of some of my questions about the specifics of training for such an event. I think he sensed the genuineness and the thirst in those questions and when the photographer and I walked down the flagstone path to the little gate, he stepped outside his bachelor cottage to extend his farewell a little longer.

Before setting up my training I wrote him a letter and he quickly replied with his suggestions, saying bluntly that what

I proposed to do would try the fiber of the most seasoned ultrarunner. Why not take a companion with me in a van for the entire trip? He thought I was a little crazy, but he wished me the best of luck. I sent him a card during the trip and when I got home I wrote a letter about how it had all been. A few months later he was dead at the age of seventy-five. When I first met him I addressed him as "Mister Gavuzzi." "None of this 'Mister' stuff," he said, "It's Pete to you."

Weston's generation, of course, is long gone, he and all the men of the 1880s and 1890s who did the six-day races and the long walks. Then there was the era of Newton, Gavuzzi, Johnny Salo, Arthur Dilks and Richard McNamara in the 1920s and the 1930s. Few of them are left. Not until the 1950s did the next real wave of ultrarunners and journey runners crop up again and many of those men are now retired from the fray —Jackie Mekler and Wally Hayward of South Africa, Bernard Gomersall of England and Ted Corbitt of America. There is now the younger generation of fanatics currently at work around the world, mixing it up with the megadistances.

For my generation of ultrarunners in the United States the patriarch is Ted Corbitt, whose modes of training—two-hundred-mile weeks, hundred-mile training runs, relentless running through sweltering New York summers and all of this when nobody had magazines and books telling you how to put your socks on, let alone how to train for fifty- or hundred-mile races. You figured it out on your own. I know that Ted had once hoped himself to run across America. The same summer that Tulloh did his run, Ted was figuring out how long it would take *him* to do the crossing just by adding up his training miles. That summer while holding down a demanding full-time job as a physical therapist at the Institute for the Crippled and Disabled, he averaged forty miles a day! I learned this ten minutes after watching Stan Cottrell, fresh-faced and smiling, run off the steps of City Hall and vanish into the indifferent southbound Broadway traffic as he headed for Los Angeles. In less than four months I would be off on my own gig. Ted's flat-voiced statement floored me.

"Do you think I should be running that far in training to get ready for this?" It was a reasonable question. It was perplexing trying to figure out how to get ready for the whole thing. There are not a lot of people around to ask.

"No," Ted said firmly. His surface manner is so understated that at times his voice blurs into inaudibility and his thin presence seems more ghostly than corporeal, but his opinions about ultrarunning are always firmly delivered. "Just run twenty miles a day. You've got the background already. It's in your legs now. Too much training now will just use up all the energy you'll need, nervous and physical energy alike, for the run. You can run yourself into road shape."

It was advice I listened to and it was just right, although most importantly it felt right at the time to do it that way. All the same, crossing America I thought about Ted and how much he had wanted to do such a run and now how unlikely it is that he will ever recover from the injuries of the years and an asthma problem. You don't always have to be told directly how much someone wants to have done something and on days when I was inclined to feel forty-odd was difficult work indeed, I would consider how it would be doing it before work, on a lunch hour, and then after work. Besides, to average a distance almost always means that frequently you run farther than that to make up for a thirty-five-mile day. And there can be a big difference between running forty-five and forty miles in a day at that kind of pitch.

Another friend, Brian Jones, an ultrarunning pal, a big husky guy whose muscular physique astonishes pedestrians and runners alike in New York, had fallen ill while I was gone. Although he is only in his thirties, he was diagnosed as having leukemia and a few of my friends who knew debated whether I should be told, worrying that it might distract me or make me feel like I should break the run off. When I did learn about it, it was a shock, but if there is anyone whose pigheadedness in running through the zero hour of hundred-milers and such had invoked my admiration, certainly Brian's attitude did. Although I liked to tease him by praising him for his "lumbering" hundred-and-ninety-pound running style, Brian was one of the guys with "the righteous stuff," as Tom Wolfe so felicitously expressed it in his recent book, *The Right Stuff,* which I read in my Chicago layover. Wolfe talks about the test-pilot days of the early astronauts and how their reckless, go-for-broke code of courage meant they were willing to "test the outside of the envelope." Those who played the edge were the ones who had the most of "the right stuff." It made me think of ultrarunners. You know who really loves the distance for its own sake. It doesn't make sense why; it doesn't have to. I mean beyond the normal childish human vanities of competitiveness and seeking after glory, there is very often a pure kind of passion in the ultra-endurance field, not more pure than in any other sport, but just responsive to this particular mode. Newton, Gavuzzi, Corbitt, all had the right stuff; so did Brian. So when I thought about that, it was clear that it mattered more than before to do the transcon and do it well, to finish strongly and in control, not to be half-wacky or a physical mess when I came in.

There is in Japan a living, nationally-honored craftsman who, when he casts bells for temples, adds to the molten mix strips of metal with the names of donors printed on them in raised characters, and pieces of paper with prayers, so that many people and the many elements of their lives—disappointments, sufferings, illnesses, hopefulness and energy—all contribute to the final uniqueness and purity of the tone. So whatever it was I expressed on the run, whatever resonance it set off in those who heard about it, I did not "own" that original energy. We all have it, but none of us owns it. Who can separate borrowing from giving? Journey running, like all things, is about living and dying, dying and living.

The Bear Comes Down the Mountain

Now it was time to come home. From the Pennsylvania border to the marathon finish line in Central Park were 421 miles left to go, or eight and a half days of running. There was no predominant mood in these last days. The earlier anticipatory bouts of sadness that had gripped me when I thought of having to end the run had been replaced by a sure sense that enough was enough. I was ready, as Smiley might have said, to come in from the cold. So I did not glance down at the flash of my feet and the blurring endless manifestation of the mottled tar road underneath and think: ah, alas! It was time to end it.

Some days, especially in New Jersey and eastern Pennsylvania, I was like a tourist whose enthusiasm for the constant flux of a novel world had worn thin. I had seen enough scenery, and enough this and that, to last for a while. A lot of that muggy frame of mind came from sheer fatigue. I regret to say that right through until the last day or two, it was still a massive effort, although I finally stepped down from the rush of fifty-plus days that had dominated my breakneck bolt across the last half of Ohio and the first two thirds of Pennsylvania.

Poor, battered Youngstown had been the grimy gateway back into the world of the East. The downtown shopping area had a shattered, empty quality. All those stores with no one going in or out through the entrance doors, all those benches in the shopping mall peopled only by white-haired pensioners and all those loudspeakers playing the fatuous sounds of Muzak orchestras as if the deaf were serenading those who had had their eyes put out. Rusting steel bridges. Empty steel plants. A man in a nearby town saying how he used to have to wait a half hour for the truck traffic to hit an ebb so he could nudge his own rig out onto the road and now . . . he gestured toward the two-lane blacktop over whose surface bright yellow maple leaves idly skittered. Later, back over in the eastern half of Pennsylvania, there was a waitress in one town who said an entire mining operation was going to close down. And what was to happen to all those black heaps of processed earth and sooty-faced men and sooty-faced buildings and all the cluster of hardware stores and lunch cafés and all the rest of life in that town? No one knew. There was a hard bitterness in some voices I heard, people who said their town was "the asshole of the earth." And who really cared? What were they to do? I wondered myself, as I ran along under the falling leaves and through the chilly heights of forested mountain roads, where concern came from. These ordinary days where cars came and went, the sun rose and set and nothing happened except the dry, tenacious rot of industrial stagnation. Economic law says some regions prosper and others falter. But when you meet people who do not feel comforted by being attached to a label or a name for a process, it makes you wonder. How can you care enough for all the struggles people go through sometimes to find work or make ends meet? There was not evidence of the kind of third-world poverty that sears the soul even of witnesses, but there was a troubled sound to voices in the industrial tier of the East that was sobering. I did not feel guilty for spending so much money on running across America, but I was reminded again and again, implicitly, that it was easier for me to do that than it was for others to do ordinary things like pay their bills.

The last range of mountains you encounter when traveling from the Pacific to the Atlantic are the Appalachians. Someone forgot to say much about them or else, like everyone else in the East, I think only the Rockies matter. Western Pennsylvania, however, remains serene in its expression of mountains, and the journey runner soon learns that not only are they to be respected after a lull of a relatively flat sixteen hundred miles, they are very beautiful as well. Although Pennsylvania was the beginning of the home stretch, its four hundred miles of westness to eastness was no trifle.

It was about the middle of October and the entire range of mountains was awake and inflamed. There was the town of Emlenton, which sits just above the Allegheny. You reach it on a plunge-down road that has been cut through steep dropaways of rock. Along the tranquil margins of the flat river are the reflected reds, rusts and yellows from the turning trees.

Between Philipsburg and Port Matilda there was a long range of Appalachian backbone to surmount. Coming down the immense slope of the mountain that seems to lead down out of the clouds in the sky was very much like leaving California and dropping down the Sierra Nevada into the state of Nevada. There were very few cars on that road. I stopped once and sat on the metal guard rail. It was a day when all the activity in the sky was a slow and somber procession of banked-up cloud cover with its gray and tender modeling on the underside slowly changing as it blew out of the north toward the south. I remember looking at the colors of the mountains and seeing the distance, looking out over the great gulf of space, and thinking how impossible it was to describe colors. Every display of ridge was another and different modulation of orange, scarlet and yellow, as carefully and tightly woven as the woodland loom could make it.

A noise came from down below the slope. About twenty meters down, among the tumble of rough rocks pitched over the side by a road crew, was a fat woodchuck. He was going about his fall business, having some errand that urged him from one clump of saplings to another. There was something sweetly comical about watching him and his spikey-colored fur rumble

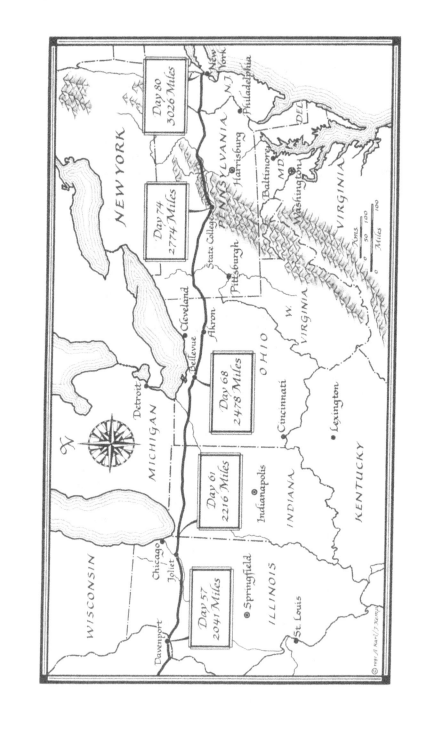

along, blissfully unaware of being watched. But it was a cold day. The hot days of the early part of the run were a dream and the cold steel metal, quicker than ambient air to anticipate the true heart of the weather, had an icy, wintry glare that sent a chill glow right into my butt. I stood up, a bit shivery already and feeling the familiar brittle stiffness in my Achilles tendons from having sat too long. It was another fifty-one-mile day, this time to State College, before being able to find a motel. The desolate west and the desolate middle earth and the desolate east! Always that long, unwanted push toward shelter. But I had a feeling as I began the familiar shuffle down the mountain, down, down, down the long descent, that I was beginning to see the end of the last real mountains. From now on would come the last occasional outbreaks of mountains and then the smaller hills of New Jersey, not insubstantial running, but somehow different. The last expressions of the mountain spirit and of as much utter solitude as I could hope to taste would be replaced for the last time by the cozy, packed-in shlock of shopping strips and busy traffic. Slowly, the bear was leaving his familiar haunts for the new life back in the home he had left.

There was a surprising quality about rural Pennsylvania, especially in the western part, a sense of some deep-rooted, mad kind of eccentricity. Those barking dogs on the end of chains guarding the lonely houses from intruders, the scruffy respectability, the sense of oddness in the way one sees a tree limb growing at some uncanny angle, pruned by a relentless wind. Certainly, the locked-in provinciality was clear at times. There was one stop in a combination gas station and grocery store on the way toward State College. The wildness had begun to vanish in this little valley of fields squeezed in between two flanks of the Appalachians. With one of those wary instincts that warn you that there is unlikely to be another place to get a bite or a drink for a few more hours, I crossed the road and went inside. I prowled the wooden shelves looking for cans of juice and candy bars. It was gray and cold outside and I felt kind of wobbly and road-sore, so there was no hurry. There was a well-set man in his forties up by the cash register in a semienclosed office space. He had a beard and was smoking a cigar that produced those flat stratosphericlike levels of blue smoke, while he and his young son kept an eye on the blue TV set. We fell to talking and got a nice conversation going. He acknowledged their rootedness, not defensively, just stating calmly that they had never been to visit any of the caves nearby. For miles there had been road signs announcing the wonders of various caverns, the display of which seemed to be the local cottage industry. Then the son, who was perhaps nine or ten, returned with two of his friends and then three little boys stood there gazing at me with a quiet kind of ardor. It is very special being a small boy and to have dodged such unfeigned admiration would have been thoughtless, so I asked their names, which they piped up with all the shy enthusiasm of their small souls, and I asked a few questions.

Then the man's wife joined in the conversation. She was the one with some not-entirely-quenched yearning. I remember her having a plain but strong face with protuberant eyes. There was a keenness and an energy in her gaze that was different from the sleepier simplicity of her easygoing husband. Was I going to write a book about it? Yes, I said.

"If it was me I would write a book about *my* adventures and send it off to a publisher," she said with such naïveté and conviction and hunger that it made me look harder at her prominent eyes as if somewhere there would be the window that would explain her. She went on to say how they have a cousin who lives in New York, but they have never been there themselves. Two hundred miles west of New York still seems backwoods. I mean it didn't matter, they were fine people, but the distance to the world of the city would always shine like an immense river between their shore and the other. They had no desire ever to comprehend it. And here was I, a regular bird of passage, drying my wings out in their shop. So when I went out I took care to say good-by again as I had been saying

good-by in little places all across America, taking special care
to say it to the three little boys who were about ready to scatter
themselves.

Once I was hitchhiking down the coast of northern Peru. At
a roadside stop under some shade trees I fell into conversation
with a small boy about that age. Soon the truck I was riding
on was about to pull out. He dashed off to the wretched shack
where he lived on the margin of the Pan-American highway
and then came sprinting back with a gift, a brown bottle filled
with some homemade soda. His mother stood in the doorway,
watching. There was just the time to grab it, thank him and
wave. He stood there waving back until the curve swallowed
him. You cannot put everything into a book by mentioning it
all. Pennsylvania and Peru—are they the same or different?

There was a day when Tom and Virginia, my brother and
sister-in-law, arrived in order to give me company as the whole
venture began to wind down, so I had the pack off for a day
and flew along at a faster clip than I should have. Tom accompanied me most of the fifty-four and a half miles on his bicycle,
but it was interesting to see how easy it was to lose control of
the run with other people around. Subtle pressures and emotions have the unsubtle result of pulling you by a ring through
your nose. Having family along fired me up. I took almost no
breaks during the day, ran without the pack, ran at a somewhat
faster pace, particularly on some downhill sections, and ran for
long periods of time. I finished well into darkness on top of a
mountain, running under an overcast night with only the occasional searing flash of headlights to break the darkness. The
next morning Virginia ran the first two miles with me and we
looked down over a drizzly morning along the orange hillside.
Suddenly they were driving off, leaving me on a wet Sunday
morning back on my own again. So as the brown VW Rabbit
dwindled to ink-blot size and then vanished altogether, the
dreaminess seemed large again. Just a moment before Virginia's gray running shoes had been keeping pace with mine
and now she had evaporated, borne by superior speed into

another dimension. Car travel. I thought back with a smile to the early days of the trip when I calculated that one day's running was equal to not quite one hour of driving. Now for someone to catch me if they retraced my route, they would have to drive for seventy-two hours without stopping.

Such recollections vanished as dizziness and a terrible tied-up feeling assaulted my thighs. It was clear that almost the whole trip I *had* been very much on the 1 percent edge and that an unregarded instinct had carefully monitored the degree of workload. I had not exceeded my previous bounds by very much, but just a minor alteration of intensity was too much.

The next three days were costly. I had the kind of beaten-up soreness and stiffness in my quads that comes after a long, hard race. It was real damage. Normally, a week of little running would be the minimum recovery time. But what could I do now except to tell myself that it was time really to accept the fact that I was a fool? Always maintain control, never surrender to the pressures of others or your own inappropriate excitement. All that time and I was still learning how to do a journey run. It wasn't much consolation as I padded along, walking and running, nursing myself over many, many hills. Overtired and underfed—it was time to be a little better to myself—even two hundred miles would need some caution.

There were the occasional breaks from routine, odd thoughts and scenes. Near Bloomsburg I took a rest on top of a hill on the grassy margin of a cemetery. It was one of those calm moments when, unassailed by thoughts of where I had come from and where I was headed, the freshness of the present moment had immense power. The speeding cars swished past with great violence, but with different readings. It seemed to me at the time that the mind of each motorist had a distinctness and individuality of feeling that communicated itself in the way they drove. Sometimes, after many hours of sitting in a zendo, staring at a small patch of floor or wall, the sounds of steps, the way in which someone coughs, the rustle of another person's robes when they stand up or sit down, communicates a powerful sense of how clear and how focused that person is. And now with the dead at rest in the field behind my back there was an added poignancy to the testiness and fearfulness and abstractedness of many who passed over this hilltop in their autos. I thought that people did not know what they were doing when they drove. They can't outdrive death or any of their problems. There is that in runners, too, feeling that it confers an immortality. We must be very careful in the middle of it all not to misunderstand speed. There were broken yellow stripes on the tar road. Sunshine. Clouds drifting by overhead.

In a nearby town there was a bookstore close to the hotel where I stayed. I wandered in looking for a good book and since I was the only person in there, could not help but hear the loud and distinctly articulated lament of the young woman on the telephone.

"He just doesn't like to drink. I mean when we go out the most he has is one beer and that just doesn't do *anything* for you. He just never lets go. He's so stiff. Listen, I've got to go. He's going to be coming in any moment now."

I stepped up to the register and she hung up and came over to ring the purchase. I found her tone abrasively immature. I felt sorry for this unknown suitor since the bitterness and bitchiness of her assault was mingled with a fierce possessiveness as if to say underneath: well, he's such a damn nuisance and maybe we'll even make a go of it and I would never really show him what I felt but he's *mine!* The coolness between us might have produced frostbite in two less leathery souls. She took my money in silence, resenting me, I thought, unfairly. If I had just wandered out again I would have been a completely anonymous eavesdropper, but the purchase threatened to bring me into focus as a human being.

"No bag," I murmured as she began to bend to get one out. "Thanks."

She said nothing and slid the book toward me an inch and a half. I had just stepped outside into the street when a young man with a mustache, wearing a suit, in his late twenties and looking quite proper, stepped into the store after throwing me the quickest of glances.

"Poor bastard," I thought.

Then came the last and final assault by fatigue. Joe Greene had driven out from New York to put in a day of relaxed picture-taking and amiability now that I was just a one hundred-odd miles from the city. Sad to say that my notes on the seventy-seventh day of the crossing refer to being tired and restless in the morning. So I dug down for sixty minutes, hating the long flattish road, the occasional spats of rain, the red gravel shoulder, but the not-stopping made things easier. Near Berwick I warmed up in a store, and really without thinking ate eight cinnamon rolls in a row and drank a can of soda pop. Normally, massive intakes of sugar had been okay, but this latest bout of frailness had made me uncommonly sensitive to diet.

In any case, a little farther on there was Joe in his father's borrowed car, the one we called the Ultramobile, since it had been to so many ultraraces in New York and New England. I hadn't seen Joe since Nevada. We kidded around, chatted about this and that, and I took my pack off and threw it in the car.

"See you in a few miles," I said. Joe nodded, did a U-turn and vanished up the road. I set off running. In a quarter of a mile I had the distinct impression someone had hit me in the head with a baseball bat. I was dizzy, nauseous, reeling. It came on so swiftly and unexpectedly that I hardly could believe it was happening to me. I tried to palliate it with words. You're just making it up, I said, thinking in a flash that perhaps I was going to blow it now with a couple of days to go. The farther you go in these ultra ventures, the harder it is to bear the last 2 percent because of that terrible fear that something might yet happen. After so far for so long, and to go through so much, only now to feel as if I were dissolving into a physical wreck. But why? "What is this!" I yelled at myself, urged myself back into a run, but the world swam as powerfully as it does in the final extremi-

ties of a heavy drunk, just when you are at the stage of doing
things that you will not be able to recall the next day. My vision
was blurred and the world seemed to swim in a softened way
in several directions and dimensions at once. I wobbled as I
walked and stumped along as best I could to the Ultramobile.
I couldn't believe that once again, getting to the car had to be
such a trial. I was most afraid of falling down and not being
able to get up and I was also afraid, since I wasn't sure where
I was in space, that a car would wallop me. The only thing I
did think of at the time was that all those little bouts of
dizziness had come to collect their due and that the lid was off
at last.

I made it to the car finally and said quietly I felt awful and
was going to nap. Joe had the wisdom not to mention how
horrible I looked; he just nodded. I fell asleep for a half hour
immediately and then in a gingerly way began to walk and run,
walk and run. In retrospect I think I understand it. Even
meeting Tom and Virginia in western Pennsylvania was still
not like getting to the end. But Joe was here when it was all
thinkable. In seventy-two hours or less I would be home. So
suddenly I could just allow myself to feel what I had not really
felt in full until that moment. I was just a desperately tired man
who could use a little sleep. So in one violent purge, the body
invaded the command post and flattened the martinet colonel
with a single blow. That was the last bad patch of the entire
trip.

"Sexy!" the teen-age girls yelled at me with a half-affection-
ate, half-mocking tone as I ran through Berwick late in the
afternoon. So it was okay again. The battered caravan wagon
just rolled on.

There was one last conversation with the folks of the world
before the relatively anonymous highways of New Jersey swallowed me up. Running on a back road through rolling hills
cluttered with trees and occasional houses, rusting barbed-wire
fences, and streams, I saw a fellow seated on the ground, legs
splayed out in front of him, bent over the drive shaft of an old

car he was working on. I asked for directions and he looked up at me, pushing his fatigue hat farther back on his brow with the back of his hand, since his fingers were black with grease. He wore a plaid shirt, a pair of old pants and work boots. Called himself Smitty of Smitty's Gap. There was a seasoned, crackly, gingery look to his tone and his eye and his face. As we spoke he started working on the universal joint and you could tell by the way he was doing that kind of thing that he loved fixing cars and that when he was a teen-ager he had been up to his elbows in it all the time, and later he confirmed as much.

"Why are you doing it, for personal satisfaction? Yeah? Well, by gee, I can appreciate that. I used to do some pretty wild things in my own day, I can tell you. I used to be a real motorcycle nut. People would say to me, Smitty, you're going to wrap yourself all over the road, but here I am.

"So when I heard at first about all these runners I thought, now who are these looney tunes? Then I said to myself, back off, Smit, who do you think *you* are? Now what it is really is a question of people doing wild things when they're younger. That's right. That's appropriate. There's a cycle for each time of your life. When you're two to four, four to ten, ten to eighteen and so on, you have your different concerns and problems. It's all okay. If I didn't have this muck on my hands, I'd shake your hand.

"I have seven kids myself. One's a hippie, kind of. He's a musician. My wife and I go round sometimes and listen to him play. Now I like that hippie stuff. At home I'll put on the earphones and listen. I hear things other people don't. I don't say I understand all of it, but I'm listening for certain things. It interests me. I like listening to lots of different things. I'm not like a lot of people who say they're only into one thing and that's it. I think you ought not to get stuck.

"You want to fill your water bottles down by the stream there. Go right ahead. Make yourselves at home. It's the best durn water in the state."

There was company every day the last few days. When Joe left, Donna came. She found me, in general, in a better mood than out West, but looking much thinner. Most of the run from then on is a blur with a few bright fragments. Donna was excited by primarily two things: the antique stores and the pretty colors of the changing leaves. I was too beat really to notice the latter. Excitement came from knowing that Don Shepherd had finished his solo run by running in on Route 46 across New Jersey.

The technical aspects of wrapping it up were a trial some-times. The next-to-last night Donna and I put up for the night with two friends at their home in Mendham, New Jersey. The long drive to their home over complicated back roads took close to an hour. And then another drive to go eat somewhere. And then a wait for a table. And then losing the telephone number of the people with whom my brother and his family were staying and worrying how they would all be able to find me the next day. And wanting in some hurt, weary way just to run in quietly to the city when I damn well felt like it, completely alone. To have to have picked the hour in advance when I would arrive, so that press could be notified and friends alerted, left me in a snarl of mixed emotions.

"You have to let people be a part of it," Innamorato coun-seled me over the phone a few days before coming in. That made me feel calmer and a little ashamed, but I couldn't help the surges of resistance to being anything other than alone. I was angry sometimes, not really at anyone or anything, but worn down, thin. Anyone who has ever watched the brave chatter of participants in a twenty-four-hour race evaporate on the hot steel of endeavor will understand. It is all you can do to concentrate on the task at hand; anything that calls you out of yourself is too much. I particularly hated the notion of the press being there, which has a fine irony coming from a some-time journalist, and someone about to spill his guts in a book about the run, and I knew that, but the book came later, on my own terms. The last day was still about the run and the run had been lonely. Well, like most crises, it wasn't worth the energy I expended on it. It didn't make any difference.

The shuttle of accompanying ghosts continued and as soon as family and friends of family arrived at a rendezvous in New Jersey, Donna vanished, off to more mundane concerns about buying cold cuts and potato salad for the party on the morrow. There was a regular troop of cyclists behind me, alongside me, ahead of me, and two cars, flitting ahead and waiting, passing with toots of salutation. It was just gray New Jersey landscape and earthscape. The hills had flattened down, the towns grew familiar and drab, and then finally the rain began to fall. By nightfall it was just my brother left on his bicycle, a dogged, miserable figure pedaling from one shelter to another, his iron-gray curls looking even curlier as the dampness stained him dark. His glasses had fogged over in the chill and the wet, and since dusk was beginning to spread, he finally packed it in. There was a bit of a tussle near Bogota, New Jersey, with my family wanting to bear with me until I came off the road for the day. I had had enough, so I insisted on finding a motel somewhere in New Jersey for the night. All the same, as the VW Rabbit puttered down the street out of sight, I felt not only relief but a mild sadness. It felt a bit forlorn after all the questions and admiration and love just to have the green pack again and to hear distinctly, instead of the thoughts in my head, the patter of rain dropping from layer to layer of leaf, falling ever downward, until spattering on the quiet streets.

Work comforts all wounds—although it can create a few of its own. So ten minutes later it seemed absolutely right that the heartiness of adventure returned. I crossed Overpeck Creek in darkness with no shoulder to run on and the ever-present threat of getting run over by two-eyed cars with their flashing yellow beams. For old-time's sake I took a final roadside piss under the night-time sky while rats scurried to and fro amid the garbage and high weeds.

Fort Lee, New Jersey, sits atop the Palisade Cliffs and is traversed by Interstate 80, which itself leads directly onto the

George Washington Bridge. I had run through here many times before, so it was like coming into my backyard as I approached from the west, seeing the last looming rise of streets, marked by the street lamps shining through the wet trees, the nimbuses of light sharp and prickly in the slight mist. On top of this dark ridge of earth, I would finally see the city again. It had been a forty-three-mile day, so I was reasonably tired and had a final debate about whether to run the three quarters of a mile up without stopping. For the last time the angry debate surged: "Just run up it, for God's sake! After all this way, you're going to get soft?" (The last sentence said in a tone of utter incredulity.) The other voice asserted that surely there had been enough mountain running to make the issue of walking or running up this last hill strictly voluntary.

The result was a somewhat resentful nonstop run to the top, or almost to the top.

I went into a florist's shop. The smell of green stems was nice. Two ladies, one young and one old, looked up. They said the nearest motels were a few miles away on one of the highways, a lousy trudge.

"Where are you coming from?" one of them asked. I explained. It was clear they thought I had come as a native Californian for the first time. It was charming the way they wished me luck, as if they thought the harsh city would swallow me and my naïve, if laudable, quest and spit me out a stone.

Finally, in a magazine and candy store, a husky fellow with a very wide open shirt, and some gold something or other hanging round his neck looking very bright against his black chest hair, frowned and said there *was* a motel nearby.

"It's not exactly luxurious," he said. I couldn't understand his look, but I protested my hardiness. "Go down by the foot of the George Washington Bridge," he said, "and you'll see it." I had run over the bridge dozens of times and had never recalled seeing a motel, but then I hadn't been looking for one, either.

It was wonderful to see the bridge for the first time, looking,

I have to admit, very much the way it had always looked, standing very straight and firm in the misty night air as the tireless concrete artery bristled with speeding demons. Ah, traffic! I paused on the underpass and watched the cars come flying in, atoms sent whirling from the far Pacific Coast to this other end of the universe.

I broke from my reverie and marched down a little hill to the motel, feeling damned strange about almost being home and yet not being there. It was peculiar really to see the lights of Washington Heights in upper Manhattan and not be there. The run was so almost over. As for the motel, it was not too bad-looking from the outside. I went into the office and stood in front of the smeared counter-to-ceiling glass window. The young attendant, in response to a question about rooms being available, replied: "The maid's cleaning one out right now."

"Ah," I said mildly, baffled by why a room would come vacant at 7 P.M. I thought no more of it.

"How long do you want it for?"

This was very odd, indeed. But light broke in when he asked his next question.

"Do you want it for an hour or the whole night?"

"The whole night," I said.

A callow youth waiting behind me sniggered and announced loudly but not derisively: "I've never rented a room here for the whole night. I get it done fast."

The youth evinced much hilarity in himself and another fellow, a very thin, very tall black man. The clerk is unmoved.

"Oh, some people spend the whole night here," he said.

I took my key and ascended. I had a western exposure from my window, which had the severe limitation of not having a lock. The bed was made with two sheets that displayed, in prominent black letters, the name of the laundry. Blankets were not visible, but were hardly necessary as four plastic ceiling grids directly over the bed spewed out a truly remarkable quantity of rank hot air. I looked around for a thermostat but found none. There were cigarette burns on the little plastic night table. A constant drip from the tiny bathroom sink announced itself, but refused to be silent when I applied myself to squeezing the taps. The kind of seeped-into-the-walls smell of urine so characteristic of underground tunnels in the New York City subway system pervaded the bathroom. But at least there was a color TV. After a bracing meal of rotten food at a nearby diner, I returned and stretched out for my last night away from home. The TV offered a colorful fare of hardcore pornography, so I watched for a longish while, enjoying the final scuzzy moments of wakefulness. There was a delicious irony of an unspecified sort to end it in a dump. The ceaseless traffic of cars and couples in the motel did not affect my sleep at all. I slept calmly and quietly, lulled by the steady swish of Interstate 80.

I perched on the rocks of the Palisades the next morning killing time until I could leave. When the time came I buckled on the pack and picked my way to the bridge. When you lean out over the railing and snuff the bright sunshine and fresh air and see the gray pile of stone towers, and it is a view you have known all your life and you have dreamed for a long eighty days of getting back to look at it one more time before you die, you feel a feeling that is very fine, very strong, very nice.

I had the same kind of feeling halfway across the bridge when I saw the old gang, the running gang, looking just as they always did: Donna, John and Lauri McBride, the two Richies, and later Michael Cleary and John Eisner. Your gang is special; you've all put in miles together, been to each other's weddings and parties, been out to Chinese restaurants together. It all seemed very normal and natural again. Soon enough we are running down Riverside Drive and the talk is the same corny talk it always is, which is fine. No need to get into all the heavy stuff about what it took to get there.

Then family appears again and my six-foot-five, fourteen-year-old nephew, Tom, is loping along beside me as we head downtown. He tells me how strong my calves look.

Then I am talking to my thirteen-year-old niece and Janice is asking: "How do you feel?"

"Fine."

"Do you feel ecstatic?"

I laugh a little, realizing that somehow she thinks I should be, which makes me wonder if I should be.

"Well, I feel happy," I say.

"But don't you feel ecstatic?" she probes.

"No," I say, "it's just a very simple, sweet feeling."

I think vaguely that I disappoint her.

As we near the entrance to Central Park there is discussion about who should run in with me, but I ask just to take in the last mile or so alone. Fred Lebow, the president of the New York Road Runners Club, has kept a group of runners and spectators from the finish of a five-mile race a little earlier that morning there, in expectation of the arrival. Word comes that Fred wants me to follow the striped blue line of the marathon. That's fine. So I run through the sunshine, holding a tiny bouquet of flowers Laurie gave me in one hand, padding on quietly, sharing the road with cyclists and other runners.

There is no particular reason why the last mile should be any more ecstatic than the previous 3,025. I was a failure. I had been way up and way down. I had attached to many ideas, many thoughts, many desires. But all the same I had not been a failure. I had tried very hard to stay in some special ground where I wasn't getting too excited or too depressed. Many times when I had wrapped the red bandanna around my clenched left fist as a signal to myself only to concentrate, I had muttered between clenched teeth: "Just steady, steady, steady." I had wanted to run through the finish rather than to it. I wanted to feel like two hours, two months or two years after the run would be good time to be in, too. I didn't want ever to look back at the run again with longing. All the same, I was riding on a very sweet, very filling sense of completion.

The more miraculous, wild flash had come the night before laboring up the hill into Fort Lee and spotting the bridge. It had been a special feeling knowing that a great enterprise was coming to an end. I had never been able to absorb it and even as I write this, I cannot say that I have swallowed the run. It seemed to happen and seemed to end the way a dream does. How do you measure 3,026 miles? It was as if the last few days I had been dying by degrees, so gradually and so increasingly transparent that there was no one left to feel affected by very much. When it is time for a leaf to fall, then it falls. So I was not ecstatic. I just felt a kind of deep appreciation.

A few people said some nice things in the last mile. The blue line that some marathon runner would follow all alone in the middle of an immense crowd in a week's time was now mine to follow all alone. I had a sense of running along Central Park South in the shadow of the great hotels, that up there around the curve where they all waited was some last necessity to match and answer before rest could come. So I kept running and my last advice to myself was not to sprint it in, not to get excited because other people would be there. I was a padder, a shuffler, a ten-minutes-a-miler and it had done the job. I would not show myself as anything other than what I was.

So I kept running and the sun kept shining and the leaves kept skimming over the asphalt and finally, there is one last hill. Always one more hill, one more mountain. When I was small I once read a story about a little boy who kept walking so he could find the place where the earth and the sky meet . . .

A friend is there, grinning and sticking his hand out. A crowd cheers. At the finish line there is a tape to breast. Faces of family and friends press in. Now it was formal. The bear was dead.

The bear went over the mountain to see what he could see. And what did he learn?

That everywhere there is sky, everywhere there is ground. At every moment, everywhere, we are home.

About the Author

JAMES SHAPIRO was born in New York City in 1946, and now lives in Manhattan. After graduating from Harvard College in 1968 he worked as a Peace Corps volunteer in the northeast of Brazil. In addition to his writing he has been a student of Zen Buddhism for the last six years, has worked at a wide variety of jobs, and has raced frequently at all distances in road running, particularly in ultramarathons.

CPSIA information can be obtained
at www.ICGtesting.com
Printed in the USA
LVHW081036090322
712934LV00013B/646

9 781635 618525